Safety Symbols

These symbols appear in laboratory activities.
They alert you to possible dangers and remind
you to work carefully.

General Safety Awareness Read all directions for an experiment several times. Follow the directions exactly as they are written. If you are in doubt, ask your teacher for assistance.

Physical Safety If the lab includes physical activity, use caution to avoid injuring yourself or others. Tell your teacher if there is a reason that you should not participate.

Safety Goggles Always wear safety goggles to protect your eyes in any activity involving chemicals, heating, or the possibility of broken glassware.

Lab Apron Wear a laboratory apron to protect your skin and clothing from harmful chemicals or hot materials.

Plastic Gloves Wear disposable plastic gloves to protect yourself from contact with chemicals that can be harmful. Keep your hands away from your face. Dispose of gloves according to your teacher's instructions.

Heating Use a clamp or tongs to hold hot objects. Test an object by first holding the back of your hand near it. If you feel heat, the object may be too hot to handle.

Heat-Resistant Gloves Hot plates, hot water, and hot glassware can cause burns. Never touch hot objects with your bare hands. Use an oven mitt or other hand protection.

Flames Tie back long hair and loose clothing, and put on safety goggles before using a burner. Follow instructions from your teacher for lighting and extinguishing burners.

No Flames If flammable materials are present, make sure there are no flames, sparks, or exposed sources of heat.

Electric Shock To avoid an electric shock, never use electrical equipment near water, or when the equipment or your hands are wet. Use only sockets that accept a three-prong plug. Be sure cords are untangled and cannot trip anyone. Disconnect equipment that is not in use.

Fragile Glassware Handle fragile glassware, such as thermometers, test tubes, and beakers, with care. Do not touch broken glass. Notify your teacher if glassware breaks. Never use chipped or cracked glassware.

Corrosive Chemical Avoid getting corrosive chemicals on your skin or clothing, or in your eyes. Do not inhale the vapors. Wash your hands after completing the activity.

Poison Do not let any poisonous chemical get on your skin, and do not inhale its vapor. Wash your hands after completing the activity.

Fumes When working with poisonous or irritating vapors, work in a well-ventilated area. Never test for an odor unless instructed to do so by your teacher. Avoid inhaling a vapor directly. Use a wafting motion to direct vapor toward your nose.

Sharp Object Use sharp instruments only as directed. Scissors, scalpels, pins, and knives are sharp and can cut or puncture your skin. Always direct sharp edges and points away from yourself and others.

Disposal All chemicals and other materials used in the laboratory must be disposed of safely. Follow your teacher's instructions.

Hand Washing Before leaving the lab, wash your hands thoroughly with soap or detergent, and warm water. Lather both sides of your hands and between your fingers. Rinse well.

Chemical Building Blocks

PRENTICE HALL **Science**
Explorer

Boston, Massachusetts
Upper Saddle River, New Jersey

Chemical Building Blocks

Book-Specific Resources

Student Edition
StudentExpress™ with Interactive Textbook
Teacher's Edition
All-in-One Teaching Resources
Color Transparencies
Guided Reading and Study Workbook
Student Edition on Audio CD
Discovery Channel School® Video
Lab Activity Video
Consumable and Nonconsumable Materials Kits

Program Print Resources

Integrated Science Laboratory Manual
Computer Microscope Lab Manual
Inquiry Skills Activity Books
Progress Monitoring Assessments
Test Preparation Workbook
Test-Taking Tips With Transparencies
Teacher's ELL Handbook
Reading Strategies for Science Content

Differentiated Instruction Resources

Adapted Reading and Study Workbook
Adapted Tests
Differentiated Instruction Guide for Labs and Activities

Program Technology Resources

TeacherExpress™ CD-ROM
Interactive Textbooks Online
PresentationExpress™ CD-ROM
ExamView®, Computer Test Bank CD-ROM
Lab zone™ Easy Planner CD-ROM
Probeware Lab Manual With CD-ROM
Computer Microscope and Lab Manual
Materials Ordering CD-ROM
Discovery Channel School® DVD Library
Lab Activity DVD Library
Web Site at PHSchool.com

Spanish Print Resources

Spanish Student Edition
Spanish Guided Reading and Study Workbook
Spanish Teaching Guide With Tests

Acknowledgments appear on page 196, which constitutes an extension of this copyright page.

Cover
Table salt and rock salt are two forms of the compound sodium chloride.

PEARSON
Prentice Hall

ISBN 0-13-201155-7

2 3 4 5 6 7 8 9 10   10 09 08 07 06

Program Authors

Michael J. Padilla, Ph.D.
Professor of Science Education
University of Georgia
Athens, Georgia

Michael Padilla is a leader in middle school science education. He has served as an author and elected officer for the National Science Teachers Association and as a writer of the National Science Education Standards. As lead author of Science Explorer, Mike has inspired the team in developing a program that meets the needs of middle grades students, promotes science inquiry, and is aligned with the National Science Education Standards.

Ioannis Miaoulis, Ph.D.
President
Museum of Science
Boston, Massachusetts

Originally trained as a mechanical engineer, Ioannis Miaoulis is in the forefront of the national movement to increase technological literacy. As dean of the Tufts University School of Engineering, Dr. Miaoulis spearheaded the introduction of engineering into the Massachusetts curriculum. Currently he is working with school systems across the country to engage students in engineering activities and to foster discussions on the impact of science and technology on society.

Martha Cyr, Ph.D.
Director of K–12 Outreach
Worcester Polytechnic Institute
Worcester, Massachusetts

Martha Cyr is a noted expert in engineering outreach. She has over nine years of experience with programs and activities that emphasize the use of engineering principles, through hands-on projects, to excite and motivate students and teachers of mathematics and science in grades K–12. Her goal is to stimulate a continued interest in science and mathematics through engineering.

Book Authors

David V. Frank, Ph.D.
Head, Department of
Physical Sciences
Ferris State University
Big Rapids, Michigan

John G. Little
Science Teacher
St. Mary's High School
Stockton, California

Steve Miller
Science Writer
State College, Pennsylvania

Contributing Writers

Thomas L. Messer
Science Teacher
Foxborough Public Schools
Foxborough, Massachusetts

Thomas R. Wellnitz
Science Teacher
The Paideia School
Atlanta, Georgia

Consultants

Reading Consultant

Nancy Romance, Ph.D.
Professor of Science
Education
Florida Atlantic University
Fort Lauderdale, Florida

Mathematics Consultant

William Tate, Ph.D.
Professor of Education and
Applied Statistics and
Computation
Washington University
St. Louis, Missouri

Reviewers

Teacher Reviewers

David R. Blakely
Arlington High School
Arlington, Massachusetts

Jane E. Callery
Two Rivers Magnet Middle
    School
East Hartford, Connecticut

Melissa Lynn Cook
Oakland Mills High School
Columbia, Maryland

James Fattic
Southside Middle School
Anderson, Indiana

Dan Gabel
Hoover Middle School
Rockville, Maryland

Wayne Goates
Eisenhower Middle School
Goddard, Kansas

Katherine Bobay Graser
Mint Hill Middle School
Charlotte, North Carolina

Darcy Hampton
Deal Junior High School
Washington, D.C.

Karen Kelly
Pierce Middle School
Waterford, Michigan

David Kelso
Manchester High School Central
Manchester, New Hampshire

Benigno Lopez, Jr.
Sleepy Hill Middle School
Lakeland, Florida

Angie L. Matamoros, Ph.D.
ALM Consulting, INC.
Weston, Florida

Tim McCollum
Charleston Middle School
Charleston, Illinois

Bruce A. Mellin
Brooks School
North Andover, Massachusetts

Ella Jay Parfitt
Southeast Middle School
Baltimore, Maryland

Evelyn A. Pizzarello
Louis M. Klein Middle School
Harrison, New York

Kathleen M. Poe
Fletcher Middle School
Jacksonville, Florida

Shirley Rose
Lewis and Clark Middle School
Tulsa, Oklahoma

Linda Sandersen
Greenfield Middle School
Greenfield, Wisconsin

Mary E. Solan
Southwest Middle School
Charlotte, North Carolina

Mary Stewart
University of Tulsa
Tulsa, Oklahoma

Paul Swenson
Billings West High School
Billings, Montana

Thomas Vaughn
Arlington High School
Arlington, Massachusetts

Susan C. Zibell
Central Elementary
Simsbury, Connecticut

Safety Reviewers

W. H. Breazeale, Ph.D.
Department of Chemistry
College of Charleston
Charleston, South Carolina

Ruth Hathaway, Ph.D.
Hathaway Consulting
Cape Girardeau, Missouri

Douglas Mandt, M.S.
Science Education Consultant
Edgewood, Washington

Activity Field Testers

Nicki Bibbo
Witchcraft Heights School
Salem, Massachusetts

Rose-Marie Botting
Broward County Schools
Fort Lauderdale, Florida

Colleen Campos
Laredo Middle School
Aurora, Colorado

Elizabeth Chait
W. L. Chenery Middle School
Belmont, Massachusetts

Holly Estes
Hale Middle School
Stow, Massachusetts

Laura Hapgood
Plymouth Community
    Intermediate School
Plymouth, Massachusetts

Mary F. Lavin
Plymouth Community
    Intermediate School
Plymouth, Massachusetts

James MacNeil, Ph.D.
Cambridge, Massachusetts

Lauren Magruder
St. Michael's Country
    Day School
Newport, Rhode Island

Jeanne Maurand
Austin Preparatory School
Reading, Massachusetts

Joanne Jackson-Pelletier
Winman Junior High School
Warwick, Rhode Island

Warren Phillips
Plymouth Public Schools
Plymouth, Massachusetts

Carol Pirtle
Hale Middle School
Stow, Massachusetts

Kathleen M. Poe
Fletcher Middle School
Jacksonville, Florida

Cynthia B. Pope
Norfolk Public Schools
Norfolk, Virginia

Anne Scammell
Geneva Middle School
Geneva, New York

Karen Riley Sievers
Callanan Middle School
Des Moines, Iowa

David M. Smith
Eyer Middle School
Allentown, Pennsylvania

Gene Vitale
Parkland School
McHenry, Illinois

Contents

Chemical Building Blocks

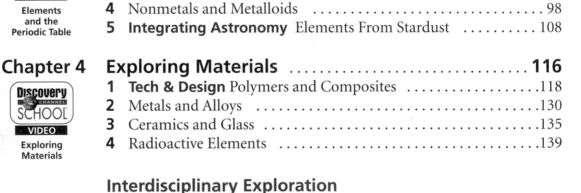

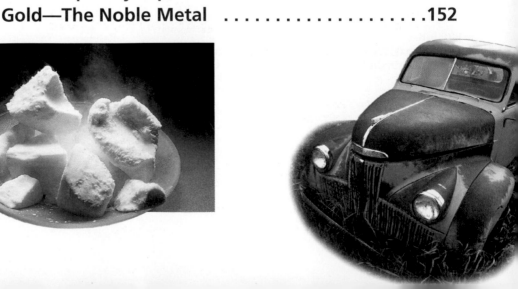

Reference Section

Enhance understanding through dynamic video.

Preview Get motivated with this introduction to the chapter content.

Field Trip Explore a real-world story related to the chapter content.

Assessment Review content and take an assessment.

Get connected to exciting Web resources in every lesson.

SciLINKS NSTA Find Web links on topics relating to every section.

Active Art Interact with selected visuals from every chapter online.

Planet Diary® Explore news and natural phenomena through weekly reports.

Science News® Keep up to date with the latest science discoveries.

Experience the complete text-book online and on CD-ROM.

Activities Practice skills and learn content.

Videos Explore content and learn important lab skills.

Audio Support Hear key terms spoken and defined.

Self-Assessment Use instant feedback to help you track your progress.

Activities

Many products, such as gasohol and plastic bottles, are made from corn-based chemicals.

From Plants to Chemicals

Can you power a car with corn? Can you drink soda from a bottle made from plants? Can you use corn to make chemicals strong enough to remove paint?

You can, thanks to scientists like Rathin Datta. Rathin is a chemical engineer at the Argonne National Laboratory in Illinois. He specializes in finding ways to get useful chemicals from plants. His discoveries will help make the environment cleaner for all of us.

For years, Rathin has been finding ways to make useful products from substances found naturally in plants. He's helped find ways to turn corn into an automobile fuel called gasohol. He's researched plants that can be used to produce powerful medicines. He has even worked on a way to use corn to make a stretchy fabric that athletes wear.

"I've always been interested in the plant and biological side of chemistry," says Rathin, who grew up in northern India. "That's because I've always been concerned about the effect of chemicals on the environment."

Talking With
Dr. Rathin Datta

Are Plant-Based Chemicals Safer?

Chemicals that come from crop plants are called *agrochemicals*, meaning "chemicals from agriculture," Rathin explains. Many agrochemicals are much less dangerous to the environment than chemicals made from petroleum, called *petrochemicals*.

Because agrochemicals are made from plant materials, nature usually recycles them, just as it recycles dead plants. Think of what happens to a tree after it falls to the ground. Tiny microbes work on its leaves and branches until the tree has rotted completely away. Much the same thing happens to products made from agrochemicals. A bag made from corn-based chemicals will break down and disappear after only a few weeks of being buried. In contrast, a plastic bag made from petrochemicals can survive hundreds of years.

Career Path

Rathin Datta was born in India. His interest in science was inspired in part by his father, who was a mathematician. Rathin came to the United States in 1970 to earn a Ph.D. in chemical engineering at Princeton University. He now works at Argonne National Laboratory in Illinois. Rathin and his team at Argonne were winners of the 1998 Presidential Green Chemistry Challenge Award for their work on the technology for the "green" solvent. Rathin plays the sitar, an Indian lute, and enjoys opera.

Converting Carbohydrates

The starting ingredients in many agrochemicals are energy-rich substances called carbohydrates. Sugar and starch are carbohydrates. Rathin converts, or changes, carbohydrates from corn into an agrochemical that can be used to make plastic. To do this, he needs help from tiny organisms—bacteria. First, he puts a special kind of bacteria in a big vat of ground-up corn. The bacteria convert the corn's carbohydrates into acids through a natural process called fermentation. Rathin then uses the acids to make plastic.

"The bacteria do all the work of converting the carbohydrates into useful molecules," says Rathin. "The hardest part for us comes afterward. The fermentation process produces a whole mix of materials. We have to find ways to separate out the one kind of material that we want to use from all the others."

Researchers Rathin Datta (right) and Mike Henry (left) developed a new, low-cost solvent. The clear substance that Rathin holds is the solvent.

Making Solvents From Corn

Rathin Datta's most recent discovery is a good example of how agrochemicals can replace petrochemicals. He and his team have found a new way to use corn to make powerful solvents. Solvents are used to dissolve other substances.

"Solvents are found everywhere," says Rathin. "For example, factories use them in many processes to clean electronic parts or to remove ink from recycled newspapers. Households use them in grease-cleaning detergents and in paint removers."

Almost 4 million tons of solvents are used in the United States every year. Most are made from petrochemicals and can be very poisonous.

Addressing the Challenge

"Scientists have known for a long time that much safer solvents can be made from agrochemicals," says Rathin. "But the process has been too expensive. It doesn't do any good to make something that is environmentally sound if it costs too much for people to use," says Rathin. "Our challenge as chemical engineers was to think about an old process in an entirely new way. We had to find a less expensive way to make these solvents."

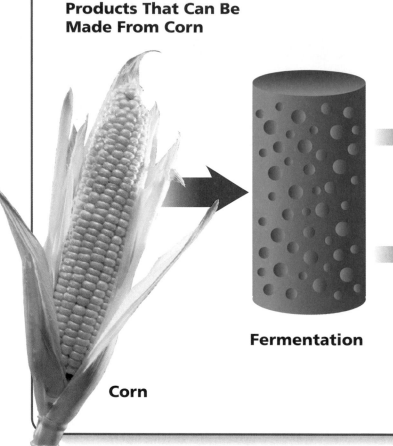

Products That Can Be Made From Corn

Corn

Fermentation

Stretchy fabric, like the material worn by this athlete, is likely to be made from corn.

Discovering a New Process

Rathin needed a new process to separate the solvents he wanted from a mixture. "I started working with a new kind of plastic that acts like a very fine filter. When we pass the fermented corn over this plastic, it captures the acids we want to keep and lets the other material pass through."

After two years of experimenting, Rathin perfected his process of making agrochemical solvents. His process works for less than half the cost of the old method. It also uses 90 percent less energy. Soon, most of the solvents used in the United States could be this cleaner, safer kind made from corn. "It even makes a great fingernail polish remover," says Datta.

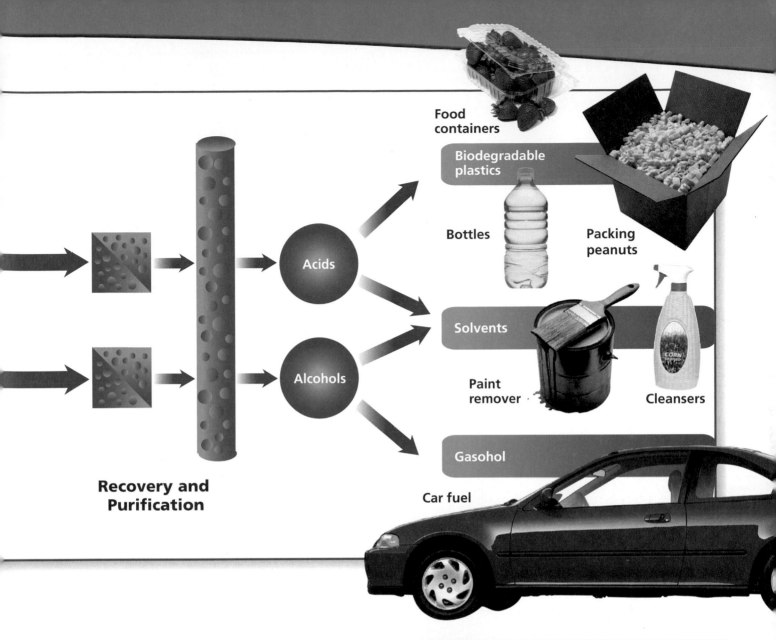

Food containers

Biodegradable plastics

Bottles

Packing peanuts

Solvents

Paint remover

Cleansers

Gasohol

Car fuel

Recovery and Purification

Making a Difference

"It's very satisfying to take a natural product like corn and use it to produce a chemical that will replace a less safe chemical," says Rathin. "It's rare to find a compound that can do everything that this corn solvent can do and still be nonpoisonous and easily break down in the environment." Rathin's projects are long term. But finally a company has formed to manufacture and sell the solvent.

Writing in Science

Career Link After years of research, Rathin and his team discovered how to make a solvent that was safe *and* inexpensive. The product is now being sold by a company. In a paragraph, describe the steps a researcher might follow to get an invention manufactured and sold.

Go Online
PHSchool.com

For: More on this career
Visit: PHSchool.com
Web Code: cgb-1000

Introduction to Matter

Chapter Preview

This "junk sculpture" of an armadillo is ▶ made entirely of metal can lids.

Introduction to Matter

▶ Video Preview
Video Field Trip
Video Assessment

Chapter **Project**

Design and Build a Density-Calculating System

How do you find the density of something if you don't have a balance to measure its mass? Suppose you can't use a graduated cylinder to measure the volume of such items as honey or table sugar. Can you build your own balance and devise a way to find the volume of items that are not easily measured with a ruler?

Your Goal To design and build a device for collecting data that can be used to calculate the density of powdered solids and liquids

To complete the project, you must

● build a device to measure accurately the masses of powdered solids and liquids

● develop a method to measure volume without using standard laboratory equipment

● obtain data you can use to calculate the density of items

● follow the safety guidelines in Appendix A

Plan It! Preview the chapter to find out how mass, volume, and density are related. Research how balances are constructed and how they work. Build a balance out of the materials supplied by your teacher. Then devise a container with a known volume that you can use to find the volumes of your test materials. When your teacher approves your plan, test your system. Redesign and retest your system to improve its accuracy and reliability.

Describing Matter

Reading Preview

Key Concepts
- What kinds of properties are used to describe matter?
- What are elements, and how do they relate to compounds?
- What are the properties of a mixture?

Key Terms
- matter • chemistry
- substance • physical property
- chemical property • element
- atom • chemical bond
- molecule • compound
- chemical formula • mixture
- heterogeneous mixture
- homogeneous mixture
- solution

Target Reading Skill
Building Vocabulary
A definition states the meaning of a word or phrase by telling its most important feature or function. After you read the section, use what you have learned to write a definition of each Key Term in your own words.

Lab zone — Discover **Activity**

What Is a Mixture?

1. Your teacher will give you a handful of objects, such as checkers, marbles, and paper clips of different sizes and colors.

2. Examine the objects. Then sort them into at least three groups. Each item should be grouped with similar items.

3. Describe the differences between the unsorted handful and the sorted groups of objects. Then make a list of the characteristics of each sorted group.

Think It Over
Forming Operational Definitions The unsorted handful of objects represents a mixture. Your sorted groups represent substances. Using your observations, infer what the terms *mixture* and *substance* mean.

You have probably heard the word *matter* many times. Think about how often you hear the phrases "As a matter of fact, …" or "Hey, what's the matter?" In science, this word has a specific meaning. **Matter** is anything that has mass and takes up space. All the "stuff" around you is matter, and you are matter too. Air, plastic, metal, wood, glass, paper, and cloth—all of these are matter.

▼ Paper, ceramic, wood, metal, and foam are all forms of matter.

Properties of Matter

Even though air and plastic are both matter, no one has to tell you they are different materials. Matter can have many different properties, or characteristics. Materials can be hard or soft, rough or smooth, hot or cold, liquid, solid, or gas. Some materials catch fire easily, but others do not burn. **Chemistry** is the study of the properties of matter and how matter changes.

The properties and changes of any type of matter depend on its makeup. Some types of matter are substances and some are not. In chemistry, a **substance** is a single kind of matter that is pure, meaning it always has a specific makeup—or composition—and a specific set of properties. For example, table salt has the same composition and properties no matter where it comes from—seawater or a salt mine. On the other hand, think about the batter for blueberry muffins. It contains flour, butter, sugar, salt, blueberries, and other ingredients shown in Figure 1. While some of the ingredients, such as sugar and salt, are pure substances, the muffin batter is not. It consists of several ingredients that can vary with the recipe.

Every form of matter has two kinds of properties— physical properties and chemical properties. A physical property of oxygen is that it is a gas at room temperature. A chemical property of oxygen is that it reacts with iron to form rust. You'll read more about physical and chemical properties in the next two pages.

FIGURE 1
Substances or Not?
Making muffin batter involves mixing together different kinds of matter. The batter itself is not a pure substance. **Classifying** *Why are salt, sugar, and baking soda pure substances?*

Pure Substances
Table salt, table sugar, and baking soda are pure substances.

Not Substances
Flour, baking powder, milk, eggs, and fruit are not pure substances.

FIGURE 2
Physical Properties

The physical properties of matter help you identify and classify matter in its different forms.
Applying Concepts *Why is melting point a physical property?*

▲ **Physical State**
Above 0°C, these icicles of solid water will change to liquid.

◄ **Texture and Color**
Bumpy texture and bright colors are physical properties of this hungry chameleon.

▲ **Flexibility**
Metal becomes a shiny, flexible toy when shaped into a flat wire and coiled.

Lab zone Skills **Activity**

Interpreting Data

Melting point is the temperature at which a solid becomes a liquid. Boiling point is the temperature at which a liquid becomes a gas. Look at the data listed below. Identify each substance's physical state at room temperature (approximately 20°C). Is it a gas, a liquid, or a solid? Explain your conclusions.

Substance	Melting Point (°C)	Boiling Point (°C)
Water	0	100
Ethanol	–117	79
Propane	–190	–42
Table salt	801	1,465

Physical Properties of Matter A **physical property** is a characteristic of a pure substance that can be observed without changing it into another substance. For example, a physical property of water is that it freezes at a temperature of 0°C. When liquid water freezes, it changes to solid ice, but it is still water. Hardness, texture, and color are some other physical properties of matter. When you describe a substance as a solid, a liquid, or a gas, you are stating another physical property. Whether or not a substance dissolves in water is a physical property, too. Sugar will dissolve in water, but iron will not. Stainless steel is mostly iron, so you can stir sugar into your tea with a stainless steel spoon.

Physical properties can be used to classify matter. For example, two properties of metals are luster and the ability to conduct heat and electricity. Some metals, such as iron, can be attracted by a magnet. Metals are also flexible, which means they can be bent into shapes without breaking. They can also be pressed into flat sheets and pulled into long, thin wires. Other materials such as glass, brick, and concrete will break into small pieces if you try to bend them or press them thinner.

FIGURE 3
Chemical Properties

The chemical properties of different forms of matter cannot be observed without changing a substance into a new substance.

◄ **New Substances, New Properties**
Gases produced during baking create spaces in freshly made bread.

◄ **Flammability**
Wood fuels a fire, producing heat, gases, and ash.

Ability to React ►
Iron can form rust, turning a once shiny car into a crumbling relic.

Chemical Properties of Matter Unlike physical properties of matter, some properties can't be observed just by looking at or touching a substance. A **chemical property** is a characteristic of a pure substance that describes its ability to change into different substances. To observe the chemical properties of a substance, you must try to change it to another substance. Like physical properties, chemical properties are used to classify substances. For example, a chemical property of methane (natural gas) is that it can catch fire and burn in air. When it burns, it combines with oxygen in the air and forms new substances, water and carbon dioxide. Burning, or flammability, is a chemical property of methane as well as the substances in wood or gasoline.

One chemical property of iron is that it will combine slowly with oxygen in air to form a different substance, rust. Silver will react with sulfur in the air to form tarnish. In contrast, a chemical property of gold is that it does *not* react easily with oxygen or sulfur. Bakers make use of a chemical property of the substances in bread dough. With the help of yeast added to the dough, some of these substances can produce a gas, which causes the bread to rise.

 **Reading Checkpoint** What must you do in order to observe a chemical property of a substance?

Figure 4

Examples of Elements
Some elements have familiar uses. Many elements are solids at room temperature, but some are gases or liquids.

Tungsten wire

Aluminum bat

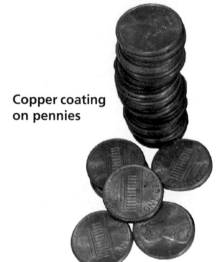

Copper coating on pennies

Elements

What is matter made of? Why is one kind of matter different from another kind of matter? Educated people in ancient Greece debated these questions. Around 450 B.C., a Greek philosopher named Empedocles proposed that all matter was made of four "elements"—air, earth, fire, and water. He thought that all other matter was a combination of two or more of these four elements. The idea of four elements was so convincing that people believed it for more than 2,000 years.

What Is an Element? In the late 1600s, experiments by the earliest chemists began to show that matter was made up of many more than four elements. Now, scientists know that all matter in the universe is made of slightly more than 100 different substances, still called elements. An **element** is a pure substance that cannot be broken down into any other substances by chemical or physical means. **Elements are the simplest substances.** Each element can be identified by its specific physical and chemical properties.

You are already familiar with some elements. Aluminum, which is used to make foil and outdoor furniture, is an element. Pennies are made from zinc, another element. Then the pennies are given a coating of copper, also an element. With each breath, you inhale the elements oxygen and nitrogen, which make up 99 percent of Earth's atmosphere. Elements are often represented by one- or two-letter symbols, such as C for carbon, O for oxygen, and H for hydrogen.

Particles of Elements—Atoms What is the smallest possible piece of matter? Suppose you could keep tearing a piece of aluminum foil in half over and over again. Would you reach a point where you have the smallest possible piece of aluminum? The answer is yes. Since the early 1800s, scientists have known that all matter is made of atoms. An **atom** is the basic particle from which all elements are made. Different elements have different properties because their atoms are different. Experiments in the early 1900s showed that an atom is made of even smaller parts. Look at the diagram of a carbon atom in Figure 5. The atom has a positively charged center, or nucleus, that contains smaller particles. It is surrounded by a "cloud" of negative charge. You will learn more about the structure of atoms in Chapter 3.

When Atoms Combine Atoms of most elements have the ability to combine with other atoms. When atoms combine, they form a **chemical bond**, which is a force of attraction between two atoms. In many cases, atoms combine to form larger particles called **molecules** (MAHL uh kyoolz)—groups of two or more atoms held together by chemical bonds. A molecule of water, for example, consists of an oxygen atom chemically bonded to two hydrogen atoms. Two atoms of the same element can also combine to form a molecule. Oxygen molecules consist of two oxygen atoms. Figure 6 shows models of three molecules. You will see similar models throughout this book.

 **Reading Checkpoint** What is a molecule?

FIGURE 5
Modeling an Atom
Pencil "lead" is made of mostly graphite, a form of carbon. Two ways to model atoms used in this book are shown here for carbon.

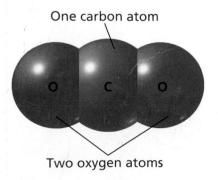

Spherical model of a carbon atom

Nucleus

Electron cloud   6e-

A cloud model of an atom shows the electron cloud and the particles in the nucleus.

FIGURE 6
Modeling Molecules
Models of molecules often consist of colored spheres that stand for different kinds of atoms.
Observing *How many atoms are in a molecule of carbon dioxide?*

Water molecule

H — Two hydrogen atoms

O   H

One oxygen atom

Oxygen molecule

O   O

Two oxygen atoms

Carbon dioxide molecule

One carbon atom

O   C   O

Two oxygen atoms

Math Skills

Ratios A ratio compares two numbers. It tells you how much you have of one item compared to how much you have of another. For example, a cookie recipe calls for 2 cups of flour to every 1 cup of sugar. You can write the ratio of flour to sugar as 2 to 1, or 2 : 1.

The chemical formula for rust, a compound made from the elements iron (Fe) and oxygen (O), may be written as Fe_2O_3. In this compound, the ratio of iron atoms to oxygen atoms is 2 : 3. This compound is different from FeO, a compound in which the ratio of iron atoms to oxygen atoms is 1 : 1.

Practice Problem What is the ratio of nitrogen atoms (N) to oxygen atoms (O) in a compound with the formula N_2O_5? Is it the same as the compound NO_2? Explain.

Compounds

All matter is made of elements, but most elements in nature are found combined with other elements. A **compound** is a pure substance made of two or more elements chemically combined in a set ratio. A compound may be represented by a **chemical formula,** which shows the elements in the compound and the ratio of atoms. For example, part of the gas you exhale is carbon dioxide. Its chemical formula is CO_2. The number *2* below the symbol for oxygen tells you that the ratio of carbon to oxygen is 1 to 2. (If there is no number after the element's symbol, the number *1* is understood.) If a different ratio of carbon atoms and oxygen atoms are seen in a formula, you have a different compound. For example, carbon monoxide—a gas produced in car engines—has the formula CO. Here, the ratio of carbon atoms to oxygen atoms is 1 to 1.

When elements are chemically combined, they form compounds having properties that are different from those of the uncombined elements. For example, the element sulfur is a yellow solid, and the element silver is a shiny metal. But when silver and sulfur combine, they form a compound called silver sulfide, Ag_2S. You would call this black compound *tarnish.* Table sugar ($C_{12}H_{22}O_{11}$) is a compound made of the elements carbon, hydrogen, and oxygen. The sugar crystals do not resemble the gases oxygen and hydrogen or the black carbon you see in charcoal.

Reading Checkpoint What information does a chemical formula tell you about a compound?

FIGURE 7
Compounds From Elements
This snail's shell is made mostly of calcium carbonate—a compound made from calcium, carbon, and oxygen.

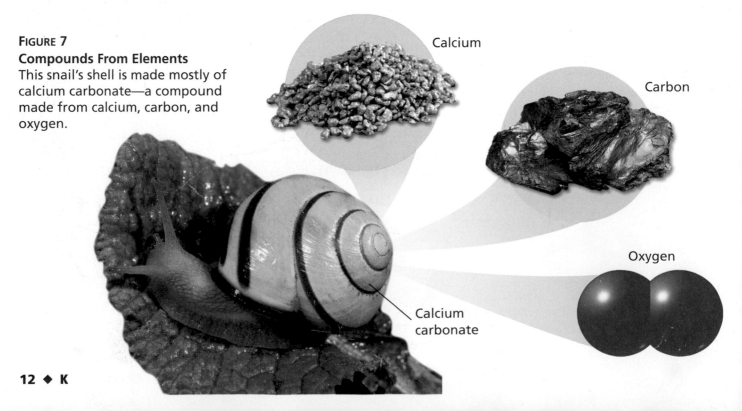

Calcium

Carbon

Oxygen

Calcium carbonate

Mixtures

Elements and compounds are pure substances, but most of the materials you see every day are not. Instead, they are mixtures. A **mixture** is made of two or more substances—elements, compounds, or both—that are together in the same place but are not chemically combined. Mixtures differ from compounds in two ways. **Each substance in a mixture keeps its individual properties. Also, the parts of a mixture are not combined in a set ratio.**

Think of a handful of moist soil such as that in Figure 8. If you look at the soil through a magnifier, you will find particles of sand, bits of clay, maybe even pieces of decaying plants. If you squeeze the soil, you might force out a few drops of water. A sample of soil from a different place probably won't contain the same amount of sand, clay, or water.

Heterogeneous Mixtures A mixture can be heterogeneous or homogeneous. In a **heterogeneous mixture** (het ur uh JEE nee us), you can see the different parts. The damp soil described above is one example of a heterogeneous mixture. So is a salad. Just think of how easy it is to see the pieces of lettuce, tomatoes, cucumbers, and other ingredients that cooks put together in countless ways and amounts.

FIGURE 8
Heterogeneous Mixture
Soil from a flowerpot in your home may be very different from the soil in a nearby park.
Interpreting Photographs
What tells you that the soil is a heterogeneous mixture?

Homogeneous Mixtures The substances in a **homogeneous mixture** (hoh moh JEE nee us), are so evenly mixed that you can't see the different parts. Suppose you stir a teaspoon of sugar into a glass of water. After stirring for a little while, the sugar dissolves, and you can no longer see crystals of sugar in the water. You know the sugar is there, though, because the sugar solution tastes sweet. A **solution** is an example of a homogeneous mixture. A solution does not have to be a liquid, however. Air is a solution of nitrogen gas (N_2) and oxygen gas (O_2), plus small amounts of a few other gases. A solution can even be solid. Brass is a solution of the elements copper and zinc.

FIGURE 9
Homogeneous Mixture
A swimmer blows bubbles of air—a homogeneous mixture of gases.

FIGURE 10

Separating a Mixture

The different physical properties of iron, sulfur, and table salt help in separating a mixture of these substances.

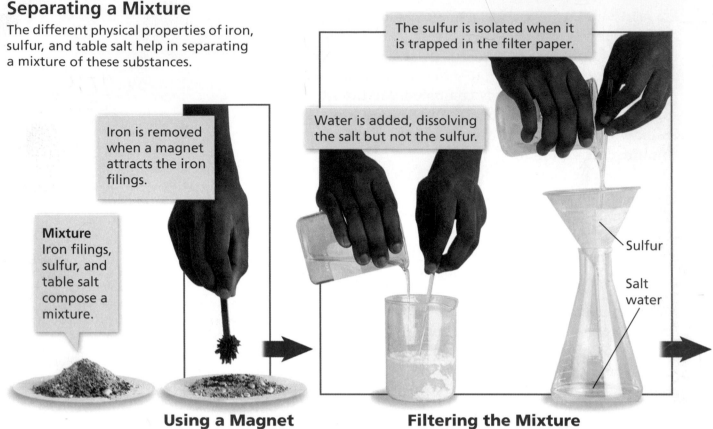

Iron is removed when a magnet attracts the iron filings.

Mixture Iron filings, sulfur, and table salt compose a mixture.

The sulfur is isolated when it is trapped in the filter paper.

Water is added, dissolving the salt but not the sulfur.

Sulfur

Salt water

Using a Magnet

Filtering the Mixture

Discovery CHANNEL **SCHOOL**™

Introduction to Matter

Video Preview
▶ **Video Field Trip**
Video Assessment

Separating Mixtures Compounds and mixtures differ in yet another way. A compound can be difficult to separate into its elements. But, a mixture is usually easy to separate into its components because each component keeps its own properties. Figure 10 illustrates a few of the ways you can use the properties of a mixture's components to separate them. These methods include magnetic attraction, filtration, distillation, and evaporation.

In the Figure, iron filings, powdered sulfur, and table salt start off mixed in a pile. Iron is attracted to a magnet, while sulfur and salt are not. Salt can be dissolved in water, but sulfur will not dissolve. So, pouring a mixture of salt, sulfur, and water through a paper filter removes the sulfur.

Now the remaining solution can be distilled. In distillation, a liquid solution is boiled. Components of the mixture that have different boiling points will boil away at different temperatures. As most of the water boils in Figure 10, it is cooled and then collected in a flask. Once the remaining salt water is allowed to dry, or evaporate, only the salt is left.

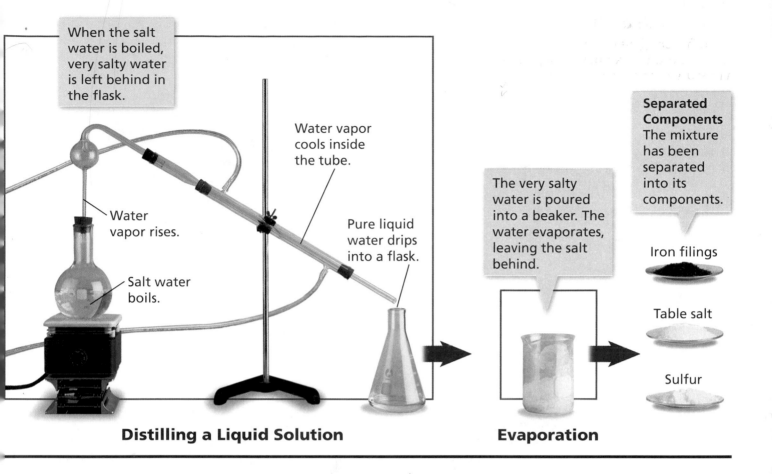

When the salt water is boiled, very salty water is left behind in the flask.

Water vapor rises.

Salt water boils.

Water vapor cools inside the tube.

Pure liquid water drips into a flask.

The very salty water is poured into a beaker. The water evaporates, leaving the salt behind.

Separated Components The mixture has been separated into its components.

Iron filings

Table salt

Sulfur

Distilling a Liquid Solution

Evaporation

Section 1 Assessment

🎯 **Target Reading Skill Building Vocabulary** Use your definitions to help answer the questions.

Reviewing Key Concepts

1. a. **Explaining** What is the difference between chemical properties and physical properties?
   b. **Classifying** A metal melts at 450°C. Is this property of the metal classified as chemical or physical? Explain your choice.
   c. **Making Judgments** Helium does not react with any other substance. Is it accurate to say that helium has no chemical properties? Explain.

2. a. **Reviewing** How are elements and compounds similar? How do they differ?
   b. **Applying Concepts** Plants make a sugar compound with the formula $C_6H_{12}O_6$. What elements make up this compound?

3. a. **Identifying** How does a heterogeneous mixture differ from a homogeneous mixture?
   b. **Drawing Conclusions** Why is it correct to say that seawater is a mixture?
   c. **Problem Solving** Suppose you stir a little baking soda into water until the water looks clear again. How could you prove to someone that the clear material is a solution, not a compound?

Math Practice

4. **Ratios** Look at the following chemical formulas: H_2O_2 and H_2O. Do these formulas represent the same compound? Explain.

Measuring Matter

Reading Preview

Key Concepts
- What is the difference between weight and mass?
- What units are used to express the amount of space occupied by matter?
- How is the density of a material determined?

Key Terms
- weight • mass
- International System of Units
- volume • density

Target Reading Skill

Asking Questions Before you read, preview the red headings. In a graphic organizer like the one below, ask a *what* or *how* question for each heading. As you read, write the answers to your questions.

Weight and Mass

Question	Answer
How are weight and mass different?	Weight is a measure of . . .

Discover Activity

Lab zone

Which Has More Mass?

1. Your teacher will provide you with some small objects. Look at the objects, but do not touch them.
2. Predict which object is lightest, which is second lightest, and so on. Record your predictions.
3. Use a triple-beam balance to find the mass of each object.
4. Based on the masses, list the objects from lightest to heaviest.

Think It Over
Drawing Conclusions How did your predictions compare with your results? Are bigger objects always heavier than smaller objects? Why or why not?

Here's a riddle for you: Which weighs more, a pound of feathers or a pound of sand? If you answered "a pound of sand," think again. Both weigh exactly the same—one pound.

There are all sorts of ways to measure matter, and you use these measurements every day. Scientists rely on measurements as well. In fact, scientists work hard to make sure their measurements are as accurate as possible.

Weight and Mass

Suppose you want to measure your weight. To find the weight, you step on a scale like the one shown in Figure 11. Your body weight presses down on the springs inside the scale. The more you weigh, the more the springs compress, causing the pointer on the scale to turn farther, giving a higher reading. However, your scale would not indicate the same weight if you took it to the moon and stepped on it. You weigh less on the moon, so the springs of the scale would not be compressed as much by your weight.

FIGURE 11
Measuring Weight
If you stood on this scale on the moon, it would show that your weight there is less than on Earth.

Weight Your **weight** is a measure of the force of gravity on you. On Earth, all objects are attracted toward the center of the planet by the force of Earth's gravity. On another planet, the force of gravity on you may be more or less than it is on Earth. On the moon, you would weigh only about one-sixth of your weight on Earth.

Mass Why do you weigh less on the moon than on Earth? The force of gravity depends partly on the mass of an object. The **mass** of an object is the measurement of the amount of matter in the object. If you travel to the moon, the amount of matter in your body—your mass—does not change. But, the mass of the moon is much less than the mass of Earth, so the moon exerts much less gravitational force on you. **Unlike weight, mass does not change with location, even when the force of gravity on an object changes.** For this reason scientists prefer to measure matter by its mass rather than its weight. The mass of an object is a physical property.

Units of Mass To measure the properties of matter, scientists use a system called the **International System of Units.** This system is abbreviated "SI" after its French name, *Système International.* The SI unit of mass is the kilogram (kg). If you weigh 90 pounds on Earth, your mass is about 40 kilograms. Although you will see kilograms used in this textbook, usually you will see a smaller unit—the gram (g). There are exactly 1,000 grams in a kilogram. A nickel has a mass of 5 grams, and a baseball has a mass of about 150 grams.

✓ **Reading Checkpoint** What is the SI unit of mass?

Go Online
PHSchool.com

For: More on measuring matter
Visit: PHSchool.com
Web Code: cgd-1012

Equating Units of Mass

1 kg = 1,000 g
1 g = 0.001 kg

A balloon and the air inside it have a combined mass of about 3 g or 0.003 kg.

A pineapple has a mass of about 1,600 g or 1.6 kg.

FIGURE 12
Measuring Mass
A triple-beam balance measures mass in grams. **Calculating** *How do you convert a mass in grams to the equivalent mass in kilograms? (Hint: Look at the table.)*

An average orange has a mass of about 230 g or 0.23 kg.

FIGURE 13
Finding Volume
The volume of a regular solid can be found by measuring its dimensions and multiplying the values.
Interpreting Tables *What volume of water in milliliters would this brick displace if submerged?*

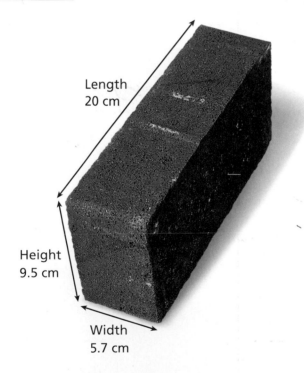

Length
20 cm

Height
9.5 cm

Width
5.7 cm

Volume = 20 cm x 9.5 cm x 5.7 cm
= 1,083 cm^3

Volume

You learned in Section 1 that all matter has mass and takes up space. The amount of space that matter occupies is called its **volume.** It's easy to see that solids and liquids take up space. Gases have volume, too. Watch a balloon as you blow into it. You're actually increasing the volume of gas in the balloon with your breath.

Units of Volume Common units of volume include the **liter (L), milliliter (mL),** and **cubic centimeter (cm^3).** Some plastic soda bottles hold 1 liter of liquid. Volumes smaller than a liter are usually given in milliliters. A milliliter is one one-thousandth of a liter and is exactly the same volume as 1 cubic centimeter. A teaspoonful of water has a volume of about 5 milliliters, and an ordinary can of soda contains 355 milliliters of liquid. In the laboratory, volumes of liquid are usually measured with a graduated cylinder.

Calculating Volume The volumes of solid objects are usually expressed in cubic centimeters. Suppose you want to know the volume of a rectangular object, such as the brick shown in Figure 13. First, you measure the brick's length, width, and height (or thickness). Then, you multiply these values.

$$\text{Volume} = \text{Length} \times \text{Width} \times \text{Height}$$

Measurements always have units. So, when you multiply the three measurements, you must multiply the units as well as the numbers.

$$\text{Units} = \text{cm} \times \text{cm} \times \text{cm} = \text{cm}^3$$

How can you measure the volume of an irregular object, such as a piece of fruit or a rock? One way is to submerge the object in water in a graduated cylinder. The water level will rise by an amount that is equal to the volume of the object in milliliters.

 **Reading Checkpoint** How are milliliters related to cubic centimeters?

Density

Samples of two different materials may have the same volume, but they don't necessarily have the same mass. Remember the riddle about the sand and the feathers? A kilogram of sand takes up much less space than a kilogram of feathers. The volumes differ because sand and feathers have different densities—an important property of matter. **Density** relates the mass of a material in a given volume. Often, density is expressed as the number of grams in one cubic centimeter. For example, the density of water at room temperature is stated as "one gram per cubic centimeter (1 g/cm^3)." This value means that every gram of water has a volume of 1 cm^3. Notice that the word *per* is replaced by the fraction bar in the units of density. **The bar tells you that you can determine the density of a sample of matter by dividing its mass by its volume.**

$$\text{Density} = \frac{\text{Mass}}{\text{Volume}}$$

Math ► Sample Problem

Calculating Density

A small block of wood floats on water. It has a mass of 200 g and a volume of 250 cm^3. What is the density of the wood?

1 **Read and Understand**
What information are you given?
Mass of block = 200 g
Volume of block = 250 cm^3

2 **Plan and Solve**
What quantity are you trying to calculate?
The density of the block = ■

What formula contains the given quantities and the unknown quantity?
$$\text{Density} = \frac{\text{Mass}}{\text{Volume}}$$

Perform the calculation.
$$\text{Density} = \frac{\text{Mass}}{\text{Volume}} = \frac{200 \text{ g}}{250 \text{ cm}^3} = 0.80 \text{ g/cm}^3$$

3 **Look Back and Check**
Does your answer make sense?
The density is lower than 1.0 g/cm^3, which makes sense because the block can float.

Math ► Practice

1. A sample of liquid has a mass of 24 g and a volume of 16 mL. What is the density of the liquid?

2. A piece of solid metal has a mass of 43.5 g and a volume of 15 cm^3. What is the density of the metal?

FIGURE 14
Density Layers
The density of water is less than corn syrup but greater than vegetable oil.

Vegetable Oil

Water

Corn Syrup

Sinking or Floating? Suppose you have a solid block of wood and a solid block of iron. When you drop both blocks into a tub of water, you can see right away that the wood floats and the iron sinks. You know the density of water is 1 g/cm³. Objects with densities greater than that of water will sink. Objects with lesser densities will float. So, the density of this wood is less than 1 g/cm³. The density of the iron is greater than 1 g/cm³.

Watch a bottle of oil-and-vinegar salad dressing after it has been shaken. You will see oil droplets rising above the vinegar. Finally, the oil forms a separate layer above the vinegar. What can you conclude? You're right if you said that the oil is less dense than vinegar.

Using Density Density is a physical property of a substance. So, density can be used to identify an unknown substance. For example, suppose you were hiking in the mountains and found a shiny, golden-colored rock. How would you know if the rock was really gold? Later at home, you could look up the density of gold at room temperature. Then measure the mass and volume of the rock and find its density. If the two densities match, you would have quite a find!

✓ **Reading Checkpoint** Why does the oil in some salad dressings rise to the top of the bottle?

Section 2 Assessment

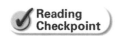

Target Reading Skill Asking Questions Use the answers you wrote in your graphic organizer about the headings to answer the questions below.

Reviewing Key Concepts

1. **a. Defining** What is mass?
   b. Explaining Why is mass more useful than weight for measuring matter?
2. **a. Identifying** What property of matter is measured in cubic centimeters?
   b. Comparing and Contrasting How are milliliters related to liters?
   c. Calculating A plastic box is 15.3 cm long, 9.0 cm wide, and 4.5 cm high. What is its volume? Include units in your answer.
3. **a. Listing** What measurements must you make to find the density of a sample of matter?

   b. Explaining How can you determine whether a solid object is more dense or less dense than water?
   c. Problem Solving Propose a way to determine the density of air.

Math Practice

4. **Calculating Density** A piece of metal has a volume of 38 cm³ and a mass of 277 g. Calculate the density of the metal, and identify it based on the information below.

   Iron 7.9 g/cm³   Tin 7.3 g/cm³
   Lead 11.3 g/cm³   Zinc 7.1 g/cm³

Making Sense of Density

Problem

Does the density of a material vary with volume?

Skills Focus

drawing conclusions, measuring, controlling variables

Materials

- balance • water • paper towels
- metric ruler • graduated cylinder, 100-mL
- wooden stick, about 6 cm long
- ball of modeling clay, about 5 cm wide
- crayon with paper removed

Procedure

1. Use a balance to find the mass of the wooden stick. Record the mass in a data table like the one shown above right.

2. Add enough water to a graduated cylinder so that the stick can be completely submerged. Measure the initial volume of the water.

3. Place the stick in the graduated cylinder. Measure the new volume of the water.

4. The volume of the stick is the difference between the water levels in Steps 2 and 3. Calculate this volume and record it.

5. The density of the stick equals its mass divided by its volume. Calculate and record its density.

6. Thoroughly dry the stick with a paper towel. Then carefully break the stick into two pieces. Repeat Steps 1 through 5 with each of the two pieces.

7. Repeat Steps 1 through 6 using the clay rolled into a rope.

8. Repeat using the crayon.

Data Table			
Object	Mass (g)	Volume Change (cm³)	Density (g/cm³)
Wooden stick			
Whole			
Piece 1			
Piece 2			
Modeling clay			
Whole			
Piece 1			
Piece 2			
Crayon			
Whole			
Piece 1			
Piece 2			

Analyze and Conclude

1. **Measuring** For each object you tested, compare the density of the whole object with the densities of the pieces of the object.

2. **Drawing Conclusions** Use your results to explain how density can be used to identify a material.

3. **Controlling Variables** Why did you dry the objects in Step 6?

4. **Communicating** Write a paragraph explaining how you would change the procedure to obtain more data. Tell how having more data would affect your answers to Questions 1 and 2 above.

Design an Experiment

Design an experiment you could use to determine the density of olive oil. With your teacher's permission, carry out your plan.

Changes in Matter

Reading Preview

Key Concepts
- What is a physical change?
- What is a chemical change?
- How are changes in matter related to changes in energy?

Key Terms
- physical change
- chemical change
- law of conservation of mass
- energy • temperature
- thermal energy
- endothermic change
- exothermic change

Target Reading Skill

Relating Cause and Effect A cause makes something happen. An effect is what happens. As you read, identify two effects caused by a chemical change. Write the information in a graphic organizer like the one below.

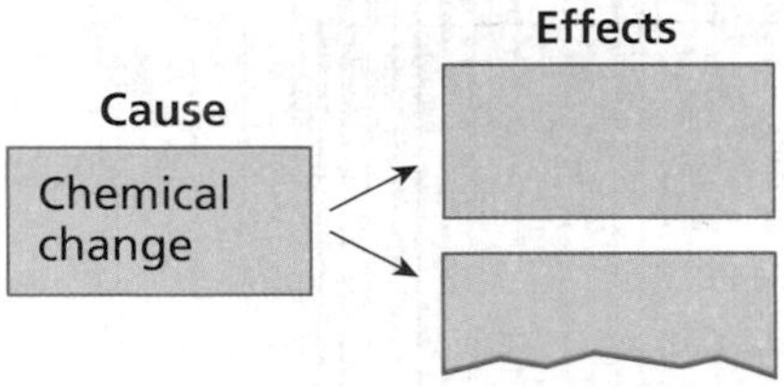

Effects

Cause

Chemical change

You look up from the sand sculpture you and your friends have been working on all afternoon. Storm clouds are gathering, and you know the sand castle may not last long. You pull on a sweatshirt to cover the start of a sunburn and begin to pack up. The gathering of storm clouds, the creation of sand art, and your sunburn are examples of changes in matter. Chemistry is mostly about changes in matter. In this section, you will read about some of those changes.

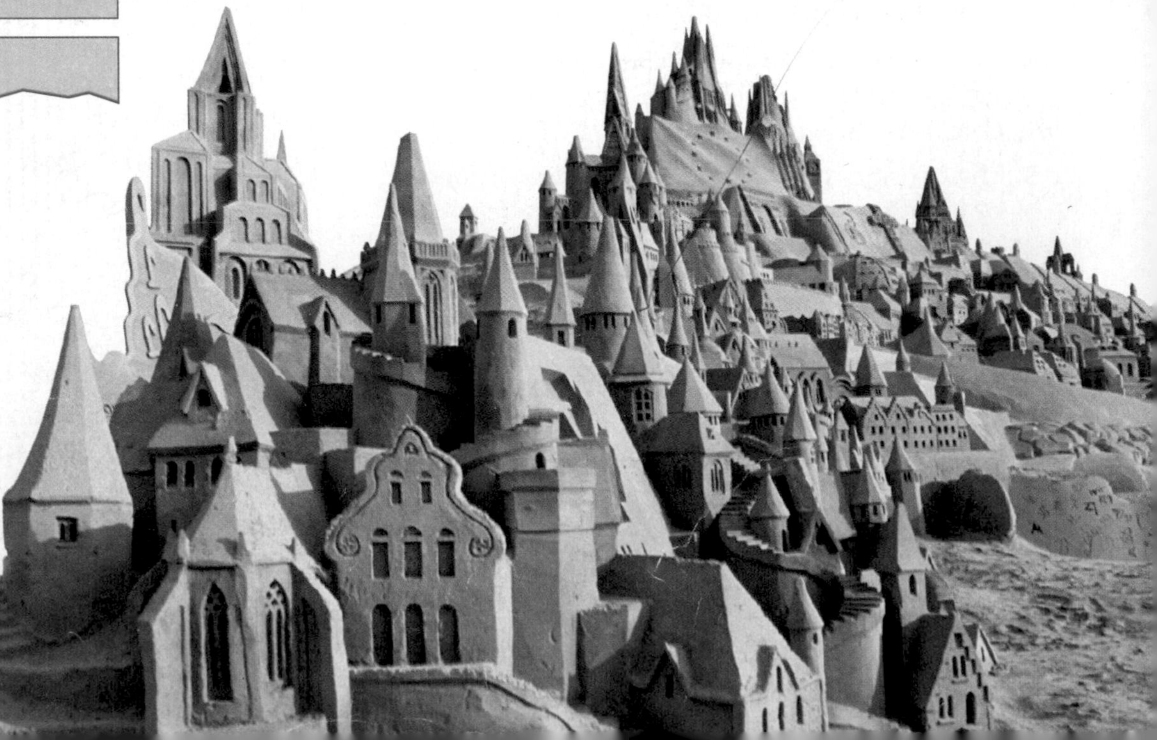

Sand has been ▶ transformed into art.

Physical Change

In what ways can matter change? A **physical change** is any change that alters the form or appearance of matter but does not make any substance in the matter into a different substance. For example, a sand artist may change a formless pile of sand into a work of art. However, the sculpture is still made of sand. **A substance that undergoes a physical change is still the same substance after the change.**

Changes of State As you may know, matter occurs in three familiar states—solid, liquid, and gas. Suppose you leave a small puddle of liquid water on the kitchen counter. When you come back two hours later, the puddle is gone. Has the liquid water disappeared? No, a physical change happened. The liquid water changed into water vapor (a gas) and mixed with the air. A change in state, such as from a solid to a liquid or from a liquid to a gas, is an example of a physical change.

Changes in Shape or Form Is there a physical change when you dissolve a teaspoon of sugar in water? To be sure, you would need to know whether or not the sugar has been changed to a different substance. For example, you know that a sugar solution tastes sweet, just like the undissolved sugar. If you pour the sugar solution into a pan and let the water dry out, the sugar will remain as a crust at the bottom of the pan. The crust may not look exactly like the sugar before you dissolved it, but it's still sugar. So, dissolving is also a physical change. Other examples of physical changes are bending, crushing, breaking, chopping, and anything else that changes only the shape or form of matter. The methods of separating mixtures—filtration and distillation—that you read about in Section 1 also involve physical changes.

 **Reading Checkpoint** Why is the melting of an ice cube called a physical change?

FIGURE 15
Change of State
At room temperature, the element iodine is a purple solid that easily becomes a gas.
Classifying *Why is the change in the iodine classified as a physical change?*

Iodine gas

Solid iodine

Table sugar

Aluminum

FIGURE 16
Change in Form
Crushing aluminum soda cans doesn't change the aluminum into another metal (left). When table sugar dissolves in a glass of water, it is still sugar (right).

FIGURE 17
Four examples of chemical change are listed in the table.
Interpreting Photographs *What fuel is undergoing combustion in the photograph?*

Chemical Change

A second kind of change occurs when a substance is transformed into a different substance. A change in matter that produces one or more new substances is a **chemical change,** or a chemical reaction. In some chemical changes, a single substance simply changes to one or more other substances. For example, when hydrogen peroxide is poured on a cut on your skin, it breaks down into water and oxygen gas.

In other chemical changes, two or more substances combine to form different substances. For example, iron metal combines with oxygen from the air to form the substance iron oxide, which you call rust. **Unlike a physical change, a chemical change produces new substances with properties different from those of the original substances.**

Examples of Chemical Change One familiar chemical change is the burning of natural gas on a gas stove. Natural gas is mostly the compound methane, CH_4. When it burns, methane combines with oxygen in the air and forms new substances. These new substances include carbon dioxide gas, CO_2, and water vapor, H_2O, which mix with air and are carried away. Both of these new substances can be identified by their properties, which are different from those of the methane. The chemical change that occurs when fuels such as natural gas, wood, candle wax, and gasoline burn in air is called combustion. Other processes that result in chemical change include electrolysis, oxidation, and tarnishing. The table in Figure 17 describes each of these kinds of chemical changes.

Combustion

Tarnished brass

Examples of Chemical Change		
Chemical Change	**Description**	**Example**
Combustion	Rapid combination of a fuel with oxygen; produces heat, light, and new substances	Gas, oil, or coal burning in a furnace
Electrolysis	Use of electricity to break a compound into elements or simpler compounds	Breaking down water into hydrogen and oxygen
Oxidation	Slow combination of a substance with oxygen	Rusting of an iron fence
Tarnishing	Slow combination of a bright metal with sulfur or another substance, producing a dark coating on the metal	Tarnishing of brass

Conservation of Mass A candle may seem to "go away" when it is burned, or water may seem to "disappear" when it changes to a gas. However, scientists long ago proved otherwise. In the 1770s, a French chemist, Antoine Lavoisier, carried out experiments in which he made accurate measurements of mass both before and after a chemical change. His data showed that no mass was lost or gained during the change. The fact that matter is not created or destroyed in any chemical or physical change is called the **law of conservation of mass.** Remember that mass measures the amount of matter. So, this law is sometimes called the law of conservation of matter.

Suppose you could collect all the carbon dioxide and water produced when methane burns, and you measured the mass of all of this matter. You would find that it equaled the mass of the original methane plus the mass of the oxygen that was used in the burning. No mass is lost, because during a chemical change, atoms are not lost or gained, only rearranged. A model for this reaction is shown in Figure 19.

 **Reading Checkpoint** Why is combustion classified as a chemical change?

Go Online
active.art

For: Conserving Matter activity
Visit: PHSchool.com
Web Code: cgp-1013

FIGURE 18
Using Methane
Natural gas, or methane, is the fuel used in many kitchen ranges. When it burns, no mass is lost.

FIGURE 19
Conserving Matter
The idea of atoms explains the law of conservation of matter. For every molecule of methane that burns, two molecules of oxygen are used. The atoms are rearranged in the reaction, but they do not disappear.

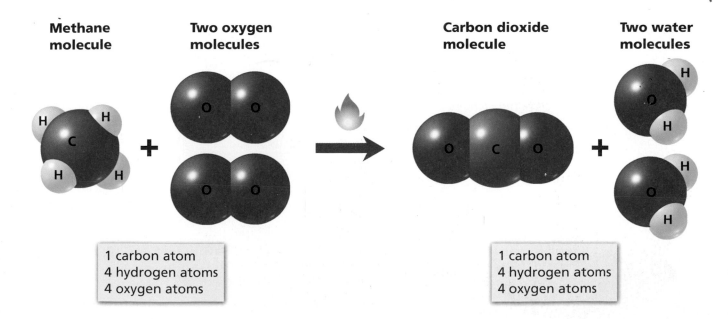

| Methane molecule | Two oxygen molecules | Carbon dioxide molecule | Two water molecules |

1 carbon atom
4 hydrogen atoms
4 oxygen atoms

1 carbon atom
4 hydrogen atoms
4 oxygen atoms

FIGURE 20
Flow of Thermal Energy
Thermal energy from a hot cup of cocoa can warm cold hands on a chilly day.
Developing Hypotheses *How will the flow of thermal energy affect the cocoa?*

Matter and Thermal Energy

Do you feel as if you are full of energy today? **Energy** is the ability to do work or cause change. **Every chemical or physical change in matter includes a change in energy.** A change as simple as bending a paper clip takes energy. When ice changes to liquid water, it absorbs energy from the surrounding matter. When candle wax burns, it gives off energy.

Temperature and Thermal Energy Think of how it feels when you walk inside an air-conditioned building from the outdoors on a hot day. Whew! Did you exclaim about the change in temperature? **Temperature** is a measure of the average energy of random motion of particles of matter. The particles of gas in the warm outside air have greater average energy of motion than the particles of air in the cool building.

   Thermal energy is the total energy of all of the particles in an object. Most often, you experience thermal energy when you describe matter—such as the air in a room—as feeling hot or cold. Temperature and thermal energy are not the same thing, but temperature is related to the amount of thermal energy an object has. Thermal energy always flows from warmer matter to cooler matter.

Thermal Energy and Changes in Matter When matter changes, the most common form of energy released or absorbed is thermal energy. For example, ice absorbs thermal energy from its surroundings when it melts. That's why you can pack food and drinks in an ice-filled picnic cooler to keep them cold. The melting of ice is an **endothermic change,** a change in which energy is taken in. Changes in matter can also occur when energy is given off. An **exothermic change** releases energy. Combustion is a chemical change that releases energy in the form of heat and light. You've taken advantage of an exothermic change if you've ever warmed your hands near a wood fire.

FIGURE 21
An Endothermic Change
An iceberg melting in the ocean absorbs thermal energy from the surrounding water.

Math ▸ Analyzing Data

Comparing Energy Changes

A student observes two different chemical reactions, one in beaker A and the other in beaker B. The student measures the temperature of each reaction every minute. The student then plots the time and temperature data and creates the following graph.

1. **Reading Graphs** What do the numbers on the *x*-axis tell you about the length of the experiment?

2. **Comparing and Contrasting** How did the change in temperature in beaker B differ from that in beaker A?

3. **Interpreting Data** Which reaction is exothermic? Explain your reasoning.

4. **Calculating** Which reaction results in a greater change in temperature over time?

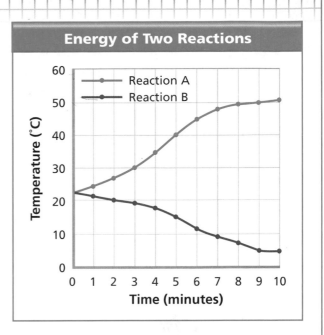

Energy of Two Reactions

Section 3 Assessment

⟳ Target Reading Skill

Relating Cause and Effect Refer to your graphic organizer about chemical change to help you answer Question 2 below.

Reviewing Key Concepts

1. **a. Listing** Identify three different kinds of physical change that could happen to a plastic spoon.
   b. Making Judgments Which of the following processes is not a physical change: drying wet clothes, cutting snowflakes out of paper, lighting a match from a matchbook?

2. **a. Defining** What evidence would you look for to determine whether a chemical change has occurred?
   b. Applying Concepts Why is the electrolysis of water classified as a chemical change but the freezing of water is not?

   c. Problem Solving Explain why the mass of a rusted nail would be greater than the mass of the nail before it rusted. Assume that all the rust is still attached to the nail. (*Hint:* The nail rusts when exposed to the air.)

3. **a. Reviewing** What is thermal energy?
   b. Explaining How can you tell whether one glass of water has more thermal energy than another, identical glass of water?
   c. Inferring How might you cause an endothermic chemical change to begin and keep going?

Writing in Science

Persuasive Letter Write a letter to persuade a friend that a change in temperature does not necessarily mean that a chemical change has occurred.

Transporting Hazardous Chemicals

Each year, millions of tons of hazardous substances criss-cross the country by truck and rail. These substances can be poisonous, flammable, and even explosive. The chemical industry tries to make the transport of hazardous substances safe, and problems are rare. But when spills do happen, these compounds can damage the environment and threaten human lives. How can hazardous substances be transported safely?

Why Do People Transport Hazardous Substances?

Useful products are made from the hazardous materials that trucks and trains carry. For example, CDs are made from plastics. To produce plastics, manufacturers use compounds such as benzene and styrene. Benzene fumes are poisonous and flammable. Styrene can explode when exposed to air. Public health experts say it is important to find safe substitutes for dangerous substances. But finding alternatives is difficult and expensive.

What Are the Risks?

Since 2000, the number of accidents in the United States involving hazardous chemical releases has dropped steadily from more than 350 to less than 20 in 2003. Still, public health experts say that some substances are too hazardous to transport on roads and railroads. An accidental release near a city could harm many people.

Some people say that vehicles carrying hazardous substances should be restricted to isolated roads. However, many factories that use the chemical compounds are located in cities. Chemicals often must be transported from where they are made to where they are used. For example, trucks and trains must transport gasoline to every neighborhood and region of the country.

Gasoline (or the crude oil from which it is made) may be transported great distances before reaching a local gas station. ▶

Gas pump

Truck

Storage tank

Train

Oil tanker

Oil rig

FLAMMABLE
3

How Should Transportation Be Regulated?

Manufacturers that use hazardous chemicals say that there already are adequate laws. The Hazardous Materials Transportation Act (1975, revised in 1994) requires carriers of hazardous substances to follow strict labeling and packaging rules. They must keep records of what they carry and where they travel. Local emergency officials in communities near transportation routes must also be trained to handle accidents involving these substances.

On the other hand, public health experts say there are not enough inspectors to check all trucks and trains and make sure rules are followed. But hiring more inspectors would cost additional tax money.

You Decide

1. Identify the Problem
In your own words, explain the problem of safely transporting hazardous substances.

2. Analyze the Options
Examine the pros and cons of greater regulation of the transport of hazardous substances. In each position, consider the effects on chemical industries and on the public.

3. Find a Solution
You are the emergency planning director in your city. Create regulations for transporting hazardous substances through your community.

Go Online
PHSchool.com

For: More on transporting hazardous chemicals
Visit: PHSchool.com
Web Code: cgh-1010

Energy and Matter

Reading Preview

Key Concepts
- What are some forms of energy that are related to changes in matter?
- How is chemical energy related to chemical change?

Key Terms
- kinetic energy
- potential energy
- chemical energy
- electromagnetic energy
- electrical energy • electrode

Target Reading Skill

Identifying Main Ideas As you read Forms of Energy, write the main idea in a graphic organizer like the one below. Then write three supporting details that give examples of the main idea.

Main Idea

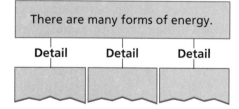

There are many forms of energy.

Detail	**Detail**	**Detail**

 Discover **Activity**

Where Was the Energy?

1. Add about 20 mL of tap water to an empty soda can. Measure the temperature of the water with a thermometer. (*Hint:* Tilt the can about 45 degrees to cover the bulb of the thermometer with water.)
2. Bend a paper clip into the shape shown in the photograph.
3. Stick a small ball of modeling clay into the center of an aluminum pie pan. Then stick the straight end of the paper clip into the ball.
4. Place one mini marshmallow on the flat surface formed by the top of the paper clip. Light the marshmallow with a match.
5. Use tongs to hold the can about 2 cm over the burning marshmallow until the flame goes out.
6. Measure the water temperature.

Think It Over

Drawing Conclusions How can you account for any change in the water's temperature? What evidence of a chemical change did you observe? What forms of energy were released when the marshmallow burned? Where did the energy come from?

Like matter, energy is never created or destroyed in chemical reactions. Energy can only be transformed—that is, changed from one form to another.

Forms of Energy

How do you know when something has energy? You would probably say that a basketball flying toward the hoop has energy because it is moving, and you'd be right. You can be sure that the player who threw the ball also has energy. Maybe you would mention light and heat from a burning candle. Again you would be right.

Energy is all around you, and it comes in many forms. **Forms of energy related to changes in matter may include kinetic, potential, chemical, electromagnetic, electrical, and thermal energy.**

Near the top of the track, the slow-moving car has more potential energy than kinetic energy.

FIGURE 22
Energy Changes
The thrills of a roller coaster ride start with the transformation of potential energy into kinetic energy. **Applying Concepts** *Where did the potential energy of the car come from?*

The car's kinetic energy increases as it gains speed on the downward track.

Kinetic Energy and Potential Energy In Section 3, you learned that energy is the ability to do work or cause change. All matter has energy of at least one form. **Kinetic energy** is the energy of matter in motion. A rolling bowling ball has kinetic energy and can do work by knocking down bowling pins. If you drop the bowling ball on your toe, you'll experience the work done by the kinetic energy of the falling ball. Even though you can't see them, the smallest particles of matter have kinetic energy because they are in constant, random motion. Recall from Section 3 that the kinetic energy of particles contributes to the thermal energy of a substance.

Suppose you push your bike to the top of a hill. That action takes energy, doesn't it? But the energy isn't wasted. In a way, it is now stored in you and in the bike. This stored energy will change to kinetic energy as you enjoy an exciting coast back down the hill. As you went up the hill, you increased the potential energy of both you and the bike. **Potential energy** is the energy an object has because of its position. When a diver climbs up to a diving board, she increases her potential energy. When you stretch a rubber band, your action gives potential energy to the rubber band to snap back and do work.

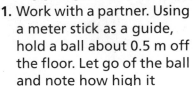

Chemical Energy The internal energy stored in the chemical bonds between atoms is a form of potential energy that is sometimes called **chemical energy**. When a chemical change occurs, these bonds are broken and new bonds are formed. If the change is exothermic, some of the chemical energy is transformed and released in a variety of other forms. As you read in Section 3, one of those forms is often thermal energy.

Electromagnetic Energy You probably know that energy reaches Earth in the form of sunlight. Energy from the sun can increase the temperature of the surface of a sidewalk or change your skin by burning it. Visible light is one example of **electromagnetic energy,** a form of energy that travels through space as waves. Radio waves, infrared "rays" from heat lamps, the waves that heat food in a microwave oven, ultraviolet rays, and X-rays are other types of electromagnetic energy.

Chemical changes can give off electromagnetic energy, such as the light from a wood fire. Also, both chemical and physical changes in matter may be *caused* by electromagnetic energy. For example, a microwave oven can change a frozen block of spaghetti and sauce into a hot meal—a physical change.

Electrical Energy Recall from Section 1 that an atom consists of a positively charged nucleus surrounded by a negatively charged cloud. This "cloud" symbolizes moving, negatively charged particles called electrons. **Electrical energy** is the energy of electrically charged particles moving from one place to another. Electrons move from one atom to another in many chemical changes.

Electrolysis—a chemical change you first read about in Section 3—involves electrical energy. In electrolysis, two metal strips called **electrodes** are placed in a solution, but the electrodes do not touch. Each electrode is attached to a wire. The wires are connected to a source of electrical energy, such as a battery. When the energy begins to flow, atoms of one kind lose electrons at one electrode in the solution. At the other electrode, atoms of a different kind gain electrons. New substances form as a result.

FIGURE 23
Electrolysis of Water
Electrical energy can be used to break down water, H_2O, into its elements. Bubbles of oxygen gas and hydrogen gas form at separate electrodes.
Drawing Conclusions *Why is the volume of hydrogen formed twice that of oxygen?*

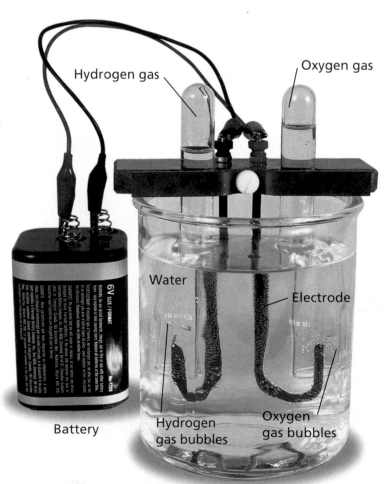

Hydrogen gas

Oxygen gas

Water

Electrode

Battery

Hydrogen gas bubbles

Oxygen gas bubbles

 **Reading Checkpoint** **Where is chemical energy stored?**

Transforming Energy

The burning of a fuel is a chemical change that transforms chemical energy and releases it as thermal energy and electromagnetic energy. When you push a bike (and yourself) up a hill, chemical energy from foods you ate is transformed into the kinetic energy of your moving muscles. Similarly, other forms of energy can be transformed, or changed, *into* chemical energy. **During a chemical change, chemical energy may be changed to other forms of energy. Other forms of energy may also be changed to chemical energy.**

One of the most important energy transformations on Earth that involves chemical energy is photosynthesis. During photosynthesis, plants transform electromagnetic energy from the sun into chemical energy as they make molecules of sugar. These plants, along with animals and other living things that eat plants, transform this chemical energy once again. It becomes the energy needed to carry out life activities. The carrots you have for dinner may supply the energy you need to go for a walk or read this book.

FIGURE 24
Photosynthesis
Photosynthesis is a series of chemical changes in which plants convert electromagnetic energy from the sun into chemical energy.

 Reading Checkpoint **What type of energy transformation occurs during photosynthesis?**

Section 4 Assessment

Target Reading Skill Identifying Main Ideas Use your graphic organizer to help you answer Question 1 below.

Reviewing Key Concepts

1. **a. Listing** What are six forms of energy related to changes in matter?
   b. Classifying Which form of energy is represented by a book lying on a desk? Which form of energy is represented by a book falling off a desk?
   c. Making Generalizations What happens to energy when matter undergoes a chemical or physical change?

2. **a. Reviewing** What happens to chemical energy during a chemical change?
   b. Relating Cause and Effect What are the two main forms of energy given off when paper burns, and where does the energy come from?
   c. Sequencing Describe the energy changes that link sunshine to your ability to turn a page in this book.

Lab zone At-Home Activity

Tracking Energy Changes
Volunteer to help cook a meal for your family. As you work, point out energy transformations, especially those that involve chemical energy. Explain to a family member what chemical energy is and what other forms of energy it can be changed into. Talk about energy sources for cooking and other tools and appliances used to prepare food. Try to identify foods that change chemically when they are cooked.

Isolating Copper by Electrolysis

Problem

How can electrical energy be used to isolate copper metal?

Skills Focus

making models, inferring, observing, interpreting data

Materials

- glass jar, about 250 mL
- two metal paper clips • 6-volt battery
- index card
- wires with alligator clips or a battery holder with wires
- copper chloride solution (0.6 *M*), 100 mL

Procedure

1. Unbend a paper clip and make a hook shape as shown in the diagram. Push the long end through an index card until the hook just touches the card.

2. Repeat Step 1 with another paper clip so that the paper clips are about 3 cm apart. The paper clips serve as your electrodes.

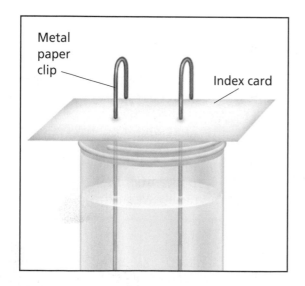

Metal paper clip

Index card

3. Pour enough copper chloride solution into a jar to cover at least half the length of the paper clips when the index card is set on top of the jar. **CAUTION:** *Copper chloride solution can be irritating to the skin and eyes. Do not touch it with your hands or get it into your mouth. The solution can stain skin and clothes.*

4. Place the index card on top of the jar. If the straightened ends of the paper clips are not at least half covered by the copper chloride solution, add more solution.

5. Attach a wire to one pole of a battery. Attach a second wire to the other pole. Attach each of the other ends of the wires to a separate paper clip, as shown in the diagram. Do not allow the paper clips to touch one another.

6. Predict what you think will happen if you allow the setup to run for 2 to 3 minutes. (*Hint:* What elements are present in the copper chloride solution?)

7. Let the setup run for 2 to 3 minutes or until you see a deposit forming on one of the electrodes. Also look for bubbles.

8. Disconnect the wires from both the battery and the paper clips. Bring your face close to the jar and gently wave your hand toward your nose. Note any odor.

9. Note whether the color of the solution has changed since you began the procedure.

10. Note the color of the ends of the electrodes.

11. Discard the solution as directed by your teacher, and wash your hands.

Analyze and Conclude

1. **Making Models** Make a labeled diagram of your laboratory setup. Indicate which electrode is connected to the positive (+) side of the battery and which is connected to the negative (−) side.

2. **Inferring** Based on your observations, what substances do you think were produced at the electrodes? On which electrode was each substance produced? Recall that one of the substances was a solid you could see and the other was a gas you could smell.

3. **Observing** Compare the properties of the substances produced to those of the copper chloride in solution.

4. **Interpreting Data** If the color of the solution changed, how can you explain the change?

5. **Inferring** Based on your observations, does electrolysis produce a chemical change? Explain your reasoning.

6. **Communicating** Write a paragraph describing what you think happened to the copper chloride solution as the electric current flowed through it.

Design an Experiment

What do you think would happen if you switched the connections to the battery without disturbing the rest of the equipment? Design an experiment to answer this question. *Obtain your teacher's permission before carrying out your investigation.*

① Describing Matter

Key Concepts

- Every form of matter has two kinds of properties—physical properties and chemical properties.

- Elements are the simplest substances.

- When elements are chemically combined, they form compounds having properties that are different from those of the uncombined elements.

- Each substance in a mixture keeps its individual properties. Also, the parts of a mixture are not combined in a set ratio.

Key Terms

matter	compound
chemistry	chemical formula
substance	mixture
physical property	heterogeneous
chemical property	mixture
element	homogeneous
atom	mixture
chemical bond	solution
molecule	

② Measuring Matter

Key Concepts

- Unlike weight, mass does not change with location, even when the force of gravity on an object changes.

- Common units of volume include the liter (L), milliliter (mL), and cubic centimeter (cm³).

- Volume = Length × Width × Height

- You can determine the density of a sample of matter by dividing its mass by its volume.

$$\text{Density} = \frac{\text{Mass}}{\text{Volume}}$$

Key Terms

weight
mass
International System of Units
volume
density

③ Changes in Matter

Key Concepts

- A substance that undergoes a physical change is still the same substance after the change.

- Unlike a physical change, a chemical change produces new substances with properties different from those of the original substances.

- Every chemical or physical change in matter includes a change in energy.

Key Terms

physical change
chemical change
law of conservation of mass
energy
temperature
thermal energy
endothermic change
exothermic change

④ Energy and Matter

Key Concepts

- Forms of energy related to changes in matter include kinetic, potential, chemical, electromagnetic, electrical, and thermal energy.

- During a chemical change, chemical energy may be changed to other forms of energy. Other forms of energy may also be changed to chemical energy.

Key Terms

kinetic energy	electromagnetic
potential energy	energy
chemical energy	electrical energy
	electrode

Review and Assessment

Organizing Information

Concept Mapping Copy the concept map about matter onto a separate sheet of paper. Then complete the map by adding in the correct missing words or phrases. (For more on Concept Mapping, see the Skills Handbook.)

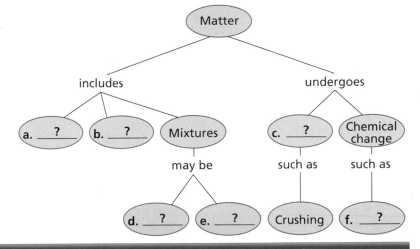

Reviewing Key Terms

Choose the letter of the best answer.

1. The ability to dissolve in water and to conduct electricity are examples of
   a. physical properties.
   b. chemical changes.
   c. chemical properties.
   d. chemical bonding.

2. Water is an example of
   a. an element.
   b. a homogeneous mixture.
   c. a compound.
   d. a heterogeneous mixture.

3. Density relates the mass of a material to the material's
   a. temperature.   **b.** volume.
   c. weight.   **d.** length.

4. New substances are always formed when matter undergoes a
   a. change in shape.
   b. physical change.
   c. change in temperature.
   d. chemical change.

5. Chemical energy is the potential energy of
   a. temperature.
   b. bonds between atoms.
   c. electricity.
   d. light.

If the statement is true, write *true*. If it is false, change the underlined word or words to make the statement true.

6. <u>Energy</u> is anything that has mass and takes up space.

7. A <u>mixture</u> is made of two or more elements that are chemically combined.

8. The <u>weight</u> of an object changes if the force of gravity changes.

9. Energy is taken in during an <u>exothermic</u> change.

10. Light is an example of <u>electromagnetic</u> energy.

Writing in Science

How-to Paragraph Suppose you are preparing for a long journey on the ocean or in space. Write a journal entry that describes your plan for having fresh, drinkable water throughout your entire trip.

Introduction to Matter
Video Preview
Video Field Trip
▶ Video Assessment

Review and Assessment

Checking Concepts

11. What are three ways that compounds and mixtures differ?

12. What two quantities do you need to measure in order to determine the density of an object?

13. What can you infer about the density of a material if a sample of it floats in water?

14. How do you know that the burning of candle wax is an exothermic change?

15. What is kinetic energy? Give an example of a use of kinetic energy that you saw today.

Thinking Critically

16. **Classifying** Which of the following is a solution: pure water, fruit punch, cereal and milk in a bowl? Explain how you know.

17. **Making Judgments** Which measurement shown in the diagram is not needed to find the volume of the box? Explain.

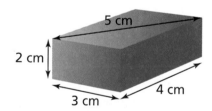

18. **Inferring** Ice has a lower density than liquid water. How does the volume of a kilogram of water change when it freezes to ice?

19. **Problem Solving** Suppose you dissolve some table salt in a glass of water. How could you prove to someone that the dissolving was a physical change, not a chemical change?

Math Practice

20. **Ratios** The elements phosphorus and oxygen form a compound with the formula P_2O_5. What is the ratio of phosphorus atoms to oxygen atoms in the compound?

21. **Calculating Density** A piece of magnesium metal has a mass of 56.5 g and a volume of 32.5 cm^3. What is the density of the magnesium?

Applying Skills

Use the information and the diagrams below to answer Questions 22–25. Some questions may have more than one answer.

Each diagram below represents a different kind of matter. Each ball represents an atom. Balls of the same color represent the same kind of atom.

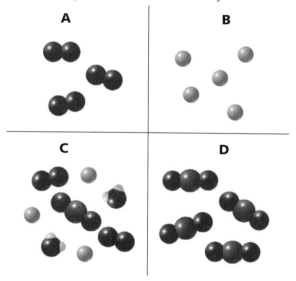

22. **Interpreting Diagrams** Which diagrams represent a single element? Explain.

23. **Classifying** Which diagrams represent pure substances? Explain.

24. **Interpreting Data** How do the molecules in diagram A differ from those in diagram D?

25. **Interpreting Diagrams** Which diagram represents a mixture? Explain.

Lab zone Chapter **Project**

Performance Assessment Present a brief summary of your experience with building your density-calculating system. Describe the most difficult part of construction. What steps were easiest? Defend the accuracy and reliability of your system, and describe its limitations.

Standardized Test Prep

Choose the letter of the best answer.
A scientist did an experiment, described by the words and symbols below, to demonstrate the law of conservation of mass. Use the information and your knowledge of science to answer Questions 1 to 2.

hydrogen + oxygen → water + energy

1. The scientist found that 2 grams of hydrogen reacted completely with 16 grams of oxygen. What was the total mass of water produced?
   A 8 grams   B 14 grams
   C 18 grams   D 32 grams

2. Which pair of terms best describes the type of change that occurred in the reaction?
   F chemical and exothermic
   G chemical and endothermic
   H physical and exothermic
   J physical and endothermic

3. What is the best title for the chart below?

?	
Helium	Colorless; less dense than air
Iron	Attracted to a magnet; melting point of 1,535°C
Oxygen	Odorless; gas at room temperature

   A The Periodic Table of the Elements
   B Gases Found in Air
   C Chemical Properties of Some Compounds
   D Physical Properties of Some Elements

4. Which diagram best represents a mixture of two kinds of gas molecules?

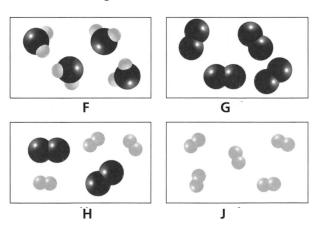

5. The density of a substance equals its mass divided by its volume. The density of sulfur is 2.0 g/cm^3. What is the mass of a sample of sulfur that has a volume of 6.0 cm^3?
   A 3.0 g   B 4.0 g
   C 8.0 g   D 12 g

Constructed Response

6. Describe three forms of energy related to changes in matter and provide an example of each.

interactive Textbook

This Japanese macaque soaks in a hot spring. In and around the spring, water exists as a liquid, solid, and gas.

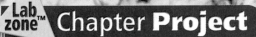
Chapter **Project**

A Story of Changes in Matter

In this chapter, you will learn how particles of matter change from a solid to a liquid to a gas. As you read this chapter, you will build a model that shows these changes.

Your Goal To create a skit or cartoon that demonstrates how particles of matter behave as they change from a solid to a liquid to a gas and then from a gas to a liquid to a solid

To complete the project, you must

● describe what happens to the particles during each change of state

● outline your skit or cartoon in a storyboard format

● illustrate your cartoon or produce your skit

Plan It! With a group of classmates, brainstorm a list of the properties of solids, liquids, and gases. You'll be working on this project as you study this chapter. When you finish Section 2, describe the particles in solids, liquids, and gases, and begin preparing a storyboard. Add information when you finish Section 3, and complete your cartoon or skit at the end of the chapter. Finally, present your completed skit or cartoon to the class.

States of Matter

Reading Preview

Key Concepts
- What are the characteristics of a solid?
- What are the characteristics of a liquid?
- What are the characteristics of a gas?

Key Terms
- solid • crystalline solid
- amorphous solid • liquid
- fluid • surface tension
- viscosity • gas

Target Reading Skill
Building Vocabulary A definition states the meaning of a word or phrase by telling about its most important feature or function. After you read the section, reread the paragraphs that contain definitions of Key Terms. Use all the information you have learned to write a definition of each Key Term in your own words.

Lab zone Discover **Activity**

What Are Solids, Liquids, and Gases?

1. Break an antacid tablet (fizzing type) into three or four pieces. Place them inside a large, uninflated balloon.
2. Fill a 1-liter plastic bottle about halfway with water. Stretch the mouth of the balloon over the top of the bottle, taking care to keep the tablet pieces inside the balloon.
3. Jiggle the balloon so that the pieces fall into the bottle. Observe what happens for about two minutes.
4. Remove the balloon and examine its contents.

Think It Over
Forming Operational Definitions Identify examples of the different states of matter—solids, liquids, and gases—that you observed in this activity. Define each of the three states in your own words.

It's a bitter cold January afternoon. You are practicing ice hockey moves on a frozen pond. Relaxing later, you close your eyes and recall the pond in July, when you and your friends jumped into the refreshing water on a scorching hot day. Was the water in July made of the same water you skated on this afternoon? Perhaps, but you're absolutely certain that solid water and liquid water do not look or feel the same. Just imagine trying to swim in an ice-covered pond in January or play hockey on liquid water in July!

FIGURE 1
A Wintry Solid
As a solid, water makes a great surface for ice hockey.
Observing *What useful property does the frozen water have here?*

Your everyday world is full of substances that can be classified as solids, liquids, or gases. (You will read about a less familiar form of matter, called plasma, in a later chapter.) Solids, liquids, and gases may be elements, compounds, or mixtures. Gold is an element. Water is a compound you've seen as both a solid and a liquid. Air is a mixture of gases. Although it's easy to list examples of these three states of matter, defining them is more difficult. To define solids, liquids, and gases, you need to examine their properties. The familiar states of matter are defined not by what they are made of but mainly by whether or not they hold their volume and shape.

Solids

What would happen if you were to pick up a solid object, such as a pen or a comb, and move it from place to place around the room? What would you observe? Would the object ever change in size or shape as you moved it? Would a pen become larger if you put it in a bowl? Would a comb become flatter if you placed it on a tabletop? Of course not. A **solid** has a definite shape and a definite volume. If your pen has a cylindrical shape and a volume of 6 cubic centimeters, then it will keep that shape and volume in any position and in any container.

FIGURE 2
Liquid Lava, Solid Rock
Hot, liquid lava flows from a volcano. When it cools to a solid, new rock will be formed.

FIGURE 3
Particle View of a Solid
Particles of a solid vibrate back
and forth but stay in place.

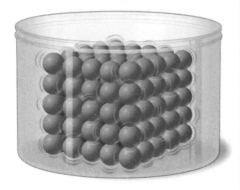

Particles in a Solid The particles that make up a solid are packed very closely together. In addition, each particle is tightly fixed in one position. **This fixed, closely packed arrangement of particles causes a solid to have a definite shape and volume.**

Are the particles in a solid completely motionless? No, not really. The particles vibrate, meaning that they move back and forth slightly. This motion is similar to a group of people running in place. The particles that make up a solid stay in about the same position, but they vibrate in place.

Types of Solids In many solids, the particles form a regular, repeating pattern. These patterns create crystals. Solids that are made up of crystals are called **crystalline solids** (KRIS tuh lin). Salt, sugar, and snow are examples of crystalline solids. When a crystalline solid is heated, it melts at a specific temperature.

In **amorphous solids** (uh MAWR fus), the particles are not arranged in a regular pattern. Plastics, rubber, and glass are amorphous solids. Unlike a crystalline solid, an amorphous solid does not melt at a distinct temperature. Instead, it may become softer and softer or change into other substances.

 **Reading Checkpoint** How do crystalline and amorphous solids differ?

FIGURE 4
Types of Solids
Solids are either crystalline
or amorphous.

 ◀ Quartz is a crystalline solid. Its particles are arranged in a regular pattern.

 ◀ Butter is an amorphous solid. Its particles are not arranged in a regular pattern.

Liquids

A **liquid** has a definite volume but no shape of its own. Without a container, a liquid spreads into a wide, shallow puddle. Like a solid, however, a liquid does have a constant volume. If you gently tried to squeeze a water-filled plastic bag, for example, the water might change shape, but its volume would not decrease or increase. Suppose that you have 100 milliliters of milk in a pitcher. If you pour it into a tall glass, you still have 100 milliliters. The milk has the same volume no matter what shape its container has.

Particles in a Liquid In general, the particles in a liquid are packed almost as closely as in a solid. However, the particles in a liquid move around one another freely. You can compare this movement to the way you might move a group of marbles around in your hand. In this comparison, the solid marbles serve as models for the particles of a liquid. The marbles slide around one another but stay in contact. **Because its particles are free to move, a liquid has no definite shape. However, it does have a definite volume.** These freely moving particles allow a liquid to flow from place to place. For this reason, a liquid is also called a **fluid,** meaning "a substance that flows."

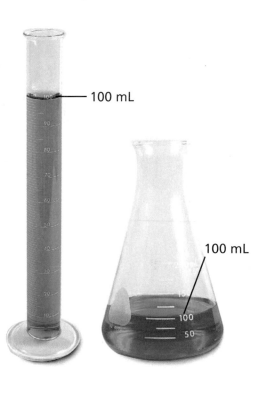

FIGURE 5
Equivalent Volumes
A liquid takes the shape of its container but its volume does not change.

100 mL

100 mL

FIGURE 6
Particle View of a Liquid
Particles in a liquid are packed close together but move freely, allowing liquids to flow.
Comparing and Contrasting *How are liquids and solids alike? How do they differ?*

FIGURE 7
Surface Tension
Water beads up on a leaf due to attractions between the water molecules. Surface tension in water is strong enough to support the weight of an insect.

Lab zone **Try This Activity**

As Thick as Honey

You can compare the viscosity of two liquids.

1. Place on a table a clear plastic jar almost filled with honey and another clear plastic jar almost filled with vegetable oil. Make sure that the tops of both jars are tightly closed.

2. Turn the jars upside down at the same time. Observe what happens.

3. Turn the two jars right-side up and again watch what happens.

Drawing Conclusions Which fluid has a greater viscosity? What evidence leads you to this conclusion?

Properties of Liquids One characteristic property of liquids is surface tension. **Surface tension** is the result of an inward pull among the molecules of a liquid that brings the molecules on the surface closer together. Perhaps you have noticed that water forms droplets and can bead up on many surfaces, such as the leaf shown in Figure 7. That's because water molecules attract one another strongly. These attractions cause molecules at the water's surface to be pulled slightly toward the water molecules beneath the surface.

Due to surface tension, the surface of water can act like a sort of skin. For example, a sewing needle floats when you place it gently on the surface of a glass of water, but it quickly sinks if you push it below the surface. Surface tension enables the water strider in Figure 7 to "walk" on the calm surface of a pond.

Another property of liquids is **viscosity** (vis KAHS uh tee)—a liquid's resistance to flowing. A liquid's viscosity depends on the size and shape of its particles and the attractions between the particles. Some liquids flow more easily than others. Liquids with high viscosity flow slowly. Honey is an example of a liquid with a particularly high viscosity. Liquids with low viscosity flow quickly. Water and vinegar have relatively low viscosities.

 **Reading Checkpoint** What property of liquids causes water to form droplets?

Gases

Like a liquid, a gas is a fluid. Unlike a liquid, however, a **gas** can change volume very easily. If you put a gas in a closed container, the gas particles will either spread apart or be squeezed together as they fill that container. Take a deep breath. Your chest expands, and your lungs fill with air. Air is a mixture of gases that acts as one gas. When you breathe in, air moves from your mouth to your windpipe to your lungs. In each place, the air has a different shape. When you breathe out, the changes happen in reverse.

What about the volume of the air? If you could see the particles that make up a gas, you would see them moving in all directions. The particles are no longer limited by the space in your body, so they move throughout the room. **As they move, gas particles spread apart, filling all the space available. Thus, a gas has neither definite shape nor definite volume.** You will read more about the behavior of gases in Section 3.

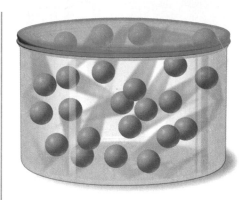

FIGURE 8
Modeling Gas Particles
The particles of a gas can be squeezed into a small volume.
Predicting *What will happen if the container lid is removed?*

 **Reading Checkpoint** How does breathing demonstrate that gases are fluids?

Section 1 Assessment

Target Reading Skill

Building Vocabulary Use your definitions to help answer the questions below.

Reviewing Key Concepts

1. a. Listing What are the general characteristics of solids?
   b. Comparing and Contrasting How do crystalline solids differ from amorphous solids?
   c. Drawing Conclusions A glass blower can bend and shape a piece of glass that has been heated. Is glass a crystalline or an amorphous solid? Explain.
2. a. Describing How may liquids be described in terms of shape and volume?
   b. Explaining How do the positions and movements of particles in a liquid help to explain the shape and volume of the liquid?
   c. Relating Cause and Effect Explain why a sewing needle can float on the surface of water in a glass.

3. a. Reviewing What determines the shape and volume of a gas inside a container?
   b. Applying Concepts Use what you know about the particles in a gas to explain why a gas has no definite shape and no definite volume.

Lab zone At-Home **Activity**

Squeezing Liquids and Gases Show your family how liquids and gases differ. Fill the bulb and cylinder of a turkey baster with water. Seal the end with your finger and hold it over the sink. Have a family member squeeze the bulb. Now empty the turkey baster. Again, seal the end with your finger and have a family member squeeze the bulb. Did the person notice any difference? Use what you know about liquids and gases to explain your observations.

Changes of State

Reading Preview

Key Concepts
- What happens to a substance during changes between solid and liquid?
- What happens to a substance during changes between liquid and gas?
- What happens to a substance during changes between solid and gas?

Key Terms
- melting • melting point
- freezing • vaporization
- evaporation • boiling
- boiling point • condensation
- sublimation

Target Reading Skill

Outlining As you read, make an outline about changes of state. Use the red headings for the main ideas and the blue headings for the supporting ideas.

Changes in State
I. Changes Between Solid and Liquid
A. Melting
B.
II. Changes Between Liquid and Gas

Lab zone **Discover Activity**

What Happens When You Breathe on a Mirror?

1. Obtain a hand mirror. Clean it with a dry cloth. Describe the mirror's surface.
2. Hold the mirror about 15 cm away from your face. Try to breathe against the mirror's surface.
3. Reduce the distance until breathing on the mirror produces a visible change. Record what you observe.

Think It Over
Developing Hypotheses What did you observe when you breathed on the mirror held close to your mouth? How can you explain that observation? Why did you get different results when the mirror was at greater distances from your face?

Picture an ice cream cone on a hot summer day. The ice cream quickly starts to drip onto your hand. You're not surprised. You know that ice cream melts if it's not kept cold. But why does the ice cream melt?

Particles of a substance at a warmer temperature have more thermal energy than particles of that same substance at a cooler temperature. You may recall that thermal energy always flows as heat from a warmer substance to a cooler substance. So, when you take ice cream outside on a hot summer day, it absorbs thermal energy from the air and your hand. The added energy changes the ice cream from a solid to a liquid.

Increased thermal energy turns an ▶ ice cream cone into a gooey mess!

Solid silver   Liquid silver

FIGURE 9
Solid to Liquid
In solid silver, atoms are in a regular, cubic pattern. Atoms in liquid (molten) silver have no regular arrangement.
Applying Concepts *How can a jewelry maker take advantage of changes in the state of silver?*

Changes Between Solid and Liquid

How does the physical state of a substance relate to its thermal energy? Particles of a liquid have more thermal energy than particles of the same substance in solid form. As a gas, the particles of this same substance have even more thermal energy. A substance changes state when its thermal energy increases or decreases sufficiently. A change from solid to liquid involves an increase in thermal energy. As you can guess, a change from liquid to solid is just the opposite: It involves a decrease in thermal energy.

Melting The change in state from a solid to a liquid is called **melting.** In most pure substances, melting occurs at a specific temperature, called the **melting point.** Because melting point is a characteristic property of a substance, chemists often compare melting points when trying to identify an unknown material. The melting point of pure water, for example, is 0°C.

What happens to the particles of a substance as it melts? Think of an ice cube taken from the freezer. The energy to melt the ice comes mostly from the air in the room. At first, the added thermal energy makes the water molecules vibrate faster, raising their temperature. **At its melting point, the particles of a solid substance are vibrating so fast that they break free from their fixed positions.** At 0°C, the temperature of the ice stops increasing. Any added energy continues to change the arrangement of the water molecules from ice crystals into liquid water. The ice melts.

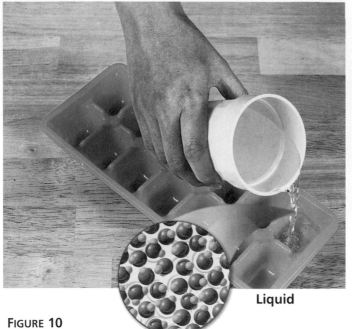

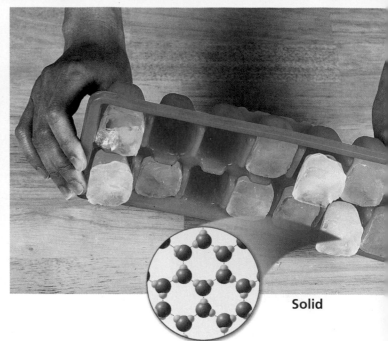

Liquid

Solid

FIGURE 10
Liquid to Solid
Just a few hours in a freezer will change liquid water into a solid.

Freezing The change of state from liquid to solid is called **freezing.** It is just the reverse of melting. **At its freezing temperature, the particles of a liquid are moving so slowly that they begin to form regular patterns.**

When you put liquid water into a freezer, for example, the water loses energy to the cold air in the freezer. The water molecules move more and more slowly as they lose energy. Over time, the water becomes solid ice. When water begins to freeze, its temperature remains at 0°C until freezing is complete. The freezing point of water, 0°C, is the same as its melting point.

> **Reading Checkpoint** What happens to the particles of a liquid as they lose more and more energy?

Changes Between Liquid and Gas

Have you ever wondered how clouds form, or why rain falls from clouds? And why do puddles dry up after a rain shower? To answer these questions, you need to look at what happens when changes occur between the liquid and gas states.

The change from a liquid to a gas is called **vaporization** (vay puhr ih ZAY shun). **Vaporization takes place when the particles in a liquid gain enough energy to form a gas.** There are two main types of vaporization—evaporation and boiling.

Evaporation Vaporization that takes place only on the surface of a liquid is called **evaporation** (ee vap uh RAY shun). A shrinking puddle is an example. Water in the puddle gains energy from the ground, the air, or the sun. The added energy enables some of the water molecules on the surface of the puddle to escape into the air, or evaporate.

Boiling Another kind of vaporization is called boiling. **Boiling** occurs when a liquid changes to a gas below its surface as well as at the surface. You see the results of this process when the boiling liquid bubbles. The temperature at which a liquid boils is called its **boiling point.** As with melting points, chemists use boiling points to help identify an unknown substance.

Boiling Point and Air Pressure The boiling point of a substance depends on the pressure of the air above it. The lower the pressure, the less energy needed for the particles of the liquid to escape into the air. In places close to sea level, the boiling point of water is 100°C. In the mountains, however, air pressure is lower and so is water's boiling point. In Denver, Colorado, where the elevation is 1,600 meters above sea level, water boils at 95°C.

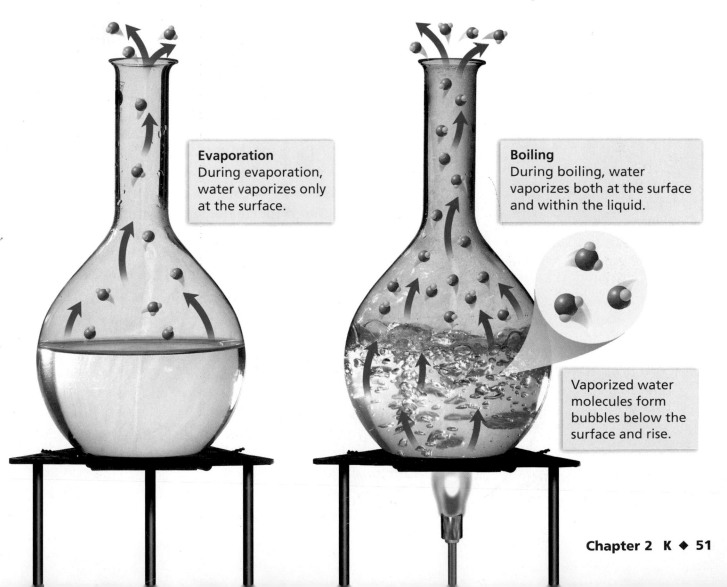

FIGURE 11
Evaporation and Boiling
Liquids can vaporize in two ways.
Interpreting Diagrams *How do these processes differ?*

Evaporation
During evaporation, water vaporizes only at the surface.

Boiling
During boiling, water vaporizes both at the surface and within the liquid.

Vaporized water molecules form bubbles below the surface and rise.

Temperature and Changes of State

A beaker of ice at −10°C was slowly heated to 110°C. The changes in the temperature of the water over time were recorded. The data were plotted on the graph shown here.

1. **Reading Graphs** What two variables are plotted on the graph?

2. **Reading Graphs** What is happening to the temperature of the water during segment C of the graph?

3. **Interpreting Data** What does the temperature value for segment B represent? For segment D?

4. **Drawing Conclusions** What change of state is occurring during segment B of the graph? During segment D?

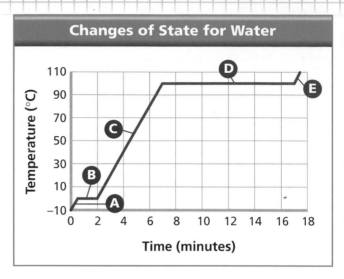

Changes of State for Water

Temperature (°C) vs *Time (minutes)*

5. **Inferring** In which segment, A or E, do the water molecules have more thermal energy? Explain your reasoning.

FIGURE 12
Condensation of Water
Water vapor from a hot shower contacts the cool surface of a bathroom mirror and condenses into a liquid.

Condensation The opposite of vaporization is called **condensation.** One way you can observe condensation is by breathing onto a mirror. When warm water vapor in your breath reaches the cooler surface of the mirror, the water vapor condenses into liquid droplets. **Condensation occurs when particles in a gas lose enough thermal energy to form a liquid.** For example, clouds typically form when water vapor in the atmosphere condenses into liquid droplets. When the droplets get heavy enough, they fall to the ground as rain.

You cannot see water vapor. Water vapor is a colorless gas that is impossible to see. The steam you see above a kettle of boiling water is not water vapor, and neither are clouds or fog. What you see in those cases are tiny droplets of liquid water suspended in air.

 **Reading Checkpoint** How do clouds typically form?

Changes Between Solid and Gas

If you live where the winters are cold, you may have noticed that snow seems to disappear even when the temperature stays well below freezing. This change is the result of sublimation. **Sublimation** occurs when the surface particles of a solid gain enough energy that they form a gas. **During sublimation, particles of a solid do not pass through the liquid state as they form a gas.**

One example of sublimation occurs with dry ice. Dry ice is the common name for solid carbon dioxide. At ordinary atmospheric pressures, carbon dioxide cannot exist as a liquid. So instead of melting, solid carbon dioxide changes directly into a gas. As it changes state, the carbon dioxide absorbs thermal energy. This property helps keep materials near dry ice cold and dry. For this reason, using dry ice is a way to keep temperature low when a refrigerator is not available. When dry ice becomes a gas, it cools water vapor in the nearby air. The water vapor then condenses into a liquid, forming fog around the dry ice.

FIGURE 13
Dry Ice
When solid carbon dioxide, called "dry ice," sublimates, it changes directly into a gas. **Predicting** *If you allowed the dry ice to stand at room temperature for several hours, what would be left in the glass dish? Explain.*

 **Reading Checkpoint** What physical state is skipped during the sublimation of a substance?

Section 2 Assessment

Target Reading Skill Outlining Use the information in your outline about changes of state to help you answer the questions below.

Reviewing Key Concepts

1. a. **Reviewing** What happens to the particles of a solid as it becomes a liquid?
   b. **Applying Concepts** How does the thermal energy of solid water change as it melts?
   c. **Making Judgments** You are stranded in a blizzard. You need water to drink, and you're trying to stay warm. Should you melt snow and then drink it, or just eat snow? Explain.
2. a. **Describing** What is vaporization?
   b. **Comparing and Contrasting** Name the two types of vaporization. Tell how they are similar and how they differ.
   c. **Relating Cause and Effect** Why does the evaporation of sweat cool your body on a warm day?

3. a. **Identifying** What process occurs as pieces of dry ice gradually get smaller?
   b. **Interpreting Photos** What is the fog you see in the air around the dry ice in Figure 13? Why does the fog form?

Writing in Science

Using Analogies Write a short essay in which you create an analogy to describe particle motion. Compare the movements and positions of people dancing with the motions of water molecules in liquid water and in water vapor.

Lab zone Skills Lab

Melting Ice

Problem

How does the temperature of the surroundings affect the rate at which ice melts?

Skills Focus

predicting, interpreting data, inferring

Materials

- stopwatch or timer
- thermometer or temperature probe
- 2 plastic cups, about 200 mL each
- 2 stirring rods, preferably plastic
- ice cubes, about 2 cm on each side
- warm water, about 40°C–45°C
- water at room temperature, about 20°C–25°C

Procedure

1. Read Steps 1–8. Based on your own experience, predict which ice cube will melt faster.

2. In your notebook, make a data table like the one below.

3. Fill a cup halfway with warm water (about 40°C to 45°C). Fill a second cup to the same depth with water at room temperature.

4. ☐ Record the exact temperature of the water in each cup. If you are using a temperature probe, see your teacher for instructions.

5. Obtain two ice cubes that are as close to the same size as possible.

Data Table

Cup	Beginning Temperature (°C)	Time to Melt (s)	Final Temperature (°C)
1			
2			

6. Place one ice cube in each cup. Begin timing with a stopwatch. Gently stir each cup with a stirring rod until the ice has completely melted.

7. Observe both ice cubes carefully. At the moment one of the ice cubes is completely melted, record the time and the temperature of the water in the cup.

8. Wait for the second ice cube to melt. Record its melting time and the water temperature.

Analyze and Conclude

1. **Predicting** Was your prediction in Step 1 supported by the results of the experiment? Explain why or why not.

2. **Interpreting Data** In which cup did the water temperature change the most? Explain.

3. **Inferring** When the ice melted, its molecules gained enough energy to overcome the forces holding them together as solid ice. What is the source of that energy?

4. **Communicating** Write a paragraph describing how errors in measurement could have affected your conclusions in this experiment. Tell what you would do differently if you repeated the procedure. (*Hint:* How well were you able to time the exact moment that each ice cube completely melted?)

Design an Experiment

When a lake freezes in winter, only the top turns to ice. Design an experiment to model the melting of a frozen lake during the spring. *Obtain your teacher's permission before carrying out your investigation.* Be prepared to share your results with the class.

Gas Behavior

Reading Preview

Key Concepts
- What types of measurements are useful when working with gases?
- How are the volume, temperature, and pressure of a gas related?

Key Terms
- pressure
- Boyle's law
- Charles's law

Target Reading Skill
Asking Questions Before you read, preview the red headings. In a graphic organizer like the one below, ask a *what* or *how* question for each heading. As you read, write the answers to your questions.

Gases

Question	Answer
What measurements are useful in studying gases?	Measurements useful in studying gases include . . .

Lab zone **Discover Activity**

How Can Air Keep Chalk From Breaking?

1. Stand on a chair and drop a piece of chalk onto a hard floor. Observe what happens to the chalk.
2. Wrap a second piece of chalk in wax paper or plastic food wrap. Drop the chalk from the same height used in Step 1. Observe the results.
3. Wrap a third piece of chalk in plastic bubble wrap. Drop the chalk from the same height used in Step 1. Observe the results.

Think It Over
Inferring Compare the results from Steps 1, 2, and 3. What properties of the air in the bubble wrap accounted for the results in Step 3?

How do you prepare a hot-air balloon for a morning ride? First, you inflate the balloon, using powerful air fans. Then you heat the air inside with propane gas burners. But the balloon and its cargo won't begin to rise until the warmer air inside is less dense than the air outside the balloon. How does this change occur? How can you keep the balloon floating safely through the atmosphere? How can you make it descend when you are ready to land? To answer these and other questions, you would need to understand the relationships between the temperature, pressure, and volume of a gas.

Before a flight, a hot-air ▶
balloon is filled with air.

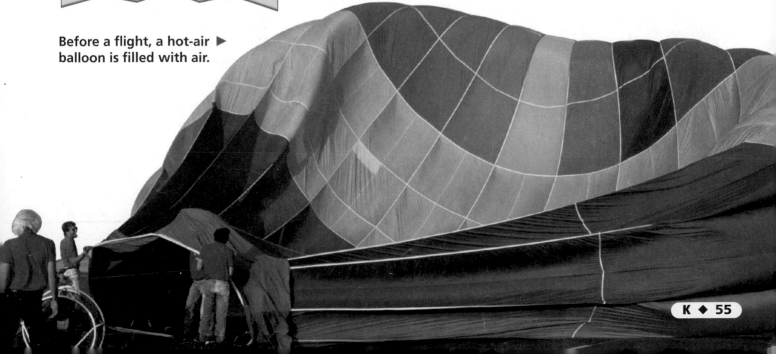

Measuring Gases

How much helium is in the tank in Figure 14? If you don't know the mass of the helium, you may think that measuring the volume of the tank will give you an answer. But gases easily contract or expand. To fill the tank, helium was compressed—or pressed together tightly—to decrease its volume. When you use the helium to fill balloons, it fills a total volume of inflated balloons much greater than the volume of the tank. The actual volume of helium you get, however, depends on the temperature and air pressure that day. **When working with a gas, it is helpful to know its volume, temperature, and pressure.** So what exactly do these measurements mean?

Volume You know that volume is the amount of space that matter fills. Volume is measured in cubic centimeters (cm^3), milliliters (mL), liters (L), and other units. Because gas particles move and fill the space available, the volume of a gas is the same as the volume of its container.

Temperature Hot soup, warm hands, cool breezes—you are familiar with matter at different temperatures. But what does temperature tell you? Recall that the particles within any substance are constantly moving. Temperature is a measure of the average energy of random motion of the particles of a substance. The faster the particles are moving, the greater their energy and the higher the temperature. You might think of a thermometer as a speedometer for molecules.

Even at ordinary temperatures, the average speed of particles in a gas is very fast. At room temperature, or about 20°C, the particles in a typical gas travel about 500 meters per second—more than twice the cruising speed of a jet plane!

FIGURE 14
How Much Helium?
A helium tank the height of this girl can fill over 500 balloons!
Interpreting Photos *How is the helium in the tank different from the helium in the balloons?*

Pressure Gas particles constantly collide with one another and with the walls of their container. As a result, the gas pushes on the walls of the container. The **pressure** of the gas is the force of its outward push divided by the area of the walls of the container. Pressure is measured in units of pascals (Pa) or kilopascals (kPa). (1 kPa = 1,000 Pa.)

$$\text{Pressure} = \frac{\text{Force}}{\text{Area}}$$

The firmness of a gas-filled object comes from the pressure of the gas. For example, the air inside a fully pumped basketball has a higher pressure than the air outside. This higher pressure is due to a greater concentration of gas particles inside the ball than in the surrounding air. (Concentration is the number of particles in a given unit of volume.)

When air leaks out of a basketball, the pressure decreases and the ball becomes softer. Why does a ball leak even when it has a tiny hole? The higher pressure inside the ball results in gas particles hitting the inner surface of the ball more often. Therefore, gas particles inside the ball reach the hole and escape more often than gas particles outside the ball reach the hole and enter. Thus, many more particles go out than in. The pressure inside drops until it is equal to the pressure outside.

 **Reading Checkpoint** What units are used to measure pressure?

Math Skills

Using Formulas
Pressure can be calculated using the formula below. Force is measured in newtons (N). If area is measured in square meters (m^2), pressure is expressed in pascals (Pa).

$$\text{Pressure} = \frac{\text{Force}}{\text{Area}}$$

For example, a machine exerts a force of 252 N on a piston having an area of 0.430 m^2. What is the pressure on the piston in Pa?

$$\text{Pressure} = \frac{252\ \text{N}}{0.430\ \text{m}^2}$$

$$= 586\ \text{Pa}$$

Practice Problem A trash compactor exerts a force of 5,600 N over an area of 0.342 m^2. What pressure does the compactor exert in Pa?

FIGURE 15
A Change in Pressure
A punctured basketball deflates as the gas particles begin to escape.

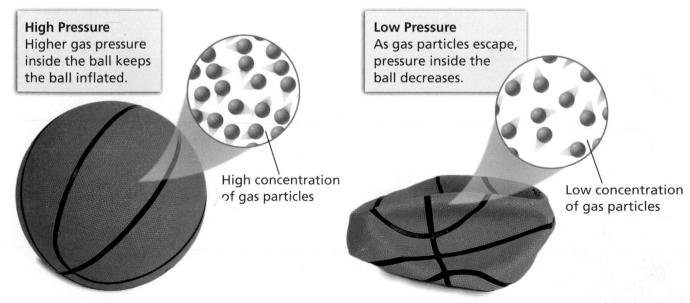

High Pressure
Higher gas pressure inside the ball keeps the ball inflated.

High concentration of gas particles

Low Pressure
As gas particles escape, pressure inside the ball decreases.

Low concentration of gas particles

Pressure and Volume

Suppose you are using a bicycle pump. By pressing down on the plunger, you force the gas inside the pump through the rubber tube and out the nozzle into the tire. What will happen if you close the nozzle and then push down on the plunger?

Boyle's Law The answer to this question comes from experiments done by the scientist Robert Boyle in an effort to improve air pumps. In the 1600s, Boyle measured the volumes of gases at different pressures. **Boyle found that when the pressure of a gas at constant temperature is increased, the volume of the gas decreases. When the pressure is decreased, the volume increases.** This relationship between the pressure and the volume of a gas is called **Boyle's law.**

Boyle's Law in Action Boyle's law plays a role in research using high-altitude balloons. Researchers fill the balloons with only a small fraction of the helium gas that the balloons can hold. As a balloon rises through the atmosphere, the air pressure around it decreases and the balloon expands. If the balloon were fully filled at takeoff, it would burst before it got very high.

Boyle's law also applies to situations in which the *volume* of a gas is changed. Then the *pressure* changes in the opposite way. A bicycle pump works this way. As you push on the plunger, the volume of air inside the pump cylinder gets smaller and the pressure increases, forcing air into the tire.

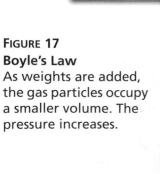

FIGURE 16
Inflating a Tire
A bicycle pump makes use of the relationship between the volume and pressure of a gas.

Reading Checkpoint What could cause a helium balloon to burst as it rises in the atmosphere?

FIGURE 17
Boyle's Law
As weights are added, the gas particles occupy a smaller volume. The pressure increases.

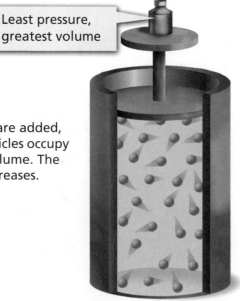

Least pressure, greatest volume

Increasing pressure, decreasing volume

Greatest pressure, least volume

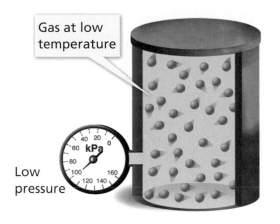

Gas at low temperature

Low pressure

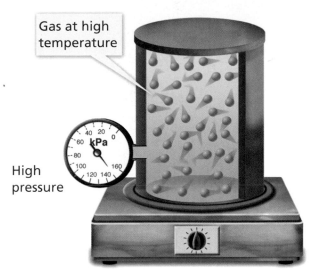

Gas at high temperature

High pressure

FIGURE 18
Gas Pressure and Temperature
When a gas is heated, the particles move faster and collide more often with each other and with the walls of their container. The pressure of the gas increases.

Pressure and Temperature

If you dropped a few grains of sand onto your hand, you would hardly feel them. But what if you were caught in a sandstorm? Ouch! The sand grains fly around very fast, and they would sting if they hit you. The faster the grains travel, the harder they hit your skin.

Although gas particles are much smaller than sand grains, a sandstorm is a good model for gas behavior. Like grains of sand in a sandstorm, gas particles travel individually and at high speeds (but randomly). The faster the gas particles move, the more frequently they collide with the walls of their container and the greater the force of the collisions.

Increasing Temperature Raises Pressure Recall from Section 2 that the higher the temperature of a substance, the faster its particles are moving. Now you can state a relationship between temperature and pressure. **When the temperature of a gas at constant volume is increased, the pressure of the gas increases. When the temperature is decreased, the pressure of the gas decreases.** (*Constant volume* means that the gas is in a closed, rigid container.)

Pressure and Temperature in Action Have you ever looked at the tires of an 18-wheel truck? Because the tires need to support a lot of weight, they are large, heavy, and stiff. The inside volume of these tires doesn't vary much. On long trips, especially in the summer, a truck's tires can become very hot. As the temperature increases, so does the pressure of the air inside the tire. If the pressure becomes greater than the tire can hold, the tire will burst. For this reason, truck drivers need to monitor and adjust tire pressure on long trips.

Go **O**nline
active art

For: Gas Laws activity
Visit: PHSchool.com
Web Code: cgp-1023

DISCOVERY CHANNEL **SCHOOL**™

Solids, Liquids, and Gases

Video Preview
▶ Video Field Trip
Video Assessment

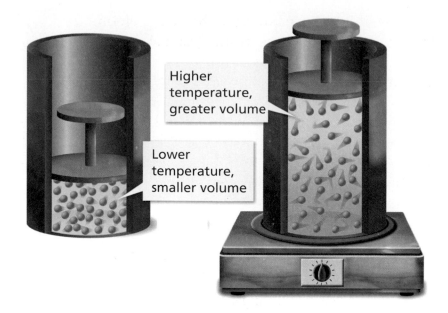

Higher temperature, greater volume

Lower temperature, smaller volume

Charles's Law

Changing the temperature of a gas at constant pressure changes its volume in a similar way.
Inferring *What happens to the gas particles in the balloon as the gas is warmed?*

▲ A gas-filled balloon is at room temperature.

▲ The balloon is lowered into liquid nitrogen at −196°C.

▲ The balloon shrinks as gas volume decreases.

Volume and Temperature

In the late 1700s, French scientist Jacques Charles helped start a new sport. He and others took to the skies in the first hydrogen balloons. Charles's interest in balloon rides led him to discover how gas temperature and volume are related.

Charles's Law Jacques Charles examined the relationship between the temperature and volume of a gas that is kept at a constant pressure. He measured the volume of a gas at various temperatures in a container that could change volume. (A changeable volume allows the pressure to remain constant.) **Charles found that when the temperature of a gas is increased at constant pressure, its volume increases. When the temperature of a gas is decreased at constant pressure, its volume decreases.** This principle is called **Charles's law.**

Charles's Law in Action In Figure 19, you can see the effects of Charles's law demonstrated with a simple party balloon. Time-lapse photos show a balloon as it is slowly lowered into liquid nitrogen at nearly −200°C, then removed. The changes to the balloon's volume result from changes in the temperature of the air inside the balloon. The pressure remains more or less constant because the air is in a flexible container.

▲ When removed from the nitrogen, the gas warms and the balloon expands.

▲ The balloon is at room temperature again.

Now think again about a hot-air balloon. Heating causes the air inside the balloon to expand. Some of the warm air leaves through the bottom opening of the balloon, keeping the pressure constant. But now, the air inside is less dense than the air outside the balloon, so the balloon begins to rise. If the pilot allows the air in the balloon to cool, the reverse happens. The air in the balloon contracts, and more air enters through the opening. The density of the air inside increases, and the balloon starts downward.

Boyle, Charles, and others often described the behavior of gases by focusing on only two factors that vary at a time. In everyday life, however, gases can show the effects of changes in pressure, temperature, and volume all at once. People who work with gases, such as tire manufacturers and balloonists, must consider these combined effects.

FIGURE 20
Hot-Air Balloon
Balloonists often use a propane burner to heat the air in a balloon.

Reading Checkpoint What factor is kept unchanged when demonstrating Charles's law?

Section 3 Assessment

Target Reading Skill Asking Questions Use the answers to the questions you wrote about the headings to help you answer the questions below.

Reviewing Key Concepts

1. **a. Defining** How is gas pressure defined?
   b. Describing Describe how the motions of gas particles are related to the pressure exerted by the gas.
   c. Relating Cause and Effect Why does pumping more air into a basketball increase the pressure inside the ball?
2. **a. Reviewing** How does Boyle's law describe the relationship between gas pressure and volume?
   b. Explaining Explain why increasing the temperature of a gas in a closed, rigid container causes the pressure in the container to increase.

   c. Applying Concepts Suppose it is the night before a big parade, and you are in charge of inflating the parade balloons. You just learned that the temperature will rise 15°C between early morning and the time the parade starts. How will this information affect the way you inflate the balloons?

Math Practice

3. **Using Formulas** Suppose the atmosphere exerts a force of 124,500 N on a kitchen table with an area of 1.5 m². What is the pressure in pascals of the atmosphere on the table?

Graphing Gas Behavior

Reading Preview

Key Concepts
- What type of relationship does the graph for Charles's law show?
- What type of relationship does the graph for Boyle's law show?

Key Terms
- graph
- origin
- directly proportional
- vary inversely

Target Reading Skill
Previewing Visuals Before you read, preview Figure 23. In a graphic organizer like the one below, write questions that you have about the diagram. As you read, answer your questions.

Graphing Charles's Law

Q.	What is the relationship between gas volume and temperature?
A.	
Q.	

Lab zone **Discover Activity**

Can You Graph Gas Behavior?

1. In an experiment, the temperature of a gas at a constant volume was varied. Gas pressure was measured after each 5°C change. Use the data in this table and follow Steps 2–4 to make a graph.
2. Show temperature on the horizontal axis with a scale from 0°C to 25°C. Show pressure on the vertical axis with a scale from 0 kPa to 25 kPa. (1 kPa = 1,000 Pa.)
3. For each pair of measurements, draw a point on the graph.
4. Draw a line to connect the points.

Temperature (°C)	Pressure (kPa)
0	8
5	11
10	14
15	17
20	20
25	23

Think It Over
Drawing Conclusions What happens to the pressure of a gas when the temperature is increased at constant volume?

Graphs are a way to tell a story with data. A **graph** is a diagram that tells how two variables, or factors that change, are related. If you did the activity above, you made a graph that helped you understand how the pressure of a gas changes when its temperature is changed. In this section, you will learn how to make and interpret graphs that relate these and other properties of gases.

A graph consists of a grid set up by two lines, one horizontal and one vertical. Each line, or axis, is divided into equal units. The horizontal axis, or x-axis, shows the manipulated variable. The vertical axis, or y-axis, shows the responding variable. Each axis is labeled with the name of the variable, the unit of measurement, and a range of values.

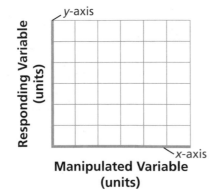

FIGURE 21
Making a Graph
The x-axis (horizontal) and the y-axis (vertical) form the "backbone" of a graph.

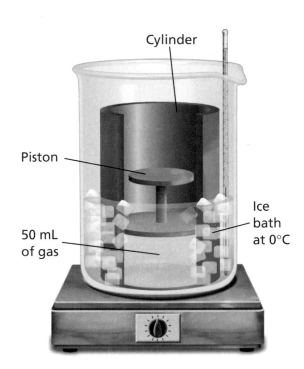

Cylinder

Piston

50 mL
of gas

Ice
bath
at 0°C

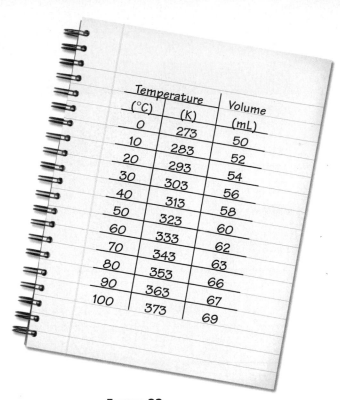

| Temperature | | Volume |
(°C)	(K)	(mL)
0	273	50
10	283	52
20	293	54
30	303	56
40	313	58
50	323	60
60	333	62
70	343	63
80	353	66
90	363	67
100	373	69

FIGURE 22
Temperature and Gas Volume
As the temperature of the water
bath increases, the gas inside the
cylinder is warmed by the water.
The data from the experiment are
recorded in the notebook table.
Calculating *How do you convert
Celsius degrees to kelvins?*

Temperature and Volume

Recall that Charles's law relates the temperature and volume of
a gas that is kept at a constant pressure. You can explore this
relationship by doing an experiment in which you change the
temperature of a gas and measure its volume. Then you can
graph the data you have recorded and interpret the results.

Collecting Data As you can see from the cutaway view in
Figure 22, the gas in the experiment is in a cylinder that has a
movable piston. The piston moves up and down freely, which
allows the gas to change volume and keep the same pressure.
To control the temperature of the gas, the cylinder is placed in
a water bath.

The experiment begins with an ice-water bath at 0°C and
the gas volume at 50 mL. Then the water bath is slowly heated.
Gradually, the temperature increases from 0°C to 100°C. Each
time the temperature increases by 10°C, the volume of the gas
in the cylinder is recorded.

You'll notice a second set of temperatures listed in the table in
Figure 22. Scientists often work with gas temperatures in units
called kelvins. To convert from Celsius degrees to kelvins (K),
add 273. The kelvin temperatures will be used to graph the data.

**Reading
Checkpoint** What units do scientists use to measure gas
temperatures?

Go Online
SC*LINKS* NSTA

For: Links on gases
Visit: www.SciLinks.org
Web Code: scn-1124

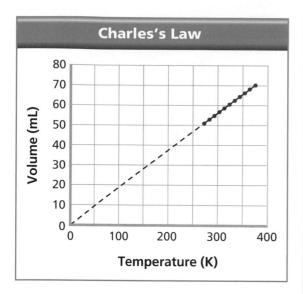

FIGURE 23
Graphing Charles's Law
A graph of the data from Figure 22 shows the relationship known as Charles's law. The dotted line predicts how the graph would look if the gas could be cooled further.

Graphing the Results Look at the graph in Figure 23. It appears as if the line would continue downward if data could be collected for lower temperatures. Such a line would pass through the point (0, 0), called the **origin.** When a graph of two variables is a straight line passing through the origin, the variables are said to be **directly proportional** to each other. **The graph of Charles's law shows that the volume of a gas is directly proportional to its kelvin temperature under constant pressure.**

In reality, the line on the graph cannot be extended as far as the origin. Remember that if a gas is cooled enough, it will condense into a liquid. After that, the volume would no longer change much. However, the line that results from the data represents a relationship that is directly proportional.

Pressure and Volume

A different experiment can show how gas pressure and volume are related when temperature is kept constant. Recall that this relationship is called Boyle's law.

Collecting Data The gas in this experiment is also contained in a cylinder with a movable piston. A gauge indicates the pressure of the gas inside the cylinder. The experiment begins with the volume of the gas at 300 mL. The pressure of the gas is 20 kPa. Next, the piston is pushed into the cylinder, making the gas volume smaller. The pressure of the gas is recorded after each 50-mL change in volume. Temperature remains constant.

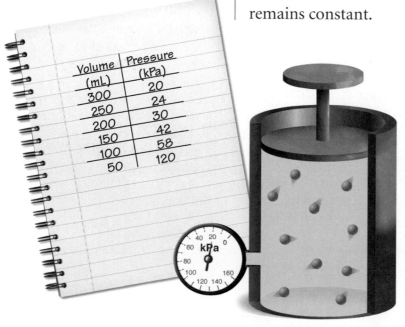

Volume (mL)	Pressure (kPa)
300	20
250	24
200	30
150	42
100	58
50	120

FIGURE 24
Pushing on the top of the piston decreases the volume of the gas. The pressure of the gas increases. The data from the experiment are recorded in the notebook table.
Predicting *What would happen if you pulled up on the piston?*

Graphing the Results In this pressure-volume experiment, the manipulated variable is volume. Volume is shown on the scale of the horizontal axis from 0 mL to 300 mL. The responding variable is pressure. Pressure is shown on the scale of the vertical axis from 0 kPa to 120 kPa.

As you can see in Figure 25, the plotted points lie on a curve. Notice that the curve slopes downward from left to right. Also notice that the curve is steep at lower volumes and becomes less steep as volume increases. When a graph of two variables forms this kind of curve, the variables are said to **vary inversely** with one another. Such a relationship means that when one variable goes up, the other variable goes down in a regular way. **The graph for Boyle's law shows that the pressure of a gas varies inversely with its volume at constant temperature.**

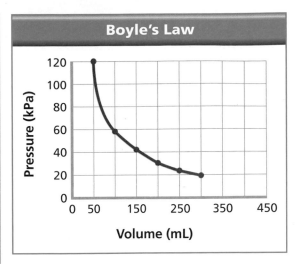

FIGURE 25
This graph of the data from Figure 24 shows the relationship between pressure and volume known as Boyle's law.

 **Reading Checkpoint** **What is the manipulated variable in the pressure-volume experiment?**

Section 4 Assessment

Target Reading Skill **Previewing Visuals** Refer to your questions and answers about Figure 23 to help you answer Question 1 below.

Reviewing Key Concepts

1. a. Classifying What term describes the relationship illustrated by the graph in Figure 23?
 b. Relating Cause and Effect How does the volume of a gas change when its temperature is increased at constant pressure?
 c. Predicting Suppose the temperature of the gas is increased to 400 kelvins (127°C). Use Figure 23 to predict the volume of the gas at this temperature.
2. a. Classifying What is the relationship between the pressure and the volume of a gas?
 b. Estimating Use the graph in Figure 25 to estimate the gas pressure when the gas volume is 125 mL.
 c. Comparing and Contrasting Compare and contrast the Charles's law and Boyle's law graphs. How can you tell the difference between a graph in which one variable is directly proportional to another and a graph in which two variables vary inversely?

Lab zone **At-Home Activity**

Finding Graphs Look for graphs in your newspaper or in magazines. Point out to members of your family which variable is the manipulated variable and which is the responding variable for each graph. Then compare any line graphs you have found to the graphs in this section. Which of your graphs show two variables that are directly proportional to each other? Do any show variables that vary inversely?

It's a Gas

Problem

How does the pressure you exert on a syringe affect the volume of the air inside it?

Skills Focus

graphing, predicting, interpreting data, drawing conclusions

Materials

- strong plastic syringe (with no needle), at least 35-cm³ capacity
- modeling clay
- 4 books of uniform weight

Procedure

1. Make a data table in your notebook like the one below.

2. Lift the plunger of the syringe as high as it will move without going off scale. The volume inside the syringe will then be as large as possible.

3. Seal the small opening of the syringe with a piece of clay. The seal must be airtight.

4. Hold the syringe upright with the clay end on the table. With the help of a partner, place one book on top of the plunger. Steady the book carefully so it does not fall.

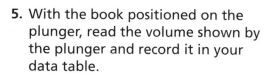

5. With the book positioned on the plunger, read the volume shown by the plunger and record it in your data table.

6. Predict what will happen as more books are placed on top of the plunger.

7. Place another book on top of the first book resting on the plunger. Read the new volume and record it in your data table.

8. One by one, place each of the remaining books on top of the plunger. After you add each book, record the volume of the syringe in your data table.

9. Predict what will happen as books are removed from the plunger one by one.

10. Remove the books one at a time. Record the volume of the syringe in your data table after you remove each book.

Data Table			
Adding Books		Removing Books	
Number of Books	Volume (cm³)	Number of Books	Volume (cm³)
0		4	
1		3	
2		2	
3		1	
4		0	

Analyze and Conclude

1. **Graphing** Make a line graph of the data obtained from Steps 5, 7, and 8. Show volume in cubic centimeters (cm³) on the vertical axis and number of books on the horizontal axis. Title this Graph 1.

2. **Graphing** Make a second line graph of the data obtained from Step 10. Title this Graph 2.

3. **Predicting** Did the results you obtained support your predictions in Steps 6 and 9? Explain.

4. **Interpreting Data** Compare Graph 2 with Graph 1. How can you explain any differences in the two graphs?

5. **Drawing Conclusions** What does Graph 1 tell you about how the volume of a gas changes with increasing pressure?

6. **Communicating** Write a paragraph explaining how the volume of the gas changed as books were added one by one. Base your explanation on what was happening to the gas particles in the syringe.

Design an Experiment

How could you use ice and warm water to show how the temperature and volume of a gas are related? Design an experiment to test the effect on the volume of a gas when you change its temperature. *Obtain your teacher's permission before carrying out your investigation.*

① States of Matter

Key Concepts

- A fixed, closely packed arrangement of particles causes a solid to have a definite shape and volume.

- Because its particles are free to move, a liquid has no definite shape. However, it does have a definite volume.

- As they move, gas particles spread apart, filling the space available. Thus, a gas has neither definite shape nor definite volume.

Key Terms

solid
crystalline solid
amorphous solid
liquid
fluid
surface tension
viscosity
gas

② Changes of State

Key Concepts

- At its melting point, the particles of a solid substance are vibrating so fast that they break free from their fixed positions.

- At its freezing temperature, the particles of a liquid are moving so slowly that they begin to form regular patterns.

- Vaporization takes place when the particles in a liquid gain enough energy to form a gas.

- Condensation occurs when particles in a gas lose enough thermal energy to form a liquid.

- During sublimation, particles of a solid do not pass through the liquid state as they form a gas.

Key Terms

melting	boiling
melting point	boiling point
freezing	condensation
vaporization	sublimation
evaporation	

③ Gas Behavior

Key Concepts

- When working with a gas, it is helpful to know its volume, temperature, and pressure.

- $\text{Pressure} = \dfrac{\text{Force}}{\text{Area}}$

- Boyle found that when the pressure of a gas at constant temperature is increased, the volume of the gas decreases. When the pressure is decreased, the volume increases.

- When the temperature of a gas at constant volume is increased, the pressure of the gas increases. When the temperature is decreased, the pressure of the gas decreases.

- Charles found that when the temperature of a gas is increased at constant pressure, its volume increases. When the temperature of a gas is decreased at constant pressure, its volume decreases.

Key Terms

pressure
Boyle's law
Charles's law

④ Graphing Gas Behavior

Key Concepts

- A graph of Charles's law shows that the volume of a gas is directly proportional to its kelvin temperature under constant pressure.

- A graph of Boyle's law shows that the pressure of a gas varies inversely with its volume at constant temperature.

Key Terms

graph
origin
directly proportional
vary inversely

Review and Assessment

Go Online
PHSchool.com
For: Self-Assessment
Visit: PHSchool.com
Web Code: cga-1020

Organizing Information

Comparing and Contrasting Copy the graphic organizer about solids, liquids, and gases onto a separate piece of paper. Complete the table and add a title. (For more on Comparing and Contrasting, see the Skills Handbook.)

State of Matter	Shape	Volume	Example (at room temperature)
a. ____?____	Definite	b. ____?____	Diamond
Liquid	c. ____?____	Definite	d. ____?____
Gas	e. ____?____	Not definite	f. ____?____

Reviewing Key Terms

Choose the letter of the best answer.

1. A substance with a definite volume but no definite shape is a(n)
   a. crystalline solid.
   b. liquid.
   c. gas.
   d. amorphous solid.

2. Unlike solids and liquids, a gas will
   a. keep its volume in different containers.
   b. keep its shape in different containers.
   c. expand to fill the space available to it.
   d. have its volume decrease when the temperature rises.

3. The process in which a gas cools and becomes a liquid is called
   a. evaporation.
   b. sublimation.
   c. boiling.
   d. condensation.

4. According to Boyle's law, the volume of a gas increases when its
   a. pressure increases.
   b. pressure decreases.
   c. temperature falls.
   d. temperature rises.

5. The vertical axis of a graph shows the
   a. responding variable.
   b. manipulated variable.
   c. constant factors.
   d. same variable as the *x*-axis.

If the statement is true, write *true*. If it is false, change the underlined word or words to make the statement true.

6. Rubber and glass, which become softer as they are heated, are examples of <u>crystalline solids</u>.

7. When you see steam, fog, or clouds, you are seeing water in the <u>liquid</u> state.

8. A substance changes from a solid to a liquid at its <u>boiling point</u>.

9. The <u>volume</u> of a gas is the force of its outward push divided by the area of the walls of the container.

10. According to <u>Boyle's law</u>, the volume of a gas varies inversely with its pressure.

Writing in Science

Explanation Write an introduction to a safety manual for deep-sea divers who use compressed air (scuba) tanks. Explain what air pressure is and what happens to gas molecules when air is compressed.

Solids, Liquids, and Gases
Video Preview
Video Field Trip
▶ Video Assessment

Review and Assessment

Checking Concepts

11. Describe the motion of particles in a solid.

12. Why are both liquids and gases called fluids?

13. Compare and contrast liquids with high and low viscosities.

14. How is the thermal energy of a substance related to its physical state?

15. Describe four examples of changes in state.

16. What happens to water molecules when water is heated from 90°C to 110°C?

17. What happens to the gas particles when the air in an inflated ball leaks out?

18. How does heating a gas in a rigid container change its pressure?

Math Practice

19. **Using Formulas** A skier exerts a force of 660 N on the snow. The surface area of the skis contacting the snow is about 0.20 m². What is the pressure in Pa of the skier on the snow?

Thinking Critically

20. **Relating Cause and Effect** Explain why placing a dented table-tennis ball in boiling water is one way to remove the dent in the ball. (Assume the ball has no holes.)

21. **Applying Concepts** When you open a solid room air freshener, the solid slowly loses mass and volume. How do you think this happens?

22. **Interpreting Data** Use the table below that shows the volume and pressure of a gas to predict how a graph of the data would look.

Volume (cm³)	Pressure (kPa)
15	222
21	159
31	108
50	67

Applying Skills

Use the table to answer Questions 23–25.

The data table tells how much mass of a compound dissolves in 100 mL of water as the temperature of the water is increased. Use the data to construct and interpret a graph.

Temperature (°C)	Mass of Compound Dissolved (g)
0	37
10	47
20	56
30	66
40	75

23. **Graphing** Label each axis of your graph with the appropriate variable, units, and range of values. Then plot the data in a line graph.

24. **Interpreting Data** What does the graph show about the effect of temperature on the amount of the compound that will dissolve in water?

25. **Predicting** Assume the amount of the compound dissolved continues to increase as the water is heated. Predict how many grams will dissolve at 50°C.

Lab zone Chapter **Project**

Performance Assessment If you prepared a cartoon, read the captions to the class and discuss the illustrations. If you prepared a skit, perform the skit in front of the class. After you finish your presentation, invite the class to ask questions about your project. Be prepared to share the decisions you made in creating your presentation.

Standardized Test Prep

Choose the letter of the best answer.

1. A wet towel is hanging on a clothesline in the sun. The towel dries by the process of

  A boiling.   **B** condensation.
  C evaporation.   **D** sublimation.

2. The pressure of a confined gas equals the force pushing on the surface divided by the area of the surface.

$$\text{Pressure} = \frac{\text{Force}}{\text{Area}}$$

What is the pressure if a force of 1,000 N acts on an area of 5.0 m^2?

  F 200 Pa   **G** 500 Pa
  H 2,000 Pa   **J** 5,000 Pa

3. The graph below shows changes in 1 kg of a solid as energy is added.

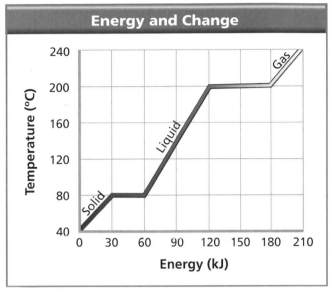

Based on the graph, what is the total amount of energy absorbed by the substance as it changes from a solid at 40°C to a gas?

  A 30 kJ
  B 60 kJ
  C 120 kJ
  D 180 kJ

4. A gas at constant temperature is confined to a cylinder with a movable piston. The piston is slowly pushed into the cylinder, decreasing the volume of the gas. The pressure increases. What are the variables in this experiment?

  F temperature and time
  G time and volume
  H volume and pressure
  J pressure and temperature

Constructed Response

5. Spray cans filled with gas usually have a warning printed on their labels that say, "Store in a cool place." Explain the danger in storing the can near a source of heat. Describe the motion of the gas molecules in the can when they gain thermal energy.

Chapter
3

Elements and the Periodic Table

Just as each spice in this Turkish bazaar has its own bin, every element has its own place in the periodic table.

interactive Textbook

Lab zone™ Chapter **Project**

Survey Properties of Metals

Chemists have a system for organizing the elements. There are more than 100 elements, and as you will learn in this chapter, about 80 of them are classified as metals. In this project, you will examine more closely the physical and chemical properties of metals.

Your Goal To survey the properties of several samples of metallic elements

To complete the project, you must

- interpret what the periodic table tells you about your samples
- design and conduct experiments that will allow you to test at least three properties of your metals
- compare and contrast the properties of your sample metals
- follow the safety guidelines in Appendix A

Plan It! Study the periodic table in Section 2 to determine which elements are metals. Brainstorm with your classmates about the properties of metals. What properties allow you to recognize a metal? How do you think metals differ from nonmetals? Your teacher will assign samples of metals to your group. You will be observing their properties in this project.

Introduction to Atoms

Reading Preview

Key Concepts
- What is the structure of an atom?
- How are elements described in terms of their atoms?
- Why are models useful for understanding atoms?

Key Terms
- nucleus • proton
- neutron • electron
- atomic number • isotope
- mass number • model

 **Target Reading Skill**

Previewing Visuals Before you read, preview Figure 2. Then write two questions you have about the diagram in a graphic organizer like the one below. As you read, answer your questions.

Structure of an Atom

Q.	What particles are in the center of an atom?
A.	
Q.	

Lab zone Discover **Activity**

What's in the Box?

1. Your teacher will give you a sealed box that contains an object. Without opening the box, move the box around to find out as much as you can about the object.
2. Make a list of your observations about the object. For example, does the object slide or roll? Is it heavy or light? Is it soft or hard? Is the object round or flat?
3. Think about familiar objects that could give you clues about what's inside the box.

Think It Over
Inferring Make a sketch showing what you think the object looks like. Tell how you inferred the properties of the object from indirect observations.

Glance at the painting below and you see people enjoying an afternoon in the park. Now look closely at the circled detail of the painting. There you'll discover that the artist used thousands of small spots of color to create these images of people and the park.

Are you surprised that such a rich painting can be created from lots of small spots? Matter is like that, too. The properties of matter that you can observe result from the properties of tiny objects that you cannot see. As you learned in Chapter 1, the tiny objects that make up all matter are atoms.

FIGURE 1

Sunday Afternoon on the Island of La Grande Jatte
This painting by artist Georges Seurat, which is made from tiny dots of paint, gives you a simple model for thinking about how matter is made of atoms.

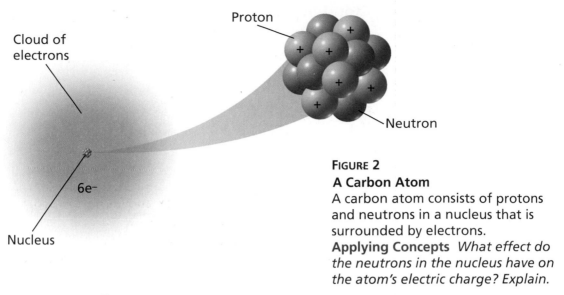

Cloud of electrons

6e⁻

Nucleus

Proton

Neutron

FIGURE 2
A Carbon Atom
A carbon atom consists of protons and neutrons in a nucleus that is surrounded by electrons.
Applying Concepts *What effect do the neutrons in the nucleus have on the atom's electric charge? Explain.*

Structure of an Atom

If you could look into a single atom, what might you see? Figuring out what atoms are made of hasn't been easy. Theories about their shape and structure have changed many times and continue to be improved even now. Until about 100 years ago, scientists thought atoms were the smallest particles of matter. Now, scientists know more. **Atoms are made of even smaller particles called protons, neutrons, and electrons.** Understanding the structure of atoms will help you understand the properties of matter.

Particles in Atoms An atom consists of a nucleus surrounded by one or more electrons. The **nucleus** (NOO klee us) (plural *nuclei*) is the very small center core of an atom. The nucleus is a group of smaller particles called protons and neutrons. **Protons** have a positive electric charge (indicated by a plus symbol, +). **Neutrons** have no charge. They are neutral. The third type of particle in an atom moves in the space outside the nucleus. **Electrons** move rapidly around the nucleus and have a negative electric charge. An electron is shown by the symbol e⁻.

Look at the model of a carbon atom in Figure 2. If you count the number of protons and electrons, you'll see there are six of each. In an atom, the number of protons equals the number of electrons. As a result, the positive charge from the protons equals the negative charge from the electrons. The charges balance, making the atom neutral.

 **Reading Checkpoint** **What kind of charge does a proton have?**

Go Online
PHSchool.com

For: More on atoms
Visit: PHSchool.com
Web Code: cgd-1031

A Cloud of Electrons Electrons move within a sphere-shaped region surrounding the nucleus. Scientists depict this region as a cloud of negative charge because electrons may be anywhere within it. Electrons with lower energy usually move in the space near the atom's nucleus. Electrons with higher energy move within the space farther from the nucleus.

Most of an atom's volume is the space in which electrons move. That space is huge compared to the space taken up by the nucleus. To picture the difference, imagine holding a pencil while standing at the pitcher's mound in a baseball stadium. If the nucleus were the size of the pencil's eraser, the electrons could be as far away as the top row of seats!

Science and History

Models of Atoms

For over two centuries, scientists have created models of atoms in an effort to understand why matter behaves as it does. As scientists have learned more, the model of the atom has changed.

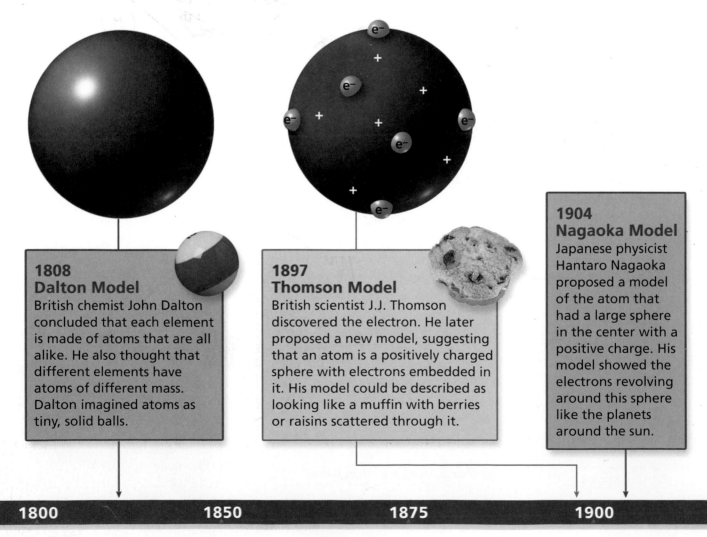

1808
Dalton Model
British chemist John Dalton concluded that each element is made of atoms that are all alike. He also thought that different elements have atoms of different mass. Dalton imagined atoms as tiny, solid balls.

1897
Thomson Model
British scientist J.J. Thomson discovered the electron. He later proposed a new model, suggesting that an atom is a positively charged sphere with electrons embedded in it. His model could be described as looking like a muffin with berries or raisins scattered through it.

1904
Nagaoka Model
Japanese physicist Hantaro Nagaoka proposed a model of the atom that had a large sphere in the center with a positive charge. His model showed the electrons revolving around this sphere like the planets around the sun.

1800   1850   1875   1900

Comparing Particle Masses Although electrons occupy most of an atom's volume, they don't account for much of its mass. It takes almost 2,000 electrons to equal the mass of just one proton. On the other hand, a proton and a neutron are about equal in mass. Together, the protons and neutrons make up nearly all the mass of an atom.

Atoms are too small to be measured in everyday units of mass, such as grams or kilograms. Instead, scientists use units known as atomic mass units (amu). A proton or a neutron has a mass equal to about one amu. The mass of an electron is about 1/2,000 amu.

Writing in Science

Research and Write Find out more about one of the scientists who worked on models of the atom. Write an imaginary interview with this person in which you discuss his work with him.

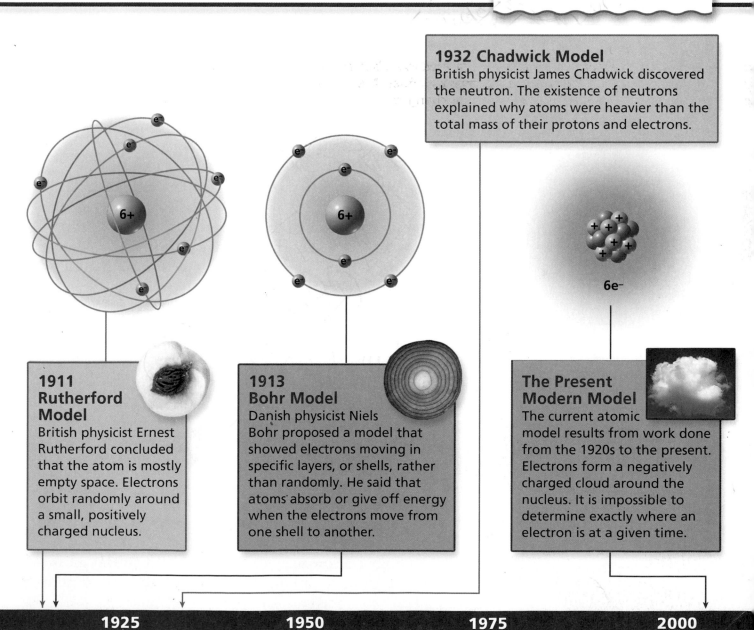

1932 Chadwick Model
British physicist James Chadwick discovered the neutron. The existence of neutrons explained why atoms were heavier than the total mass of their protons and electrons.

1911 Rutherford Model
British physicist Ernest Rutherford concluded that the atom is mostly empty space. Electrons orbit randomly around a small, positively charged nucleus.

1913 Bohr Model
Danish physicist Niels Bohr proposed a model that showed electrons moving in specific layers, or shells, rather than randomly. He said that atoms absorb or give off energy when the electrons move from one shell to another.

The Present Modern Model
The current atomic model results from work done from the 1920s to the present. Electrons form a negatively charged cloud around the nucleus. It is impossible to determine exactly where an electron is at a given time.

1925   1950   1975   2000

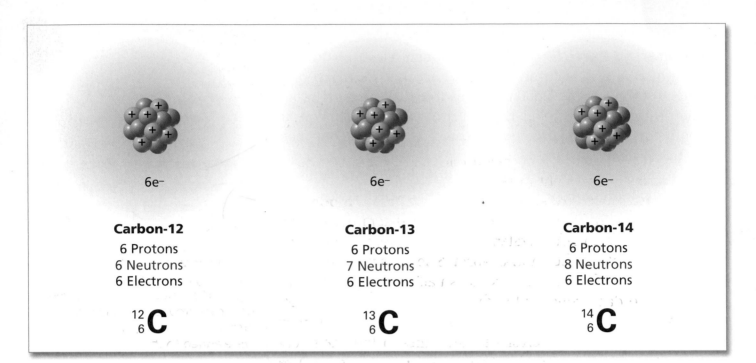

Carbon-12
6 Protons
6 Neutrons
6 Electrons

$^{12}_{6}$**C**

Carbon-13
6 Protons
7 Neutrons
6 Electrons

$^{13}_{6}$**C**

Carbon-14
6 Protons
8 Neutrons
6 Electrons

$^{14}_{6}$**C**

FIGURE 3
Isotopes
Atoms of all isotopes of carbon contain 6 protons, but they differ in their number of neutrons. Carbon-12 is the most common isotope. **Interpreting Diagrams** *Which isotope of carbon has the largest mass number?*

Atoms and Elements

Each element consists of atoms that differ from the atoms of all other elements. **An element can be identified by the number of protons in the nucleus of its atoms.**

Atomic Number Every atom of an element has the same number of protons. For example, the nucleus of every carbon atom contains 6 protons. Every oxygen atom has 8 protons, and every iron atom has 26 protons. Each element has a unique **atomic number**—the number of protons in its nucleus. Carbon's atomic number is 6, oxygen's is 8, and iron's is 26.

Isotopes Although all atoms of an element have the same number of protons, their number of neutrons can vary. Atoms with the same number of protons and a different number of neutrons are called **isotopes** (EYE suh tohps). Three isotopes of carbon are illustrated in Figure 3. Each carbon atom has 6 protons, but you can see that the number of neutrons is 6, 7, or 8.

An isotope is identified by its **mass number,** which is the sum of the protons and neutrons in the nucleus of an atom. The most common isotope of carbon has a mass number of 12 (6 protons + 6 neutrons) and may be written as "carbon-12." Two other isotopes are carbon-13 and carbon-14. As shown in Figure 3, a symbol with the mass number above and the atomic number below may also be used to represent an isotope. Although these carbon atoms have different mass numbers, all carbon atoms react the same way chemically.

Modeling Atoms

Atoms are hard to study because they are amazingly small. The smallest visible speck of dust may contain 10 million billion atoms! Even a sheet of paper is about a million atoms thick. Powerful microscopes can give a glimpse of atoms, such as the one shown in Figure 4. But they do not show the structure of atoms or how they might work.

Because atoms are so small, scientists create models to describe them. In science, a **model** may be a diagram, a mental picture, a mathematical statement, or an object that helps explain ideas about the natural world. Scientists use models to study objects and events that are too small, too large, too slow, too fast, too dangerous, or too far away to see. These models are used to make and test predictions. For example, you may know that engineers use crash-test dummies to test the safety of new car designs. The dummies serve as models for live human beings. In chemistry, models of atoms are used to explain how matter behaves. The modern atomic model explains why most elements react with other elements, while a few elements hardly react at all.

FIGURE 4
Imaging Atoms
This image was made by a scanning tunneling microscope. It shows a zigzag chain of cesium atoms (red) on a background of gallium and arsenic atoms (blue). The colors were added to the image.

 **Reading Checkpoint** What are three types of situations for which models can be useful?

Section 1 Assessment

Target Reading Skill Previewing Visuals Compare your questions and answers about Figure 2 with those of a partner.

Reviewing Key Concepts

1. **a. Reviewing** What are the three main particles in an atom?
   b. Comparing and Contrasting How do the particles of an atom differ in electric charge?
   c. Relating Cause and Effect Why do atoms have no electric charge even though most of their particles have charges?
2. **a. Defining** What is the atomic number of an element?
   b. Explaining How can atomic numbers be used to distinguish one element from another?
   c. Applying Concepts The atomic number of the isotope nitrogen-15 is 7. How many protons, neutrons, and electrons make up an atom of nitrogen-15?

3. **a. Reviewing** What is the main reason that scientists use models to study atoms?
   b. Making Generalizations What kind of information do scientists seek when using models to study atoms?

Lab zone At-Home **Activity**

Modeling Atoms Build a three-dimensional model of an atom to show to your family. The model could be made of beads, cotton, small candies, clay, plastic foam, and other simple materials. Describe how the mass of the nucleus compares to the mass of the electrons. Explain what makes atoms of different elements different from one another. Emphasize that everything in your home is made of atoms in different combinations.

Organizing the Elements

Reading Preview

Key Concepts
- How did Mendeleev discover the pattern that led to the periodic table?
- What data about elements are found in the periodic table?
- How is the organization of the periodic table useful for predicting the properties of elements?

Key Terms
- atomic mass
- chemical symbol
- group
- periodic table
- period

Target Reading Skill

Asking Questions Before you read, preview the red headings. In a graphic organizer like the one below, ask a *what* or *how* question for each heading. As you read, write the answers to your questions.

Patterns in the Elements

Question	Answer
What pattern of elements did Mendeleev discover?	Patterns appeared when . . .

Lab zone Discover **Activity**

Which Is Easier?
1. Make 4 sets of 10 paper squares, using a different color for each set. Number the squares in each set from 1 through 10.
2. Place all of the squares on a flat surface, numbered side up. Don't arrange them in order.
3. Ask your partner to name a square by color and number. Have your partner time how long it takes you to find this square.
4. Repeat Step 3 twice, choosing different squares each time. Calculate the average value of the three times.
5. Rearrange the squares into four rows, one for each color. Order the squares in each row from 1 to 10.
6. Repeat Step 3 three times. Calculate an average time.
7. Trade places with your partner and repeat Steps 2 through 6.

Think It Over
Inferring Which average time was shorter, the one produced in Step 4 or Step 6? Why do you think the times were different?

You wake up, jump out of bed, and start to get dressed for school. Then you ask yourself a question: Is there school today? To find out, you check the calendar. There's no school today because it's Saturday.

The calendar arranges the days of the month into horizontal periods called weeks and vertical groups called days of the week. This arrangement follows a repeating pattern that makes it easy to keep track of which day it is. The chemical elements can also be organized into something like a calendar. The name of the "chemists' calendar" is the periodic table.

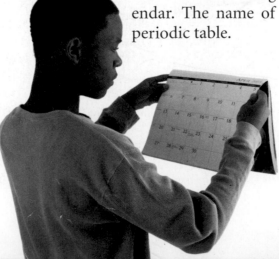

◀ A calendar organizes the days of the week into a useful, repeating pattern.

Patterns in the Elements

By 1869, a total of 63 elements had been discovered. These elements had a wide variety of properties. A few were gases. Two were liquids. Most were solid metals. Some reacted explosively as they formed compounds. Others reacted more slowly. Scientists wondered if the properties of elements followed any sort of pattern. A Russian scientist, Dmitri Mendeleev (men duh LAY ef), discovered a set of patterns that applied to all the elements.

Mendeleev's Work Mendeleev knew that some elements have similar chemical and physical properties. For example, both fluorine and chlorine are gases that irritate the lungs and form similar compounds. Silver and copper, shown in Figure 5, are both shiny metals that tarnish if exposed to air. Mendeleev thought these similarities were important clues to a hidden pattern.

To try to find that pattern, Mendeleev wrote each element's melting point (M.P.), density, and color on individual cards. He also included the element's atomic mass and the number of chemical bonds it could form. The **atomic mass** of an element is the average mass of all the isotopes of that element. Mendeleev tried various arrangements of cards. **He noticed that a pattern of properties appeared when he arranged the elements in order of increasing atomic mass.**

Mendeleev's Periodic Table Mendeleev found that the properties of elements repeated. After fluorine (F), for instance, the next heaviest element he knew was sodium (Na). (Neon had not yet been discovered.) Sodium reacted with water the same way that lithium (Li) and potassium (K) did. So he placed the cards for these elements into a group. He did the same with other similar elements.

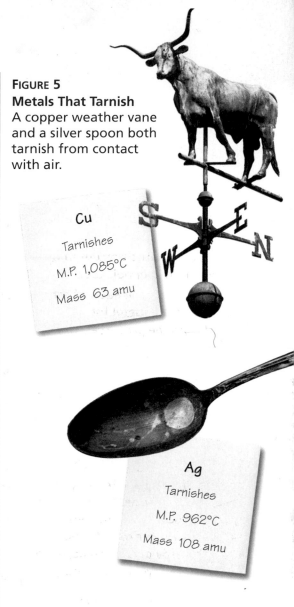

FIGURE 5
Metals That Tarnish
A copper weather vane and a silver spoon both tarnish from contact with air.

Cu
Tarnishes
M.P. 1,085°C
Mass 63 amu

Ag
Tarnishes
M.P. 962°C
Mass 108 amu

FIGURE 6
Metals That React With Water
Lithium and sodium both react with water. **Interpreting Photographs** *Which metal reacts more vigorously with water?*

Na
Reacts with water
M.P. 98°C
Mass 23 amu

Li
Reacts with water
M.P. 180°C
Mass 7 amu

FIGURE 7
Mendeleev's Periodic Table
When Mendeleev published his first periodic table, he left question marks in some places. Based on the properties and atomic masses of surrounding elements, he predicted that new elements with specific properties would be discovered.

				Ti $=50$	Zr $=90$	$?=180.$
				V $=51$	Nb $=94$	Ta $=182.$
				Cr $=52$	Mo $=96$	W $=186.$
				Mn $=55$	Rh $=104,4$	Pt $=197,4$
				Fe $=56$	Ru $=104,4$	Ir $=198.$
			Ni $=$ Co $=59$		Pl $=106{\tiny 6},$	Os $=199.$
H $=1$				Cu $=63,4$	Ag $=108$	Hg $=200.$
	Be $=9,4$	Mg $=24$		Zn $=65,2$	Cd $=112$	
	B $=11$	Al $=27,4$		$?=68$	Ur $=116$	Au $=197?$
	C $=12$	Si $=28$		$?=70$	Sn $=118$	
	N $=14$	P $=31$		As $=75$	Sb $=122$	Bi $=210$
	O $=16$	S $=32$		Se $=79,4$	Te $=128?$	
	F $=19$	Cl $=35,5$		Br $=80$	I $=127$	
Li $=7$	Na $=23$	K $=39$		Rb $=85,4$	Cs $=133$	Tl $=204$
		Ca $=40$		Sr $=57,6$	Ba $=137$	Pb $=207.$
		$?=45$		Ce $=92$		
		?Er $=56$		La $=94$		
		?Yt $=60$		Di $=95$		
		?In $=75,6$		Th $=118?$		

Lab zone  **Skills Activity**

Classifying

Choose any ten elements and assign them letters from *A* to *J*. On an index card for each element, write the letter for the element and list some of its properties. You may list properties that you learn about in this chapter or properties presented in another reference source.

Exchange cards with a classmate. Can you identify each element? Can you identify elements that have similar properties? Which properties are most helpful in identifying elements?

Predicting New Elements Mendeleev found that arranging the known elements strictly by increasing atomic mass did not always group similar elements together. So, he moved a few of his element cards into groups where the elements did have similar properties. After arranging all 63 elements, three blank spaces were left. Mendeleev predicted that the blank spaces would be filled by elements that had not yet been discovered. He even predicted the properties of those new elements.

In 1869, Mendeleev published the first periodic table. It looked something like the one shown in Figure 7. Within 16 years, chemists discovered the three missing elements—scandium, gallium, and germanium. Their properties are close to those that Mendeleev had predicted.

The Modern Periodic Table In the **periodic table** used today, the properties of the elements repeat in each period—or row—of the table. (The word *periodic* means "in a regular, repeated pattern.") The periodic table has changed a little since Mendeleev's time. New elements were added as they were discovered. Also, an important change occurred in the early 1900s. In 1913, Henry Moseley, a British scientist, discovered a way to measure the positive charge on an atom's nucleus—in other words, the atomic number. Not long after, the table was rearranged in order of atomic number, not atomic mass. As a result, a few of the elements shifted position, and some of the patterns of properties became more regular. An up-to-date version of the table appears on pages 84 and 85.

Finding Data on Elements

The periodic table has one square for each element. **In this book, each square includes the element's atomic number, chemical symbol, name, and atomic mass.**

Atomic Number Look at the periodic table on the next two pages and find the square for iron. That square is reproduced below in Figure 8. The first entry in the square is the number 26, the atomic number of iron. From Section 1, you know that the atomic number tells you that every iron atom has 26 protons in its nucleus. Because it has 26 protons, an iron atom also has 26 electrons.

Chemical Symbols and Names Just below the atomic number are the letters Fe—the **chemical symbol** for iron. Most chemical symbols contain either one or two letters. Often, an element's symbol is an abbreviation of the element's name in English. For example, zinc's symbol is Zn, the symbol for calcium is Ca, and the symbol for silicon is Si. Other elements, especially those that were known in ancient times, have symbols that are abbreviations of their Latin names. For example, the Latin name of sodium is *natrium*, so its symbol is Na. The Latin name of potassium is *kalium*, so its symbol is K. The symbol Au for gold stands for *aurum*. Fe for iron stands for *ferrum*, and Pb for lead stands for *plumbum*.

Average Atomic Mass The last number in the square is the average atomic mass. For iron, this value is 55.847 amu. The atomic mass is an average because most elements consist of a mixture of isotopes. For example, iron is a mixture of four isotopes. About 92 percent of iron atoms are iron-56 (having 30 neutrons). The rest are a mixture of iron-54, iron-57, and iron-58. The average atomic mass of iron is determined from the combined percentages of all its isotopes.

Reading Checkpoint Why is the atomic mass of an element an average?

Atomic number ———— 26

Chemical symbol ———— **Fe**

Element name ———— **Iron**

Atomic mass ———— **55.847**

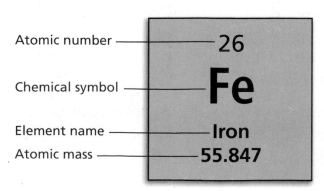

FIGURE 8
iron
Bok choy is a green, leafy vegetable used in Asian cooking. It is rich in iron.
Interpreting Diagrams *What does atomic number 26 in the square tell you about iron?*

FIGURE 9
Periodic Table of the Elements

The periodic table includes over 100 elements. Many of the properties of an element can be predicted by its position in the table.

Go Online
active art

For: Periodic Table activity
Visit: PHSchool.com
Web Code: cgp-1032

Key	
C	Solid
Br	Liquid
H	Gas
Tc	Not found in nature

Symbol
One- or two-letter symbols identify most elements. Some periodic tables also list the names of the elements.

To make the table easier to read, the lanthanides and the actinides are printed below the rest of the elements. Follow the blue shading to see how they fit in the table.

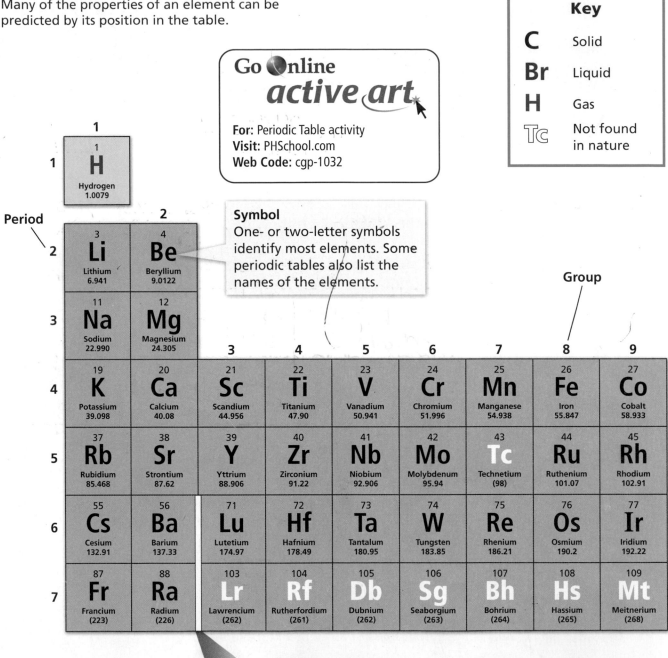

Lanthanides

Actinides

Key

- Metal
- Metalloid
- Nonmetal
- Properties not established

Atomic Number
The atomic number is the number of protons in an atom's nucleus.

Atomic Mass
Atomic mass is the average mass of an element's atoms. Atomic masses in parentheses are those of the most stable isotope.

Many periodic tables include a zigzag line that separates the metals from the nonmetals.

			13	14	15	16	17	18
								2 **He** Helium 4.0026
			5 **B** Boron 10.81	6 **C** Carbon 12.011	7 **N** Nitrogen 14.007	8 **O** Oxygen 15.999	9 **F** Fluorine 18.998	10 **Ne** Neon 20.179
10	11	12	13 **Al** Aluminum 26.982	14 **Si** Silicon 28.086	15 **P** Phosphorus 30.974	16 **S** Sulfur 32.06	17 **Cl** Chlorine 35.453	18 **Ar** Argon 39.948
28 **Ni** Nickel 58.71	29 **Cu** Copper 63.546	30 **Zn** Zinc 65.38	31 **Ga** Gallium 69.72	32 **Ge** Germanium 72.59	33 **As** Arsenic 74.922	34 **Se** Selenium 78.96	35 **Br** Bromine 79.904	36 **Kr** Krypton 83.80
46 **Pd** Palladium 106.4	47 **Ag** Silver 107.87	48 **Cd** Cadmium 112.41	49 **In** Indium 114.82	50 **Sn** Tin 118.69	51 **Sb** Antimony 121.75	52 **Te** Tellurium 127.60	53 **I** Iodine 126.90	54 **Xe** Xenon 131.30
78 **Pt** Platinum 195.09	79 **Au** Gold 196.97	80 **Hg** Mercury 200.59	81 **Tl** Thallium 204.37	82 **Pb** Lead 207.2	83 **Bi** Bismuth 208.98	84 **Po** Polonium (209)	85 **At** Astatine (210)	86 **Rn** Radon (222)
110 **Ds** Darmstadtium (269)	111 ***Uuu** Unununium (272)	112 ***Uub** Ununbium (277)		114 ***Uuq** Ununquadium				

*Name not officially assigned

63 **Eu** Europium 151.96	64 **Gd** Gadolinium 157.25	65 **Tb** Terbium 158.93	66 **Dy** Dysprosium 162.50	67 **Ho** Holmium 164.93	68 **Er** Erbium 167.26	69 **Tm** Thulium 168.93	70 **Yb** Ytterbium 173.04
95 **Am** Americium (243)	96 **Cm** Curium (247)	97 **Bk** Berkelium (247)	98 **Cf** Californium (251)	99 **Es** Einsteinium (252)	100 **Fm** Fermium (257)	101 **Md** Mendelevium (258)	102 **No** Nobelium (259)

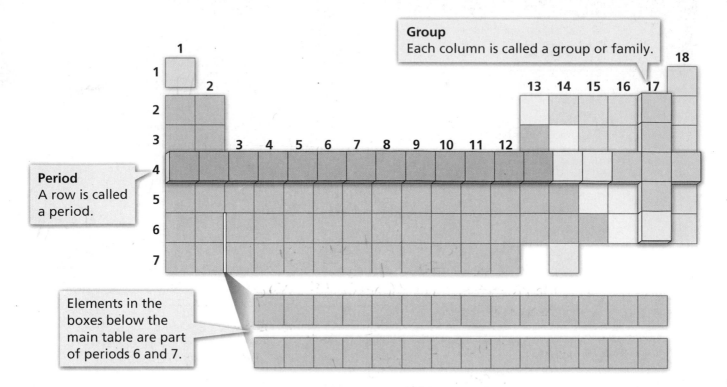

Group
Each column is called a group or family.

Period
A row is called a period.

Elements in the boxes below the main table are part of periods 6 and 7.

FIGURE 10
Periods and Groups
The 18 columns of the periodic table reflect a repeating pattern of properties that generally occur across a period. **Interpreting Tables** *How many periods are in the periodic table?*

Organization of the Periodic Table

Remember that the periodic table is arranged by atomic number. Look over the entire table, starting at the top left with hydrogen (H), which has atomic number 1. Follow the atomic numbers as they increase from left to right, and read across each row.

The properties of an element can be predicted from its location in the periodic table. As you look at elements across a row, the elements' properties change in a predictable way. This predictability is the reason that the periodic table is so useful to chemists.

Periods The table is arranged in horizontal rows called **periods.** A period contains a series of different elements, just as a week on a calendar has a series of seven days. As you move across a period from left to right, properties of the elements change according to a pattern.

As an example, look at the fourth period of the periodic table in Figure 10. The elements on the left of this period are highly reactive metals, such as potassium (K) and calcium (Ca). Elements in the center of the period are relatively unreactive metals, such as nickel (Ni) and copper (Cu). Elements to the right of these include metalloids such as arsenic (As) and the nonmetals selenium (Se) and bromine (Br). The last element in a period is always a very unreactive gas. In this period, that element is krypton (Kr).

Groups The modern periodic table has 7 periods, which form 18 vertical columns. The elements in a column are called a **group.** Groups are also known as families. The groups are numbered, from Group 1 on the left of the table to Group 18 on the right. Group 17 is highlighted in Figure 10. Most groups are named for the first element in the column. Group 14, for example, is the carbon family. Group 15 is the nitrogen family.

Because the pattern of properties of elements repeats in each new period, the elements in each group have similar characteristics. The elements in Group 1 are all metals that react violently with water, while the metals in Group 2 all react with water slowly or not at all. Group 17 elements react violently with elements from Group 1. Group 18 elements rarely react at all.

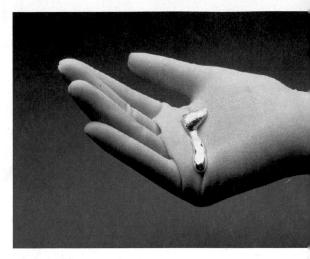

FIGURE 11
Group 13 Element
This sample of gallium metal is an element in Group 13.

 **Reading Checkpoint** | **How many groups are in the modern periodic table?**

Section 2 Assessment

Target Reading Skill **Asking Questions** Use your graphic organizer about the section headings to help you answer the questions below.

Reviewing Key Concepts

1. **a. Reviewing** In what order did Mendeleev arrange the elements in the first periodic table?
   b. Explaining What pattern did Mendeleev discover when he arranged the elements?
   c. Comparing and Contrasting Describe two differences between Mendeleev's periodic table and the modern periodic table.
2. **a. Identifying** List three kinds of information about an element that can be found in a square of the periodic table.
   b. Interpreting Tables What element has 47 protons in its nucleus?
   c. Making Generalizations Why aren't the atomic masses of most elements whole numbers?

3. **a. Describing** What does an element's location in the periodic table tell you about that element?
   b. Predicting Use the periodic table to name two elements that you would expect to have properties very much like those of calcium.

Writing in Science

Advertisement Write an advertisement that you could use to sell copies of Mendeleev's periodic table to chemists in 1869. Be sure to emphasize the benefits of the table to the chemical profession. Remember, the chemists have never seen such a table.

Metals

Reading Preview

Key Concepts
- What are the physical properties of metals?
- How does the reactivity of metals change across the periodic table?
- How are elements that follow uranium in the periodic table produced?

Key Terms
- metal • malleable • ductile
- conductivity • reactivity
- corrosion
- alkali metal
- alkaline earth metal
- transition metal • alloy
- particle accelerator

🎯 Target Reading Skill
Using Prior Knowledge Before you read, write what you know about metals in a graphic organizer like the one below. As you read, write what you learn.

What You Know
1. Metals are shiny.
2.

What You Learned
1.
2.

Lab zone · Discover **Activity**

Why Use Aluminum?

1. Examine several objects made from aluminum, including a can, a disposable pie plate, heavy-duty aluminum foil, foil-covered wrapping paper, and aluminum wire.
2. Compare the shape, thickness, and general appearance of the objects.
3. Observe what happens if you try to bend and unbend each object.
4. For what purpose is each object used?

Think It Over
Inferring Use your observations to list as many properties of aluminum as you can. Based on your list of properties, infer why aluminum was used to make each object. Explain your answer.

Metals are all around you. The cars and buses you ride in are made of steel, which is mostly iron. Airplanes are covered in aluminum. A penny is made of zinc coated with copper. Copper wires carry electricity into lamps, stereos, and computers. It's hard to imagine modern life without metals.

Properties of Metals

What is a metal? Take a moment to describe a familiar metal, such as iron, copper, gold, or silver. What words did you use—*hard, shiny, smooth*? Chemists classify an element as a **metal** based on its properties. Look again at the periodic table in Section 2. All of the elements in blue-tinted squares to the left of the zigzag line are metals.

Physical Properties The physical properties of metals include shininess, malleability, ductility, and conductivity. A **malleable** (MAL ee uh bul) material is one that can be hammered or rolled into flat sheets and other shapes. A **ductile** material is one that can be pulled out, or drawn, into a long wire. For example, copper can be made into thin sheets and wire because it is malleable and ductile.

Conductivity is the ability of an object to transfer heat or electricity to another object. Most metals are good conductors. In addition, a few metals are magnetic. For example, iron (Fe), cobalt (Co), and nickel (Ni) are attracted to magnets and can be made into magnets like the one in Figure 12. Most metals are also solids at room temperature. However, one metal— mercury (Hg)—is a liquid at room temperature.

Chemical Properties The ease and speed with which an element combines, or reacts, with other elements and compounds is called its **reactivity.** Metals usually react by losing electrons to other atoms. Some metals are very reactive. For example, sodium (Na) reacts strongly when exposed to air or water. To prevent a reaction, sodium and metals like it must be stored under oil in sealed containers. By comparison, gold (Au) and platinum (Pt) are valued for their *lack* of reactivity and because they are rare.

The reactivities of other metals fall somewhere between those of sodium and gold. Iron, for example, reacts slowly with oxygen in the air, forming iron oxide, or rust. If iron is not protected by paint or plated with another metal, it will slowly turn to reddish-brown rust. The destruction of a metal through this process is called **corrosion.**

 **Reading Checkpoint** **What are three physical properties of metals?**

FIGURE 12
Properties of Metals

Metals have certain physical and chemical properties. **Classifying** *Categorize each of the properties of metals that are shown as either physical or chemical.*

▼ **Malleability**
Gold can be pounded into coins.

Magnetism ▲
Many metals are attracted to magnets.

Reactivity ▶
This iron chain is coated with rust after being exposed to air.

◀ Potassium is highly reactive with air, so it is stored in oil.

Bananas are a good source of potassium in a healthful diet. ▶

▲ The reactions of some compounds containing potassium help get fireworks off the ground.

1
3 **Li** Lithium
11 **Na** Sodium
19 **K** Potassium
37 **Rb** Rubidium
55 **Cs** Cesium
87 **Fr** Francium

FIGURE 13
Alkali Metals

Potassium is an alkali metal.
Making Generalizations *What characteristics do other Group 1 elements share with potassium?*

Metals in the Periodic Table

The metals in a group, or family, have similar properties, and these family properties change gradually as you move across the table. **The reactivity of metals tends to decrease as you move from left to right across the periodic table.**

Alkali Metals The metals in Group 1, from lithium to francium, are called the **alkali metals.** Alkali metals react with other elements by losing one electron. These metals are so reactive that they are never found as uncombined elements in nature. Instead, they are found only in compounds. In the laboratory, scientists have been able to isolate alkali metals from their compounds. As pure, uncombined elements, some of the alkali metals are shiny and so soft that you can cut them with a plastic knife. You can see pieces of potassium in Figure 13.

The two most important alkali metals are sodium and potassium. Sodium compounds are found in large amounts in seawater and salt beds. Your diet includes foods that contain compounds of sodium and potassium, elements important for life. Another alkali metal, lithium, is used in batteries and some medicines.

Alkaline Earth Metals Group 2 of the periodic table contains the **alkaline earth metals.** Each is fairly hard, gray-white, and a good conductor of electricity. Alkaline earth metals react by losing two electrons. These elements are not as reactive as the metals in Group 1, but they are more reactive than most other metals. Like the Group 1 metals, the Group 2 metals are never found uncombined in nature.

The two most common alkaline earth metals are magnesium and calcium. Mixing magnesium and a small amount of aluminum makes a strong but lightweight material used in ladders, airplane parts, automobile wheels, and other products. Calcium compounds are an essential part of teeth and bones. Calcium also helps muscles work properly. You get calcium compounds from milk and other dairy products, as well as from green, leafy vegetables.

2
4 **Be** Beryllium
12 **Mg** Magnesium
20 **Ca** Calcium
38 **Sr** Strontium
56 **Ba** Barium
88 **Ra** Radium

▲ Without calcium, muscles and bones cannot grow and function.

FIGURE 14
Alkaline Earth Metals
Calcium is one of the Group 2 elements.

Math ▶ Analyzing Data

Melting Points in a Group of Elements

The properties of elements within a single group in the periodic table often vary in a certain pattern. The following graph shows the melting points of Group 1 elements (alkali metals) from lithium to francium.

1. **Reading Graphs** As you look at Group 1 from lithium to francium, describe how the melting points of the alkali metals change.

2. **Predicting** If element number 119 were synthesized, it would fall below francium in Group 1 of the periodic table. Predict the approximate melting point of new element 119.

3. **Interpreting Data** Room temperature is usually about 22°C. Human body temperature is 37°C. Which of the alkali metals are liquids at room temperature? Which might melt if you could hold them in your hand?

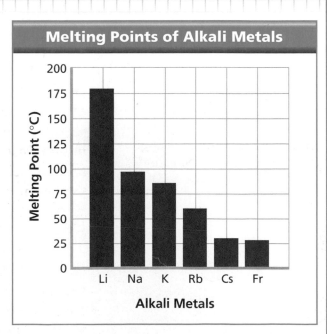

Melting Points of Alkali Metals

(Bar graph with y-axis "Melting Point (°C)" from 0 to 200, and x-axis "Alkali Metals" with Li, Na, K, Rb, Cs, Fr)

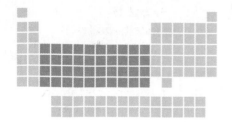

Transition Metals The elements in Groups 3 through 12 are called the **transition metals.** The transition metals include most of the familiar metals, such as iron, copper, nickel, silver, and gold. Most of the transition metals are hard and shiny. All of the transition metals are good conductors of electricity. Many of these metals form colorful compounds.

The transition metals are less reactive than the metals in Groups 1 and 2. This lack of reactivity is the reason ancient gold coins and jewelry are as beautiful and detailed today as they were thousands of years ago. Even when iron reacts with air and water, forming rust, it sometimes takes many years to react completely. Some transition metals are important to your health. For example, you would not survive without iron. It forms the core of a large molecule called hemoglobin, which carries oxygen in your bloodstream.

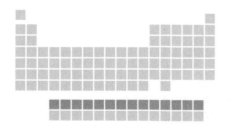

Metals in Mixed Groups Only some of the elements in Groups 13 through 15 of the periodic table are metals. These metals are not nearly as reactive as those on the left side of the table. The most familiar of these metals are aluminum, tin, and lead. Aluminum is the lightweight metal used in beverage cans and airplane bodies. A thin coating of tin protects steel from corrosion in some cans of food. Lead was once used in paints and water pipes. But lead is poisonous, so it is no longer used for these purposes. Now, its most common uses are in automobile batteries and weights for balancing tires.

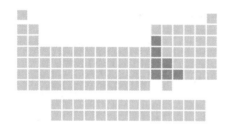

Lanthanides Two rows of elements are placed below the main part of the periodic table. This makes the table more compact. The elements in the top row are called the lanthanides (LAN thuh nydz). Lanthanides are soft, malleable, shiny metals with high conductivity. They are mixed with more common metals to make alloys. An **alloy** is a mixture of a metal with at least one other element, usually another metal. Different lanthanides are usually found together in nature. They are difficult to separate from one another because they all share very similar properties.

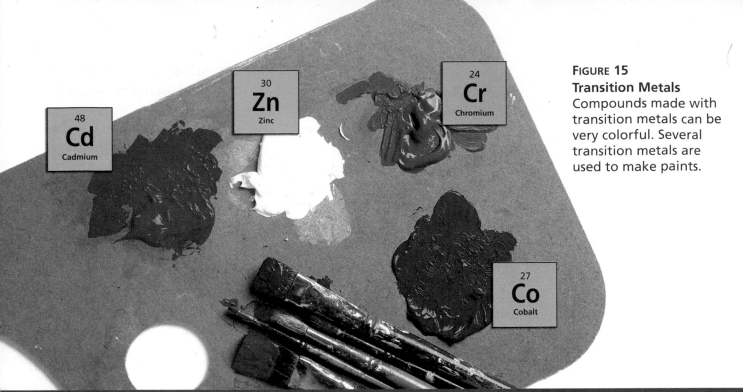

FIGURE 15
Transition Metals
Compounds made with transition metals can be very colorful. Several transition metals are used to make paints.

FIGURE 16
Metals in Groups 13, 14, and 15
Lead can be used in the borders around the glass sections in stained glass objects. Tin can be fashioned into artistic objects, such as picture frames.

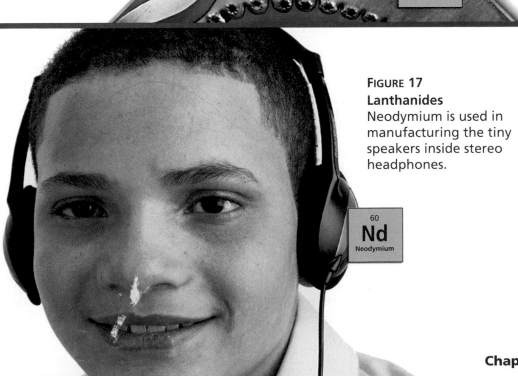

FIGURE 17
Lanthanides
Neodymium is used in manufacturing the tiny speakers inside stereo headphones.

Actinides The elements below the lanthanides are called actinides (AK tuh nydz). Of these, only actinium (Ac), thorium (Th), protactinium (Pa), and uranium (U) occur naturally on Earth. Uranium is used to produce energy in nuclear power plants. All of the elements heavier than uranium were created artificially in laboratories. The nuclei of these elements are unstable, meaning that they break apart quickly into smaller nuclei. In fact, many of these elements are so unstable that they last for only a fraction of a second after they are made.

 Reading Checkpoint Where are the actinides located in the periodic table?

FIGURE 18
Mars Exploration Rover
Curium, one of the actinide elements, is used as a source of high-energy particles that heat and provide power for certain scientific equipment aboard the Mars Exploration Rover.
Posing Questions *Based on this information, write a question about curium.*

Synthetic Elements

Elements with atomic numbers higher than 92 are sometimes described as synthetic elements because they are not found naturally on Earth. **Instead, elements that follow uranium are made—or synthesized—when nuclear particles are forced to crash into one another.** For example, plutonium is made by bombarding nuclei of uranium-238 with neutrons in a nuclear reactor. Americium-241 (Am-241) is made by bombarding plutonium nuclei with neutrons.

To make even heavier elements (with atomic numbers above 95), scientists use powerful machines called particle accelerators. **Particle accelerators** move atomic nuclei faster and faster until they have reached very high speeds. If these fast-moving nuclei crash into the nuclei of other elements with enough energy, the particles can sometimes combine into a single nucleus. Curium (Cm) was the first synthetic element to be made by colliding nuclei. In 1940, scientists in Chicago synthesized curium by colliding helium nuclei with plutonium nuclei.

In general, the difficulty of synthesizing new elements increases with atomic number. So, new elements have been synthesized only as more powerful particle accelerators have been built. For example, German scientists synthesized element 112 in 1996 by accelerating zinc nuclei and crashing them into lead. Element 112, like other elements with three-letter symbols, has been given a temporary name and symbol. In the future, scientists around the world will agree on permanent names and symbols for these elements.

 Reading Checkpoint Which elements are described as synthetic elements and why?

Americium-241 is produced in nuclear reactors. It is widely used in smoke detectors.

The heaviest synthetic elements are synthesized in particle accelerators.

FIGURE 19
Synthetic Elements
Synthetic elements are not found naturally on Earth.

Section 3 Assessment

Target Reading Skill Using Prior Knowledge
Review your graphic organizer about metals and revise it based on what you learned in the section.

Reviewing Key Concepts

1. **a. Defining** What properties of metals do the terms *conductivity* and *ductility* describe?
   b. Classifying Give an example of how the ductility of metal can be useful.
   c. Inferring What property of metals led to the use of plastic or wood handles on many metal cooking utensils? Explain.
2. **a. Identifying** What family of elements in the periodic table contains the most reactive metals?
   b. Applying Concepts What area of the periodic table is the best place to look for a metal that could be used to coat another metal to protect it from corrosion?

   c. Predicting If scientists could produce element 120, what predictions would you make about its reactivity?
3. **a. Describing** Describe the general process by which new elements are synthesized.
   b. Applying Concepts How is plutonium made?

Lab zone At-Home **Activity**

Everyday Metals Make a survey of compounds in your home that contain metals. Look at labels on foods, cooking ingredients, dietary supplements, medicines, and cosmetics. Also look for examples of how metals are used in your home, such as in cookware and wiring. Identify for your family the ways that the properties of metals make them useful in daily life.

Consumer **Lab**

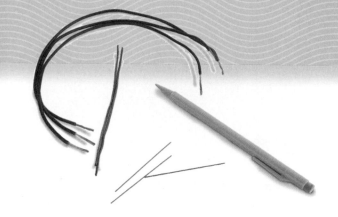

Copper or Carbon? That Is the Question

Problem

Materials scientists work to find the best materials for different products. In this lab, you will look for an answer to the following problem: How do the properties of copper and graphite determine their uses? You will compare the properties of a copper wire and a pencil lead. Pencil lead is made mostly of graphite, a form of the nonmetal element carbon.

Skills Focus

observing, classifying, controlling variables, drawing conclusions

Materials

- 1.5-V dry cell battery
- 250-mL beaker • stopwatch
- flashlight bulb and socket
- 3 lengths of insulated wire
- thin copper wire with no insulation, about 5–6 cm long
- 2 graphite samples (lead from a mechanical pencil), each about 5–6 cm long
- hot plate
- water

Procedure 🥽 🧤 🔥

1. Fill a 250-mL beaker about three-fourths full with water. Heat it slowly on a hot plate. Let the water continue to heat as you complete Part 1 and Part 2 of the investigation.

PART 1 **Physical Properties**

2. Compare the shininess and color of your copper and graphite samples. Record your observations.

3. Bend the copper wire as far as possible. Next, bend one of the graphite samples as far as possible. Record the results of each test.

PART 2 **Electrical Conductivity**

4. Place a bulb into a lamp socket. Use a piece of insulated wire to connect one pole of a dry cell battery to the socket, as shown in the photo below.

5. Attach the end of a second piece of insulated wire to the other pole of the dry cell battery. Leave the other end of this wire free.

6. Attach the end of a third piece of insulated wire to the other pole of the lamp socket. Leave the other end of this wire free.

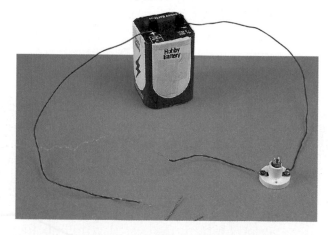

7. Touch the free ends of the insulated wire to the ends of the copper wire. Record your observations of the bulb.

8. Repeat Step 7 using a graphite sample instead of the copper wire.

PART 3 Heat Conductivity

9. Turn off the hot plate.

10. Hold one end of a graphite sample between the fingertips of one hand. Hold one end of the copper wire between the fingertips of the other hand. **CAUTION:** *Be careful not to touch the beaker.*

11. Dip both the graphite and copper wire into the hot water at the same time. Allow only about 1 cm of each piece to reach under the water's surface. From your fingertips to the water, the lengths of both the graphite sample and the copper wire should be approximately equal.

12. Time how long it takes to feel the heat in the fingertips of each hand. Record your observations.

Analyze and Conclude

1. **Observing** Compare the physical properties of copper and graphite that you observed.

2. **Classifying** Based on the observations you made in this lab, explain why copper is classified as a metal.

3. **Controlling Variables** In Step 11, why was it important to use equal lengths of copper wire and graphite?

4. **Drawing Conclusions** Which of the two materials, graphite or copper, would work better to cover the handle of a frying pan? Explain your choice.

5. **Communicating** Write a paragraph explaining why copper is better than graphite for electrical wiring. Include supporting evidence from your observations in this lab.

More to Explore

Research other uses of copper in the home and in industry. For each use, list the physical properties that make the material a good choice.

Nonmetals and Metalloids

Reading Preview

Key Concepts
- What are the properties of nonmetals?
- How are the metalloids useful?

Key Terms
- nonmetal
- diatomic molecule • halogen
- noble gas • metalloid
- semiconductor

⟳ Target Reading Skill

Using Prior Knowledge Before you read, write what you know about the properties of nonmetals and metalloids in a graphic organizer like the one below. As you read, write what you learn.

What You Know
1. Nonmetals are not shiny.
2.

What You Learned
1.
2.

Life on Earth depends on certain nonmetal elements. The air you and other animals breathe contains several nonmetals, including oxygen. And all living organisms are made from compounds of the nonmetal carbon. Yet, while many compounds containing nonmetals are useful to life, some nonmetals by themselves are poisonous and highly reactive. Still other nonmetals are completely unreactive. Compared to metals, nonmetals have a much wider variety of properties. However, nonmetals do have several properties in common.

These bears, the grass ▶ behind them, and all life on Earth is based on carbon, a nonmetal.

FIGURE 20
**Physical Properties
of Nonmetals**

Nonmetals have properties
that are the opposite of metals.
Comparing and Contrasting
*Contrast the properties of these
nonmetals with those of metals.*

▲ The helium filling this
blimp is a gas at room
temperature.

◄ Sulfur crumbles
into a powder.

Nonmetals are good
insulators. Carbon
compounds are found
in the plastic insulating
these copper wires. ▶

Properties of Nonmetals

A **nonmetal** is an element that lacks most of the properties of a
metal. **Most nonmetals are poor conductors of electricity and
heat and are reactive with other elements. Solid nonmetals
are dull and brittle.** Look at the periodic table in Section 2. All
of the elements in green-tinted boxes are nonmetals. Many of
the nonmetals are common elements on Earth.

Physical Properties Ten of the 16 nonmetals are gases at
room temperature. The air you breathe is mostly a mixture of
two nonmetals, nitrogen (N) and oxygen (O). Other nonmetal
elements, such as carbon (C), iodine (I), and sulfur (S), are solids at room temperature. Bromine (Br) is the only nonmetal
that is liquid at room temperature.

Look at examples of nonmetals in Figure 20. In general, the
physical properties of nonmetals are the opposite of those of the
metals. Solid nonmetals are dull, meaning not shiny, and brittle, meaning not malleable or ductile. If you hit most solid nonmetals with a hammer, they break or crumble into a powder.
Nonmetals usually have lower densities than metals. And nonmetals are also poor conductors of heat and electricity.

Chemical Properties

Most nonmetals are reactive, so they readily form compounds. In fact, fluorine (F) is the most reactive element known. Yet, Group 18 elements hardly ever form compounds.

Atoms of nonmetals usually gain or share electrons when they react with other atoms. When nonmetals and metals react, electrons move from the metal atoms to the nonmetal atoms, as shown by the formation of salt, shown in Figure 21. Another example is rust—a compound made of iron and oxygen (Fe_2O_3). It's the reddish, flaky coating you might see on an old piece of steel or an iron nail.

Many nonmetals can also form compounds with other nonmetals. The atoms share electrons and become bonded together into molecules.

> **Reading Checkpoint** In which portion of the periodic table do you find nonmetals?

Families of Nonmetals

Look again at the periodic table. Notice that only Group 18 contains elements that are all nonmetals. In Groups 14 through 17, there is a mix of nonmetals and other kinds of elements.

The Carbon Family Each element in the carbon family has atoms that can gain, lose, or share four electrons when reacting with other elements. In Group 14, only carbon is a nonmetal. What makes carbon especially important is its role in the chemistry of life. Compounds made of molecules containing long chains of carbon atoms are found in all living things.

Most of the fuels that are burned to yield energy contain carbon. Coal, for example, is mostly the element carbon. Gasoline is made from crude oil, a mixture of carbon compounds with chains of 5 to 50 or more carbon atoms in their molecules.

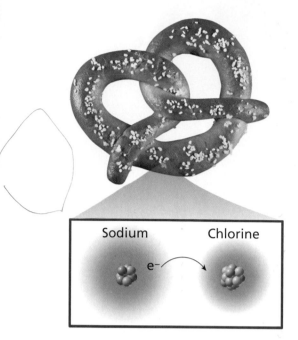

FIGURE 21
Reactions of Nonmetals
The table salt on a pretzel is mined from deposits found on Earth. The same compound can also be formed from a reaction between the metal sodium and the nonmetal chlorine.

FIGURE 22
Carbon
Charcoal is one form of carbon, the only nonmetal in Group 14.

The Nitrogen Family Group 15, the nitrogen family, contains two nonmetals, nitrogen and phosphorus. These nonmetals usually gain or share three electrons when reacting with other elements. To introduce yourself to nitrogen, take a deep breath. The atmosphere is almost 80 percent nitrogen gas (N_2). Nitrogen does not readily react with other elements, so you breathe out as much nitrogen as you breathe in.

Nitrogen is an example of an element that occurs in nature in the form of diatomic molecules, as N_2. A **diatomic molecule** consists of two atoms. In this form, nitrogen is not very reactive. Although living things need nitrogen, most of them are unable to use nitrogen from the air. However, certain kinds of bacteria can use this nitrogen to form compounds. This process is called nitrogen fixation. Plants can then take up these nitrogen compounds formed in the soil by the bacteria. Farmers also add nitrogen compounds to the soil in the form of fertilizers. Like all animals, you get the nitrogen you need from the food you eat—from plants, or from animals that ate plants.

Phosphorus is the other nonmetal in the nitrogen family. Phosphorus is much more reactive than nitrogen, so phosphorus in nature is always found in compounds. A compound containing phosphorus is used to make matches, because it can react with oxygen in the air.

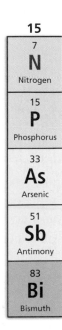

FIGURE 23
The Nitrogen Family
Nitrogen and phosphorus are grouped in the same family of the periodic table, Group 15. **Making Generalizations** *How do atoms of both these elements change when they react?*

▼ Nitrogen is a key ingredient of fertilizers.

▲ Match heads contain a highly reactive phosphorus compound that ignites easily.

Show Me the Oxygen

How can you test for the presence of oxygen?

1. 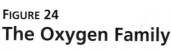 Pour about a 3-cm depth of hydrogen peroxide (H_2O_2) into a test tube.

2. Add a pea-sized amount of manganese dioxide (MnO_2) to the test tube.

3. Observe the test tube for about 1 minute.

4. When instructed by your teacher, set a wooden splint on fire.

5. Blow the splint out after 5 seconds and immediately plunge the glowing splint into the mouth of the test tube. Avoid getting the splint wet.

Observing Describe the change in matter that occurred in the test tube. What evidence indicates that oxygen was produced?

The Oxygen Family Group 16, the oxygen family, contains three nonmetals—oxygen, sulfur, and selenium. These elements usually gain or share two electrons when reacting with other elements.

You are using oxygen right now. With every breath, oxygen travels into your lungs. There, it is absorbed into your bloodstream, which distributes it all over your body. You could not live without a steady supply of oxygen. Like nitrogen, the oxygen you breathe is a diatomic molecule (O_2). In addition, oxygen sometimes forms a triatomic (three-atom) molecule, which is called ozone (O_3). Ozone collects in a layer in the upper atmosphere, where it screens out harmful radiation from the sun. However, ozone is a dangerous pollutant at ground level because it is highly reactive.

Because oxygen is highly reactive, it can combine with almost every other element. It also is the most abundant element in Earth's crust and the second-most abundant element in the atmosphere. (The first is nitrogen.)

Sulfur is the other common nonmetal in the oxygen family. If you have ever smelled the odor of a rotten egg, then you are already familiar with the smell of some sulfur compounds. Sulfur is used in the manufacture of rubber for rubber bands and automobile tires. Most sulfur is used to make sulfuric acid (H_2SO_4), one of the most important chemicals used in industry.

FIGURE 24

The Oxygen Family

Oxygen and sulfur are the most common of the three nonmetals in Group 16.
Interpreting Tables *What is the atomic number of each Group 16 element?*

▲ Some of the oxygen needed by a frog enters through its skin.

16
8
O
Oxygen
16
S
Sulfur
34
Se
Selenium
52
Te
Tellurium
84
Po
Polonium

◄ The rubber in these tires contains sulfur.

The Halogen Family Group 17 contains fluorine, chlorine, bromine, iodine, and astatine. These elements are also known as the **halogens,** which means "salt forming." All but astatine are nonmetals, and all share similar properties. A halogen atom typically gains or shares one electron when it reacts with other elements.

All of the halogens are very reactive, and the uncombined elements are dangerous to humans. Fluorine is so reactive that it reacts with almost every other known substance. Even water and powdered glass will burn in fluorine. Chlorine gas is extremely dangerous, but it is used in small amounts to kill bacteria in water supplies.

Though the halogen elements are dangerous, many of the compounds that halogens form are quite useful. Compounds of carbon and fluorine make up the nonstick coating on cookware. Small amounts of fluorine compounds that are added to water supplies help prevent tooth decay. Chlorine is one of the elements in ordinary table salt (the other is sodium). Another salt of chlorine, calcium chloride, is used to help melt ice on roads and walkways. Bromine reacts with silver to form silver bromide, which is used in photographic film.

Go Online
SciLINKS NSTA

For: Links on nonmetals
Visit: www.SciLinks.org
Web Code: scn-1134

FIGURE 25
The Halogens
The Group 17 elements are the most reactive nonmetals. Atoms of these elements easily form compounds by sharing or gaining one electron with atoms of other elements.

◄ Bromine is highly reactive, and will burn skin on contact.

▲ Fluorine-containing compounds are found in toothpaste.

FIGURE 26
The Noble Gases
Electricity makes the Group 18 elements glow brightly inside glass tubes. **Applying Concepts** *Why are neon and the other noble gases so unreactive?*

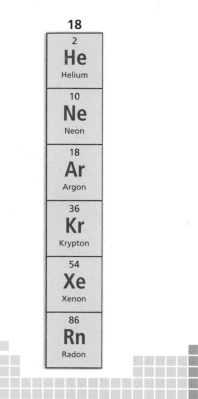

The Noble Gases The elements in Group 18 are known as the **noble gases.** They do not ordinarily form compounds because atoms of noble gases do not usually gain, lose, or share electrons. As a result, the noble gases are usually unreactive. Even so, scientists have been able to form some compounds of the heavy noble gases (Kr, Xe) in the laboratory.

All the noble gases exist in Earth's atmosphere, but only in small amounts. Because they are so unreactive, the noble gases were not discovered until the late 1800s. Helium was discovered by a scientist who was studying not the atmosphere but the sun.

Have you made use of a noble gas? You have if you have ever purchased a floating balloon filled with helium. Noble gases are also used in glowing electric lights. These lights are commonly called neon lights, even though they are often filled with argon, xenon, or other noble gases.

Hydrogen Alone in the upper left corner of the periodic table is hydrogen—the element with the simplest and smallest atoms. Each hydrogen atom has one proton and one electron. Some hydrogen atoms also have neutrons. Because the chemical properties of hydrogen differ very much from those of the other elements, it really cannot be grouped into a family. Although hydrogen makes up more than 90 percent of the atoms in the universe, it makes up only 1 percent of the mass of Earth's crust, oceans, and atmosphere. Hydrogen is rarely found on Earth as a pure element. Most hydrogen is combined with oxygen in water (H_2O).

Reading Checkpoint Why were the noble gases undiscovered until the late 1800s?

FIGURE 27
Importance of Hydrogen
Water is a compound of hydrogen and oxygen. Without liquid water, life on Earth would be impossible.

The Metalloids

Along the border between the metals and the nonmetals are seven elements called metalloids. These elements are shown in the yellow squares in the periodic table in Section 2. The **metalloids** have some characteristics of both metals and nonmetals. All are solids at room temperature. They are brittle, hard, and somewhat reactive.

The most common metalloid is silicon (Si). Silicon combines with oxygen to form silicon dioxide (SiO_2). Ordinary sand, which is mostly SiO_2, is the main component of glass. A compound of boron (B) and oxygen is added during the process of glassmaking to make heat-resistant glass. Compounds of boron are also used in some cleaning materials.

The most useful property of the metalloids is their varying ability to conduct electricity. Whether or not a metalloid conducts electricity can depend on temperature, exposure to light, or the presence of small amounts of impurities. For this reason, metalloids such as silicon, germanium (Ge), and arsenic (As) are used to make semiconductors. **Semiconductors** are substances that can conduct electricity under some conditions but not under other conditions. Semiconductors are used to make computer chips, transistors, and lasers.

 **Reading Checkpoint** What is the most common metalloid, and where is it found?

FIGURE 28
Silicon
A silicon computer chip is dwarfed by an ant, but the chip's properties as a semiconductor make it a powerful part of modern computers.

14
Si
Silicon

Section 4 Assessment

⊙ **Target Reading Skill** Using Prior Knowledge Review your graphic organizer about nonmetals and metalloids, and revise it based on what you learned in the section.

Reviewing Key Concepts

1. a. **Reviewing** What physical and chemical properties are found among the nonmetals?
   b. **Making Generalizations** What happens to the atoms of most nonmetals when they react with other elements?
   c. **Comparing and Contrasting** How do the physical and chemical properties of the halogens compare with those of the noble gases?

2. a. **Identifying** Where in the periodic table are the metalloids found?
   b. **Describing** What are three uses of metalloids?
   c. **Applying Concepts** What property makes certain metalloids useful as "switches" to turn a small electric current on and off?

Lab zone At-Home Activity

Halogen Hunt Identify compounds in your home that contain halogens. Look at labels on foods, cooking ingredients, cleaning materials, medicines, and cosmetics. The presence of a halogen is often indicated by the words *fluoride*, *chloride*, *bromide*, and *iodide* or the prefixes *fluoro-*, *chloro-*, *bromo-*, and *iodo-*. Show your family these examples and describe properties of the halogens.

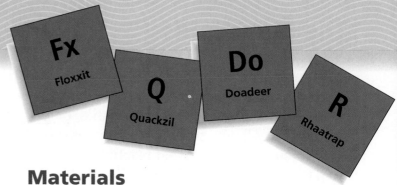

Alien Periodic Table

Problem

Imagine that inhabitants of another planet send a message to Earth that contains information about 30 elements. However, the message contains different names and symbols for these elements than those used on Earth. Which elements on the periodic table do these "alien" names represent?

Skills Focus

drawing conclusions, classifying, interpreting data, inferring

Materials

• ruler
• periodic table from text for reference

Procedure

1. Copy the blank periodic table on page 107 into your notebook.

2. Listed below are data on the chemical and physical properties of the 30 elements. Place the elements in their proper position in the blank periodic table.

Alien Elements

  The noble gases are **bombal (Bo)**, **wobble (Wo)**, **jeptum (J)**, and **logon (L)**. Among these gases, wobble has the greatest atomic mass and bombal the least. Logon is lighter than jeptum.

 The most reactive group of metals are **xtalt (X)**, **byyou (By)**, **chow (Ch)**, and **quackzil (Q)**. Of these metals, chow has the lowest atomic mass. Quackzil is in the same period as wobble.

The **apstrom (A)**, **vulcania (V)**, and **kratt (Kt)** are nonmetals whose atoms typically gain or share one electron. Vulcania is in the same period as quackzil and wobble.

 The metalloids are **ernst (E)**, **highho (Hi)**, **terriblum (T)**, and **sississ (Ss)**. Sississ is the metalloid with the greatest atomic mass. Ernst is the metalloid with the lowest atomic mass. Highho and terriblum are in Group 14. Terriblum has more protons than highho. **Yazzer (Yz)** touches the zigzag line, but it's a metal, not a metalloid.

 The lightest element of all is called **pfsst (Pf)**. The heaviest element in the group of 30 elements is **eldorado (El)**. The most chemically active nonmetal is apstrom. Kratt reacts with byyou to form table salt.

 The element **doggone (D)** has only 4 protons in its atoms.

 Floxxit (Fx) is important in the chemistry of life. It forms compounds made of long chains of atoms. **Rhaatrap (R)** and **doadeer (Do)** are metals in the fourth period, but rhaatrap is less reactive than doadeer.

 Magnificon (M), **goldy (G)**, and sississ are all members of Group 15. Goldy has fewer electrons than magnificon.

 Urrp (Up), **oz (Oz)**, and **nuutye (Nu)** all gain 2 electrons when they react. Nuutye is found as a diatomic molecule and has the same properties as a gas found in Earth's atmosphere. Oz has a lower atomic number than urrp.

 The element **anatom (An)** has atoms with a total of 49 electrons. **Zapper (Z)** and **pie (Pi)** lose two electrons when they react. Zapper is used to make lightweight alloys.

Alien Periodic Table

	1								18
1		2		13	14	15	16	17	
2									
3									
4									
5									

Analyze and Conclude

1. **Drawing Conclusions** List the Earth names for the 30 alien elements in order of atomic number.

2. **Classifying** Were you able to place some elements within the periodic table with just a single clue? Explain using examples.

3. **Interpreting Data** Why did you need two or more clues to place other elements? Explain using examples.

4. **Inferring** Why could you use clues about atomic mass to place elements, even though the table is now based on atomic numbers?

5. **Communicating** Write a paragraph describing which groups of elements are not included in the alien periodic table. Explain whether or not you think it is likely that an alien planet would lack these elements.

More to Explore

Notice that Period 5 is incomplete on the alien periodic table. Create names and symbols for each of the missing elements. Then, compose a series of clues that would allow another student to identify these elements. Make your clues as precise as possible.

▼ Radio telescopes in New Mexico

Elements From Stardust

Reading Preview

Key Concepts
- How are elements created in stars?
- What are the results of fusion in large stars?

Key Terms
- plasma
- nuclear fusion
- nebula
- supernova

Target Reading Skill

Sequencing As you read, make a flowchart like the one below that shows how elements are formed in stars. Write the steps in separate boxes in the flowchart in the order in which they occur.

Formation of Elements

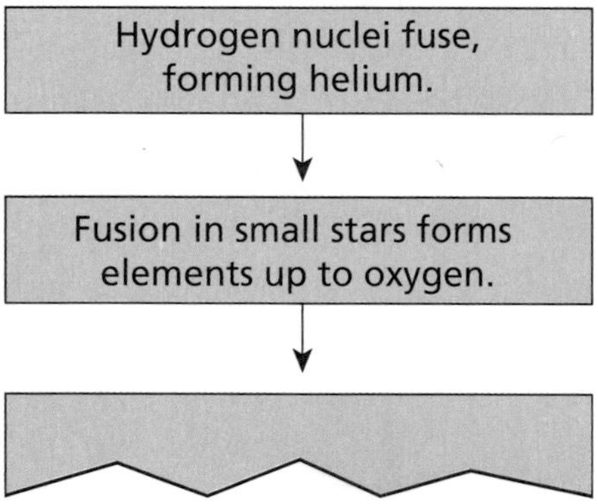

Hydrogen nuclei fuse, forming helium.

↓

Fusion in small stars forms elements up to oxygen.

↓

Lab zone

Discover **Activity**

Can Helium Be Made From Hydrogen?

1. A hydrogen atom has a nucleus of 1 proton surrounded by an electron. Most hydrogen nuclei do not contain neutrons, but one isotope of hydrogen contains 1 neutron, and another isotope contains 2 neutrons. Draw models of each of the three isotopes of hydrogen.

2. All helium atoms have 2 protons and 2 electrons, and almost all have 2 neutrons. Draw a model of a typical helium atom.

Think It Over

Developing Hypotheses How might the hydrogen atoms you drew combine to form a helium atom? Draw a diagram to illustrate your hypothesis. Why would hydrogen nuclei with neutrons be important for this process?

Have you wondered where the elements come from, or why some elements are common here on Earth, while others are much more rare? To answer questions such as these, scientists have looked in a place that might surprise you: stars. They have looked not only at distant stars, but also at the nearest star, the sun. By studying the sun and other stars, scientists have formed some interesting models of how the stars shine and theories about the origins of matter here on Earth.

How Elements Form in Stars

Like many other stars, the sun is made mostly of one element—hydrogen. This hydrogen exists at tremendously high pressures and hot temperatures. How hot is it? The temperature in the sun's core is about 15 million degrees Celsius.

FIGURE 29
The Sun
Hot plasma streams into space from the surface of the sun.

Plasma At the extreme temperatures found in the sun and other stars, matter does not exist as a solid, a liquid, or a gas. Instead, it exists in a state called plasma. The **plasma** state of matter consists of a gas-like mixture of free electrons and atoms stripped of electrons. Plasmas don't exist just in stars. A comet's tail is made partly of plasma. Plasmas also can be produced by high-voltage electricity or even an electric spark. A plasma forms inside a fluorescent light when it is switched on. Plasmas are also used to generate light inside flat-panel TV screens that you can hang on a wall. The difference between a plasma in a fluorescent light and plasma in the sun is that the sun's plasma is under extremely high pressure.

When Nuclei Combine Remember that atomic nuclei contain protons, which means that nuclei are positively charged. Usually, positively charged nuclei repel one another. But in stars, the pressure is so high that nuclei are squeezed close together and collide with one another.

As in particle accelerators, when colliding nuclei have enough energy, they can join together, as shown in Figure 31. **Nuclear fusion** is a process in which two atomic nuclei combine to form a larger nucleus, releasing huge amounts of energy in the process. **Nuclear fusion, which occurs in stars on a huge scale, combines smaller nuclei into larger nuclei, creating heavier elements.**

Figure 30
Plasma in Comets
The glowing tail of a comet consists partly of plasma that forms as the comet comes closer to the sun.

FIGURE 31
Nuclear Fusion
During nuclear fusion, two atomic nuclei collide and fuse. **Applying Concepts** *How can nuclear fusion result in the production of a different element?*

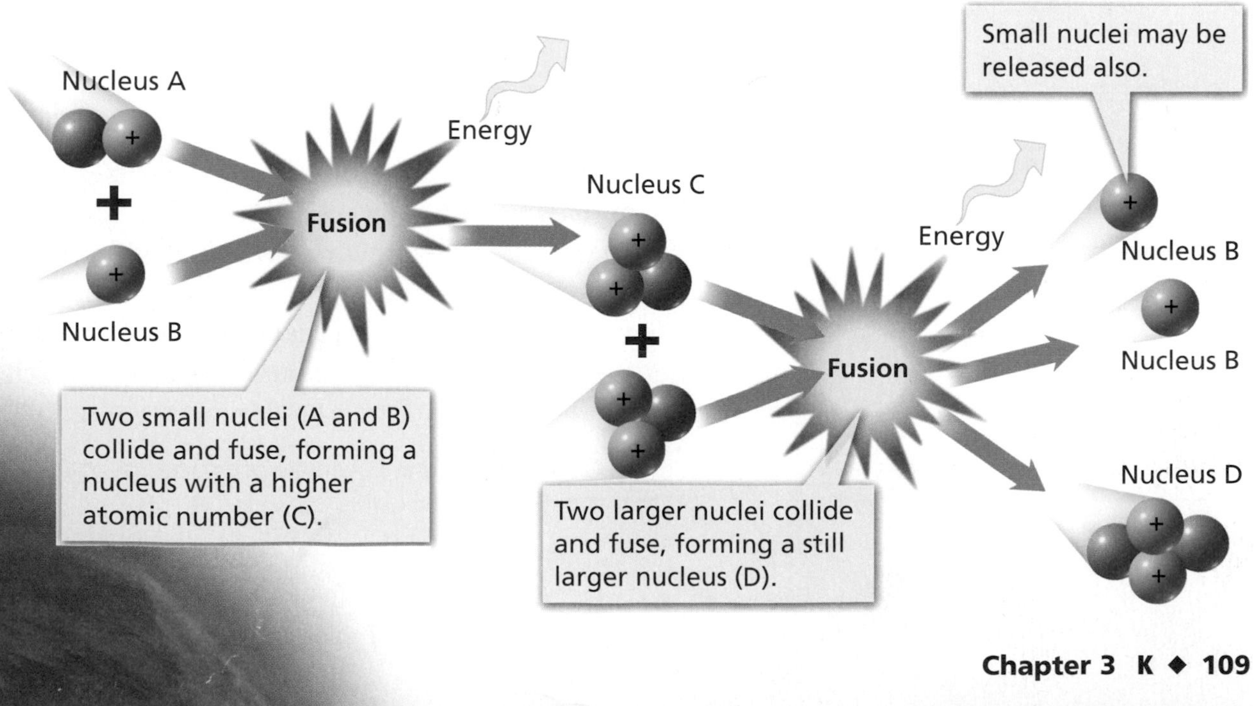

Nucleus A

Energy

Fusion

Nucleus C

Nucleus B

Two small nuclei (A and B) collide and fuse, forming a nucleus with a higher atomic number (C).

Two larger nuclei collide and fuse, forming a still larger nucleus (D).

Fusion

Energy

Small nuclei may be released also.

Nucleus B

Nucleus B

Nucleus D

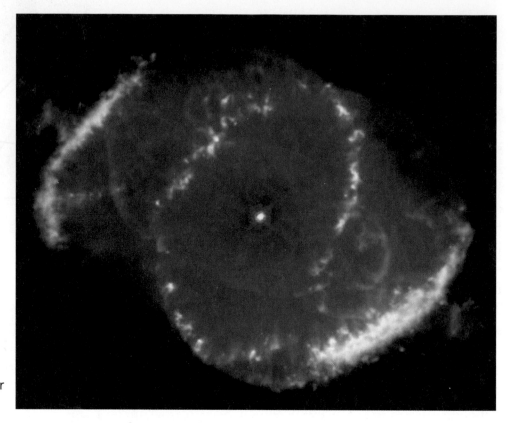

FIGURE 32
Planetary Nebula
The Cat's Eye Nebula is the remains of a star similar to the sun. Energy from the star causes the gases to glow.

For: Links on nuclear fusion
Visit: www.SciLinks.org
Web Code: scn-1135

New Elements From Fusion What are the steps of nuclear fusion in the sun and other stars? In the sun, different isotopes of hydrogen fuse, producing nuclei of helium. This reaction produces a huge amount of energy and is the most important source of the energy in the sun. In other words, hydrogen is the fuel that powers the sun. Scientists estimate that the sun has enough hydrogen to last another 5 billion years.

As helium builds up in the core of a star, its temperature and volume change. New fusion reactions occur. Over time, these fusion reactions can form nuclei of slightly heavier elements, such as carbon, nitrogen, and oxygen. For example, carbon can form as the result of a series of steps in the fusion of three helium nuclei. Yet another helium nucleus and a carbon nucleus can fuse, forming oxygen. Nitrogen may form when a carbon nucleus fuses with a hydrogen nucleus. Stars the size of the sun do not contain enough energy to produce elements heavier than oxygen. Eventually, a star like the sun shrinks, and its elements spread into space. It forms a **nebula**—or cloudlike region of gases—similar to the one shown in Figure 32.

 **Reading Checkpoint** What elements can be produced by stars the size of the sun?

Elements From Large Stars

As they age, larger stars become even hotter than the sun. These stars have enough energy to produce heavier elements, such as magnesium and silicon. In more massive stars, fusion continues until the core is almost all iron.

Find iron on the periodic table in Section 2. You can see that there are many other elements heavier than iron. How are elements heavier than iron produced? In the final hours of the most massive stars, scientists have observed an event called a supernova. A **supernova** is a huge explosion that breaks apart a massive star, producing temperatures up to 1 billion degrees Celsius. **A supernova provides enough energy for the nuclear fusion reactions that create the heaviest elements.** These and other elements are blown off into space as the star burns out.

Most astronomers agree that the matter in the sun and the planets around it, including Earth, originally came from a gigantic supernova that occurred billions of years ago. If so, this means that the matter all around you was created in a star, and all matter on Earth is a form of stardust.

FIGURE 33
Supernova
The Crab Nebula is the supernova of a massive star first observed on Earth in the year 1054 by Chinese astronomers.
Making Generalizations *What elements may have formed in this supernova that would not have formed in a smaller star?*

 **Reading Checkpoint** Where are elements heavier than iron produced?

Section 5 Assessment

Target Reading Skill Sequencing Refer to your flowchart about the formation of elements in stars as you answer Question 1.

Reviewing Key Concepts

1. **a. Identifying** What is the process that produces elements in stars?
   b. Explaining How are the elements carbon, nitrogen, and oxygen produced in stars like the sun?
   c. Applying Concepts Why can elements be produced in the sun but not in Earth's atmosphere?
2. **a. Defining** What is a supernova?
   b. Describing What conditions of a supernova cause elements that are heavier than iron to form?
   c. Developing Hypotheses Earth has abundant amounts of iron, but also has many elements heavier than iron. Form a hypothesis to explain the presence of these heavier elements.

Writing in Science

How-to Paragraph Suppose you are the science officer on a spaceship. Your mission is to collect and analyze samples of matter from various sites as the ship travels around the Milky Way Galaxy. You and your assistants are able to identify the elements present in a sample. You want to know whether the sample could have come from a star like the sun, a more massive star, or a supernova. Write a set of instructions telling your assistants how to decide on the origin of the samples.

1 Introduction to Atoms

Key Concepts

- Atoms are made of even smaller particles called protons, neutrons, and electrons.
- An element can be identified by the number of protons in the nucleus of its atoms.
- Because atoms are so small, scientists create models to describe them.

Key Terms

nucleus
proton
neutron
electron
atomic number
isotope
mass number
model

2 Organizing the Elements

Key Concepts

- Mendeleev noticed that a pattern of properties appeared when he arranged the elements in order of increasing atomic mass.
- Each square in the periodic table includes the element's atomic number, chemical symbol, name, and atomic mass.
- The properties of an element can be predicted from its location in the periodic table.

Key Terms

atomic mass	period
periodic table	group
chemical symbol	

3 Metals

Key Concepts

- The physical properties of metals include shininess, malleability, ductility, and conductivity.
- The reactivity of metals tends to decrease as you move from left to right across the periodic table.
- Elements that follow uranium in the periodic table are made—or synthesized—when nuclear particles are forced to crash into one another.

Key Terms

metal	alkali metal
malleable	alkaline earth metal
ductile	transition metal
conductivity	alloy
reactivity	particle accelerator
corrosion	

4 Nonmetals and Metalloids

Key Concepts

- Most nonmetals are poor conductors of heat and electricity and are reactive with other elements. Solid nonmetals are dull and brittle.
- The most useful property of the metalloids is their varying ability to conduct electricity.

Key Terms

nonmetal	noble gas
diatomic molecule	metalloid
halogen	semiconductor

5 Elements From Stardust

Key Concepts

- Nuclear fusion, which occurs in stars on a huge scale, combines smaller nuclei into larger nuclei, creating heavier elements.
- A supernova provides enough energy for the nuclear fusion reactions that create the heaviest elements.

Key Terms

plasma	nebula
nuclear fusion	supernova

Review and Assessment

Organizing Information

Concept Mapping Copy the concept map about the periodic table onto a sheet of paper. Then complete it and add a title. (For more on Concept Mapping, see the Skills Handbook.)

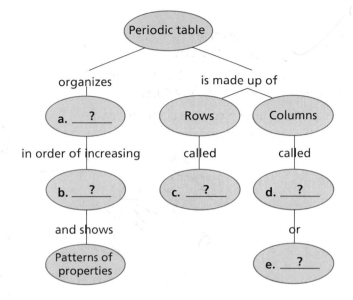

Reviewing Key Terms

Choose the letter of the best answer.

1. The atomic number of an atom is determined by the number of
   a. protons.   **b.** electrons.
   c. neutrons.   **d.** isotopes.

2. In the modern periodic table, elements are arranged
   a. according to atomic mass.
   b. according to atomic number.
   c. in alphabetical order.
   d. according to the number of neutrons in their nuclei.

3. Of the following, the group that contains elements that are the most reactive is the
   a. alkali metals.
   b. alkaline earth metals.
   c. carbon family.
   d. noble gases.

4. Unlike metals, many nonmetals are
   a. good conductors of heat and electricity.
   b. malleable and ductile.
   c. gases at room temperature.
   d. shiny.

5. At the hot temperatures of stars, electrons are stripped away from nuclei. This process forms a state of matter called
   a. a heavy element.   **b.** liquid.
   c. plasma.   **d.** supernova.

6. Inside the sun, nuclear fusion creates helium nuclei from
   a. oxygen nuclei.
   b. beryllium nuclei.
   c. carbon nuclei.
   d. hydrogen nuclei.

Writing in Science

News Report Imagine you are writing an article for a space magazine about the life cycle of a star. Which elements are produced in a star at different stages? How are these elements distributed into space?

Elements and the Periodic Table
Video Preview
Video Field Trip
▶ Video Assessment

Review and Assessment

Checking Concepts

7. How do two isotopes of an element differ from one another?

8. What element has an average atomic mass nearest to 31?

9. Use the periodic table to name two elements that have properties similar to those of chlorine (Cl).

10. Which two elements in Group 14 on the periodic table are most likely to be malleable and good conductors of electricity?

11. Of the elements oxygen (O), zinc (Zn), and iodine (I), which one would you predict to be a poor conductor of electricity and a brittle solid at room temperature?

12. Why are elements heavier than oxygen *not* produced in stars like the sun?

Thinking Critically

13. **Comparing and Contrasting** List the three kinds of particles that make up atoms, and compare their masses and their locations in an atom.

14. **Applying Concepts** Below is a square taken from the periodic table. Identify the type of information given by each labeled item.

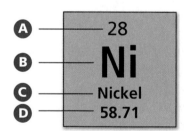

15. **Applying Concepts** Explain how particle accelerators are used to synthesize elements with atomic numbers above 95.

16. **Inferring** What property of the materials used in computer chips makes them useful as switches that turn electricity on and off?

17. **Relating Cause and Effect** Why is extremely high pressure required to cause atomic nuclei to crash into one another in stars?

Applying Skills

Use the table to answer Questions 18–22.

The table below list properties of five elements.

Element	Appearance	Atomic Mass	Conducts Electricity
A	Invisible gas	14.007	No
B	Invisible gas	39.948	No
C	Hard, silvery solid	40.08	Yes
D	Silvery liquid	200.59	Yes
E	Shiny, bluish-white solid	207.2	Slightly

18. **Classifying** Classify each element in the table as a metal or a nonmetal. Explain your answers.

19. **Inferring** Both elements B and C have an atomic mass close to 40. How is this similarity possible?

20. **Drawing Conclusions** Use the periodic table to identify the five elements.

21. **Predicting** Would you expect elements A and B to have similar chemical properties? Why or why not?

22. **Predicting** Would you expect to find element C uncombined in nature? Explain.

Lab zone Chapter Project

Performance Assessment Display the chart showing the metals you studied. Be ready to discuss which properties are common to all metals. Describe other properties of metals you could not test. List all the properties that could be used to find out whether an unknown element is a metal.

Standardized Test Prep

Choose the letter of the best answer.

1. Elements that are gases at room temperature are likely to be classified as which of the following?
   A metals
   B nonmetals
   C metalloids
   D unreactive

2. Which property of aluminum makes it a suitable metal for soft drink cans?
   F It has good electrical conductivity.
   G It can be hammered into a thin sheet (malleability).
   H It can be drawn into long wires (ductility).
   J It can reflect light (shininess).

Use the table below to answer Questions 3–5.

8	9	10
O	**F**	**Ne**
Oxygen 15.999	Fluorine 18.998	Neon 20.179
16	17	18
S	**Cl**	**Ar**
Sulfur 32.06	Chlorine 35.453	Argon 39.948

3. Which element has an atomic number of 18?
   A hydrogen
   B oxygen
   C fluorine
   D argon

4. An atom of fluorine has 10 neutrons. What is the total number of other subatomic particles in this atom?
   F 9 protons and 9 electrons
   G 9 protons and 19 electrons
   H 10 protons and 10 electrons
   J 19 protons and 19 electrons

5. Which combination of elements represents part of a group, or family, of the periodic table?
   A oxygen, fluorine, and neon
   B sulfur, chlorine, and argon
   C fluorine and chlorine
   D oxygen and chlorine

Constructed Response

6. Describe the modern model of the atom. Your discussion should include the three main types of particles that make up an atom and the charge and location of each. Include an explanation of the overall charge on an atom.

Chapter
4

Exploring Materials

Chapter Preview

Navajo women weave wool, ▶ a natural polymer.

◢ Lab zone™ **Chapter Project**

Material Profiles

In this chapter, you will explore the properties of different types of materials. As you read this chapter, you will survey different materials found around you.

Your Goal To collect and investigate different materials found around you

To complete the project, you must

● collect at least eight material samples from at least three different locations
● identify several properties of each material
● create an informative display about these materials
● follow the safety guidelines in Appendix A

Plan It! With a group of classmates, brainstorm a list of the properties of various materials and how you might test these properties. You'll be working on this project as you study this chapter. When you finish Section 1, describe some polymers and composites you chose to collect and begin preparing a showcase. Add information when you finish Section 2, and complete your list of materials at the end of the chapter. Finally, present your completed showcase to the class.

Polymers and Composites

Reading Preview

Key Concepts
- How do polymers form?
- What are composites made of?
- What benefits and problems relate to the use of synthetic polymers?

Key Terms
- polymer • monomer • plastic
- composite

Target Reading Skill
Asking Questions Before you read, preview the red headings. In a graphic organizer like the one below, ask a *how* or *why* question for each heading. As you read, write the answers to your questions.

Question	Answer
How do polymers form?	Polymers form when chemical bonds link . . .

Lab zone ## Discover **Activity**

What Did You Make?

1. Look at a sample of borax solution and write down the properties you observe. Do the same with white glue.
2. Put about 2 tablespoons of borax solution into a paper cup.
3. Stir the solution as you add about 1 tablespoon of white glue.
4. After 2 minutes, record the properties of the material in the cup. Wash your hands when you are finished.

Think It Over
Observing What evidence of a chemical reaction did you observe? How did the materials change? What do you think you made?

Delectable foods and many other interesting materials surround you every day. Have you ever wondered what makes up these foods and materials? You might be surprised to learn that many are partly or wholly polymers. A **polymer** (PAHL uh mur) is a large, complex molecule built from smaller molecules joined together in a repeating pattern.

The starches in pancakes and the proteins in meats and eggs are natural polymers. Many other polymers, however, are manufactured or synthetic. These synthetic polymers include polyester and nylon clothing, and plastics. Whether synthetic or natural, most polymers rely on the element carbon for their fundamental structures.

FIGURE 1
Polymers
The clothing, boots, goggles, and helmet worn by this climber are all made of polymers.

Forming Polymers

Food materials, living things, and plastic have something in common. All are made of carbon compounds. Carbon compounds contain atoms of carbon bonded to each other and to other kinds of atoms. Carbon is present in several million known compounds, and more carbon-containing compounds are being discovered or invented every day.

Carbon's Chains and Rings Carbon's unique ability to form so many compounds comes from two properties. First, a carbon atom can form four bonds. Second, it can bond to other carbon atoms in straight and branched chains and ring-shaped groups, as you can see in Figure 2. These structures form the "backbones" to which other atoms attach.

Hydrogen is the most common element found in compounds with carbon. Other elements include oxygen, nitrogen, phosphorus, sulfur, and the halogens—especially chlorine.

Carbon Compounds and Polymers Molecules of some carbon compounds can bond together, forming larger molecules, such as polymers. The smaller molecules from which polymers are built are called **monomers** (MAHN uh murz). **Polymers form when chemical bonds link large numbers of monomers in a repeating pattern.** A polymer may consist of hundreds or even thousands of monomers.

Many polymers consist of a single kind of monomer that repeats over and over again. You could think of these monomers as linked like the identical cars of a long passenger train. In other cases, two or three monomers may join in an alternating pattern. Sometimes links between monomer chains occur, forming large webs or netlike molecules. The chemical properties of a polymer depend on the monomers from which it is made.

 **Reading Checkpoint** What are the patterns in which monomers come together to form polymers?

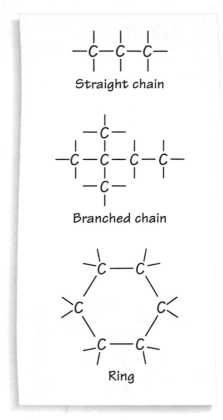

FIGURE 2
Carbon's Bonds
Carbon atoms can form structures like those shown above. In these drawings, lines represent bonds.
Interpreting Diagrams *How many bonds are shown for each carbon atom?*

FIGURE 3
Building Polymers
Like chains made of similar or different paper clips, polymers can form from similar or different kinds of monomers.

Polymer made of one kind

Polymer made of two

119

FIGURE 4
Natural Polymers

Cellulose, the proteins in snake venom, and spider's silk are three examples of natural polymers.

▲ The cellulose in fruits and vegetables serves as dietary fiber that keeps the human digestive system healthy.

A spider's web is a silken polymer that is one of the strongest materials known. ▶

▲ Snake venom is a mixture containing approximately 90 percent proteins.

Polymers and Composites

Polymers have been around as long as life on Earth. Plants, animals, and other living things produce many natural materials made of large polymer molecules.

Natural Polymers Cellulose (SEL yoo lohs) is a flexible but strong natural polymer found in the cell walls of fruits and vegetables. Cellulose is made in plants when sugar molecules are joined into long strands. Humans cannot digest cellulose. But plants also make digestible polymers called starches, formed from sugar molecules that are connected in a different way. Starches are found in pastas, breads, and many vegetables.

You can wear polymers made by animals. Silk is made from the fibers of the cocoons spun by silkworms. Wool is made from sheep's fur. These polymers can be woven into thread and cloth. Your own body makes polymers, too. For example, your fingernails and muscles are made of polymers called proteins. Within your body, proteins are assembled from combinations of monomers called amino acids. The properties of a protein depend on which amino acids are used and in what order. One combination builds the protein that forms your fingernails. Yet another combination forms the protein that carries oxygen in your blood.

Synthetic Polymers Many polymers you use every day are synthesized—or made—from simpler materials. The starting materials for many synthetic polymers come from coal or oil. **Plastics**, which are synthetic polymers that can be molded or shaped, are the most common products. But there are many others. Carpets, clothing, glue, and even chewing gum can be made of synthetic polymers.

Figure 5 lists just a few of the hundreds of polymers people use. Although the names seem like tongue twisters, see how many you recognize. You may be able to identify some polymers by their initials printed on the bottoms of plastic bottles.

Compare the uses of polymers shown in the figure with their characteristics. Notice that many products require materials that are flexible, yet strong. Others must be hard or lightweight. When chemical engineers develop a new product, they have to think about how it will be used. Then they synthesize a polymer with properties to match.

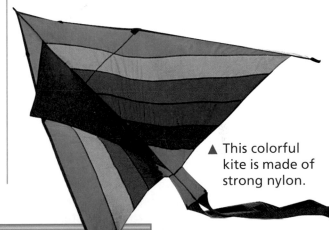

▲ This colorful kite is made of strong nylon.

Some Synthetic Polymers You Use		
Name	**Properties**	**Uses**
Low-density polyethylene (LDPE)	Flexible, soft, melts easily	Plastic bags, squeeze bottles, electric wire insulation
High-density polyethylene (HDPE)	Stronger than LDPE; higher melting temperatures	Detergent bottles, gas cans, toys, milk jugs
Polypropylene (PP)	Hard, keeps its shape	Toys, car parts, bottle caps
Polyvinyl chloride (PVC)	Tough, flexible	Garden hoses, imitation leather, plumbing pipes
Polystyrene (PS)	Lightweight, can be made into foam	Foam drinking cups, insulation, furniture, "peanut" packing material
Nylon	Strong, can be drawn into flexible thread	Stockings, parachutes, fishing line, fabric
Teflon (polytetrafluoroethylene)	Nonreactive, low friction	Nonstick coating for cooking pans

FIGURE 5
The properties of synthetic polymers make them ideal starting materials for many common objects.
Applying Concepts
Which synthetic polymer would you use to make a cover for a picnic table?

Exploring Materials

Video Preview
▶ Video Field Trip
Video Assessment

Comparing Polymers Synthetic polymers are often used in place of natural materials that are too expensive or wear out too quickly. Polyester and nylon fabrics, for example, are frequently used instead of wool, silk, and cotton to make clothes. Laminated countertops and vinyl floors replace wood in many kitchens. Other synthetic polymers have uses for which there is no suitable natural material. Compact discs, computer parts, artificial heart valves, and even bicycle tires couldn't exist without synthetic polymers.

Composites Every substance has its desirable and undesirable properties. What would happen if you could take the best properties of two substances and put them together? A **composite** combines two or more substances in a new material with different properties.

• Tech & Design in History •

The Development of Polymers
The first synthetic polymers were made by changing natural polymers in some way. Later, crude oil and coal became the starting materials. Now, new polymers are designed regularly in laboratories.

1839 Synthetic Rubber
Charles Goodyear invented a process that turned natural rubber into a hard, stretchable polymer. It did not get sticky and soft when heated or become brittle when cold, as natural rubber does. Bicycle tires were an early use.

1869 Celluloid
Made using cellulose, celluloid became a substitute for ivory in billiard balls and combs and brushes. It was later used to make movie film. Because celluloid is very flammable, other materials have replaced it for almost all purposes.

1909 Bakelite
Bakelite was the first commercial polymer made from compounds in coal tar. Bakelite doesn't get soft when heated, and it doesn't conduct electricity. These properties made it useful for handles of pots and pans, for telephones, and for parts in electrical outlets.

1800　　**1850**　　**1900**

By combining the useful properties of two or more substances in a composite, chemists can make a new material that works better than either one alone. **Many composite materials include one or more polymers.** The idea of putting two different materials together to get the advantages of both was inspired by the natural world. Many synthetic composites are designed to imitate a common natural composite—wood.

Wood is made of long fibers of cellulose, held together by another plant polymer called lignin. Cellulose fibers are flexible and can't support much weight. Lignin is brittle and would crack under the weight of the tree branches. But the combination of the two polymers makes a strong tree trunk.

Reading Checkpoint Why is wood a composite?

Writing in Science

Research and Write Find out more about the invention of one of these polymers. Write a newspaper headline announcing the invention. Then write the first paragraph of the news report telling how the invention will change people's lives.

1934
Nylon
A giant breakthrough came with a synthetic fiber that imitates silk. Nylon replaced expensive silk in women's stockings and fabric for parachutes and clothing. It can also be molded to make objects like buttons, gears, and zippers.

1971
Kevlar
Kevlar is five times stronger than steel. Kevlar is tough enough to substitute for steel ropes and cables in offshore oil rigs but light enough to use in spacecraft parts. It is also used in protective clothing for firefighters and police officers.

2002
Light-Emitting Polymers
Discovered accidentally in 1990, light-emitting polymers (LEPs) are used commercially in products such as MP3 audio players and electric shavers with display screens. LEPs give off light when exposed to low-voltage electricity. Newer, more colorful LEPs may be useful as flexible monitors for computers, TV screens, and watch-sized phones.

1950   2000   2050

FIGURE 6
Synthetic Composites
The composites in the fishing rod above make it flexible so that it will not break when reeling in a fish. Fiberglass makes the snowboard at right both lightweight and strong.

Uses of Composites The idea of combining the properties of two substances to make a more useful one has led to many new products. Fiberglass composites are one example. Strands of glass fiber are woven together and strengthened with a liquid plastic that sets like glue. The combination makes a strong, hard solid that can be molded around a form to give it shape. These composites are lightweight but strong enough to be used as a boat hull or car body. Also, fiberglass will not rust as metal does.

Many other useful composites are made from strong polymers combined with lightweight ones. Bicycles, automobiles, and airplanes built from such composites are much lighter than the same vehicles built from steel or aluminum. Some composites are used to make fishing rods, tennis rackets, and other sports equipment that needs to be flexible but strong.

 **Reading Checkpoint** What are two examples of composites?

Too Many Polymers?

You can hardly look around without seeing something made of synthetic polymers. They have replaced many natural materials for several reasons. **Synthetic polymers are inexpensive to make, strong, and last a long time.**

But synthetic polymers have caused some problems, too. Many of the disadvantages of using plastics come from the same properties that make them so useful. **For example, it is often cheaper to throw plastics away and make new ones than it is to reuse them. As a result, plastics increase the volume of trash.**

Go Online
PHSchool.com

For: More on polymers
Visit: PHSchool.com
Web Code: cgd-1041

One of the reasons that plastics last so long is that most plastics don't react very easily with other substances. As a result, plastics don't break down—or degrade—into simpler materials in the environment. In contrast, natural polymers do. Some plastics are expected to last thousands of years. How do you get rid of something that lasts that long?

Is there a way to solve these problems? One solution is to use waste plastics as raw material for making new plastic products. You know this idea as recycling. Recycling has led to industries that create new products from discarded plastics. Bottles, fabrics for clothing, and parts for new cars are just some of the many items that can come from waste plastics. A pile of empty soda bottles can even be turned into synthetic wood. Look around your neighborhood. You may see park benches or "wooden" fences made from recycled plastics. Through recycling, the disposal problem is eased and new, useful items are created.

 **Reading Checkpoint** **Why do plastic materials often increase the volume of trash?**

FIGURE 7
Recycling Plastics
Plastics can be recycled to make many useful products. This boardwalk, for example, is made of recycled plastics. **Making Judgments** *What advantages or disadvantages does this material have compared to wood?*

Section 1 Assessment

🎯 **Target Reading Skill** **Asking Questions** Use your graphic organizer about the section headings to help answer the questions below.

Reviewing Key Concepts

1. a. **Defining** What are polymers made of?
   b. **Identifying** What properties enable carbon atoms to form polymers and so many other compounds?
   c. **Interpreting Diagrams** How do the two kinds of polymers modeled in Figure 3 differ?
2. a. **Reviewing** Distinguish between natural polymers, synthetic polymers, and composites.
   b. **Classifying** Make a list of polymers you can find in your home. Classify them as natural or synthetic.
   c. **Drawing Conclusions** Why are composites often more useful than the individual materials from which they are made?

3. a. **Listing** List two benefits and two problems associated with the use of synthetic polymers.
   b. **Making Judgments** Think of something plastic that you have used today. Is there some other material that would be better than plastic for this use?

Writing in Science

Advertisement You are a chemist. You invent a polymer that can be a substitute for a natural material such as wood, cotton, or leather. Write an advertisement for your polymer, explaining why you think it is a good replacement for the natural material.

Technology Lab

Lab zone

· Tech & Design ·

Design and Build a Polymer Package

Problem

Can you design and build packaging made of polymers that is suitable for mailing a breakable object to a friend?

Design Skills

designing a solution, building a prototype, evaluating the design

Materials

- water
- hand lens
- weights (or books)
- scissors
- packaging tape
- thermometer
- balance
- hot plate
- clock or timer
- containers (20 beakers, trays, or plastic cups)
- iodine solution, 1% solution (10 mL)
- cookies or hard-boiled eggs
- polymers used in packaging (paper, Tyvek, plastic foam, ecofoam, cardboard, fabric, popcorn, sawdust, wood shavings, plastic)

Procedure

PART 1   Research and Investigate

1. Make a list of all the ways you can think of to test the properties of polymers. Think about properties including:
   - ability to protect a fragile object
   - reaction to water   • appearance
   - heat insulation   • strength
   - reaction to iodine   • mass

   Note: Iodine turns a dark blue-black color when starch is present. (Starch may attract insects or other pests.)

2. Select a property you wish to test. Choose a method that you think would be the best way to test that property.

3. Design a step-by-step procedure for the test. Do the same for each of the other properties you decide to investigate. Be sure that you change only one variable at a time. Include any safety directions in your procedure.

4. Predict which polymers you think will perform best in each test you plan.

5. After your teacher has approved your procedure, perform the tests on each polymer.

6. Record your observations in a table similar to the one shown.

Data Table				
Polymer	Brief Description of Test 1	Brief Description of Test 2	Brief Description of Test 3	Brief Description of Test 4
A				
B				
C				

PART 2 Design and Build

7. Using what you learned in Part 1, design packaging that
   - could be used to completely enclose a hard-boiled egg or cookie.
   - can drop a distance of 1.5 m without breaking the egg or cookie.
   - is strong and inexpensive to make.

8. Sketch your design on a sheet of paper, and list the materials you will need. Design an experiment to test the packaging.

9. Obtain your teacher's approval for your design. Then construct the packaging.

PART 3 Evaluate and Redesign

10. Test your packaging to evaluate how well the packaging meets the criteria in Step 7.

11. Based on the results of your tests, decide how you could improve your packaging. Then make any needed changes and test how the packaging performs again.

Analyze and Conclude

1. **Building a Prototype** What properties of polymers that you identified in Part 1 proved most useful when you designed your prototype in Part 2?

2. **Evaluating the Design** Did your packaging protect the object inside? What characteristics of your design do you think led to this result?

3. **Designing a Solution** How did your testing and evaluation of your prototype help you to redesign it?

4. **Evaluating the Impact on Society** How might people change their behavior if stronger and cheaper packaging material becomes available?

5. **Working With Design Constraints** Suppose the constraints on your design are changed. Now, your packaging must also be able to support a 10-kilogram weight. How would this affect your choice of materials and your design?

Communicate

Write an advertisement to market your packaging. In your ad, explain why your packaging does the best job of protecting the objects inside.

Polyester Fleece

Would you go hiking in the freezing Antarctic wearing a bunch of plastic beverage bottles? If you are like most serious hikers, you would. Polyester fleece is a lightweight, warm fabric made from plastic, including recycled soda bottles. The warmth of the fabric is due to its ability to trap and hold air. Polyester fleece is easy to wash and requires less energy to dry than wool or goose down.

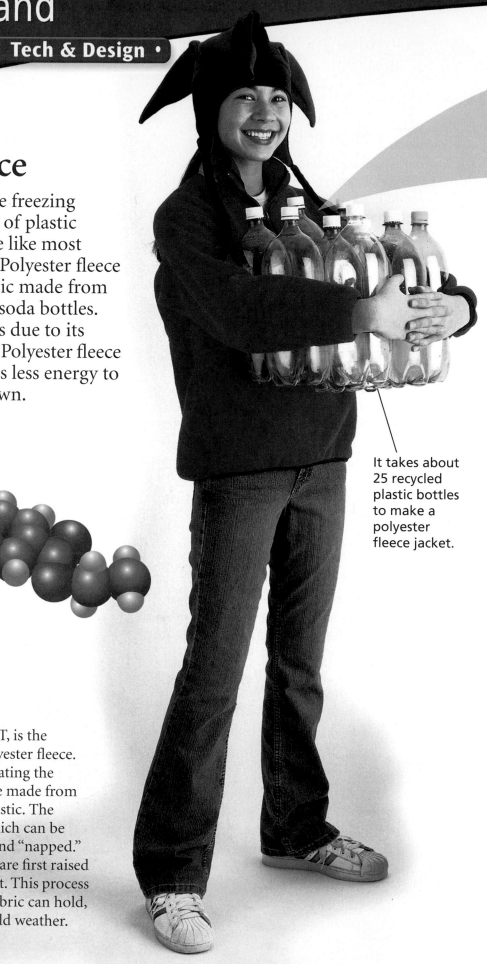

It takes about 25 recycled plastic bottles to make a polyester fleece jacket.

Molecular Model
A simplified molecular model of the polymer used to create polyester fleece is shown here. The molecules form long, straight chains.

Making Polyester Fleece

Polyethylene terephthalate, or PET, is the polymer that is used to make polyester fleece. The first step in the process is creating the polyester fiber or thread. It can be made from raw materials or recycled PET plastic. The thread is then knit into fabric, which can be dyed or printed. It is then dried and "napped." In the napping process, the fibers are first raised and then clipped to an even height. This process increases the amount of air the fabric can hold, which helps keep you warm in cold weather.

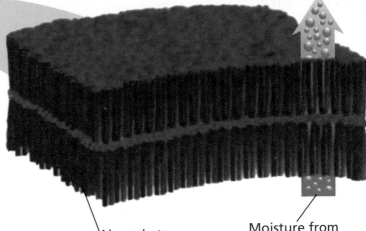

▲ Fleece Fabric
Similar to yarn in a sweater, fleece fibers are knit together to create a stretchy, dense fabric that is soft, lightweight, and durable.

Air pockets between fibers trap body heat.

Moisture from the body passes through the fabric.

Polyester Fleece and the Environment

Making polyester fleece fabric uses water and energy, like other fabric-making processes. Using recycled materials to create polyester fleece saves energy and reduces wastes. One trade-off involves the safety of workers in the fleece factories. The clipping process creates dust particles in the air that workers then breathe. Some companies that produce fleece are developing technology that should reduce dust in the workplace, as well as technologies that conserve and reuse energy and water.

Plastic Bottle Granules
PET plastic bottles are chipped to create granules like those shown here. The granules can be used in making polyester fleece. ▼

Weigh the Impact

1. Identify the Need
What are some benefits of using polyester fleece to make clothing and blankets?

2. Research
Use the Internet to find companies that make or sell polyester fleece made from recycled plastic. Identify ways in which this form of recycling helps the environment.

3. Write
Create a pamphlet to encourage your classmates to recycle plastics. Describe how PET plastic can be used to create polyester fleece.

For: More on polyester fleece
Visit: PHSchool.com
Web Code: cgh-1040

Reading Preview

Key Concepts
- How do the properties of metals and alloys compare?
- How are steels and other alloys made and used?

Key Term
- alloy

Target Reading Skill

Outlining As you read, make an outline about metals and alloys that you can use for review. Use the red section headings for the main topics and the blue headings for the subtopics.

Metals and Alloys
I. Comparing metals and alloys
A. Properties of metals
B.
II. Making and using alloys
A.

More than 6,000 years ago, people learned to make copper tools that were sharper than stone tools. Later, people also used tin for tools. But copper and tin are soft, so they bend easily and are hard to keep sharp. About 5,000 years ago, metal makers discovered a way to make better tools.

Comparing Metals and Alloys

Copper and tin mixed together in the right amounts make a stronger, harder metal that keeps its sharp edge after long use. This discovery marked the beginning of the Bronze Age. It also was the invention of the first alloy. An **alloy** is a mixture made of two or more elements that has the properties of metal. In every alloy, at least one of the elements is a metal.

Properties of Metals You know a piece of metal when you see it. It's usually hard and shiny. At room temperature, all metallic elements (except mercury) are solids. Metals share other properties, too. You may recall that metals can conduct electricity. They are ductile—that is, they can be drawn out into thin wire. For example, copper made into wire carries electric current to the outlets in your home. Metals are also malleable—that is, they can be hammered into a sheet. Aluminum, rolled flat, makes aluminum foil.

▲ A brass euphonium

Properties of Alloys The properties of an alloy can differ greatly from those of its individual elements. Pure gold, for example, is soft and easily bent. For that reason, gold jewelry and coins are made of an alloy of gold with another metal, such as copper or silver. These gold alloys are much harder than pure gold but still let its beauty show. Even after thousands of years, objects made of gold alloys do not change. They still look exactly the same as when they were first made.

Alloys are used much more than pure metals because they are generally stronger and less likely to react with air or water. Iron, for example, is often alloyed with one or more other elements to make steel. And steel is used in many tools because of its superior strength and hardness. You have seen iron objects rust when they are exposed to air and water. But forks and spoons made of stainless steel can be washed over and over again without rusting. That's because stainless steel—an alloy of iron, carbon, nickel, and chromium—does not react with air and water as iron does.

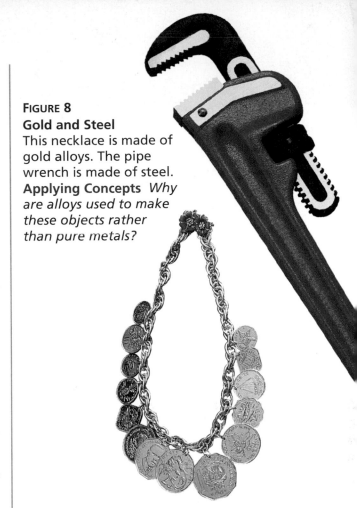

FIGURE 8
Gold and Steel
This necklace is made of gold alloys. The pipe wrench is made of steel.
Applying Concepts *Why are alloys used to make these objects rather than pure metals?*

✓ Reading Checkpoint) **Why is most jewelry made of gold alloys rather than pure gold?**

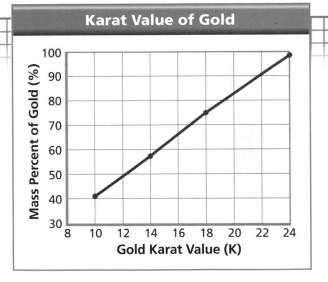

Math ▶ Analyzing Data

Calculating Karat Value
Gold is often alloyed with other metals, such as silver, to improve its hardness and durability. The mass percent of gold in such an alloy is usually expressed by its karat value. Gold karat values and mass percent data are plotted on the graph shown here.

1. **Reading Graphs** Which axis has values that describe the mass of gold relative to the mass of the alloy?

2. **Reading Graphs** How does the mass percent of gold change as the karat value increases?

3. **Interpreting Data** What is the mass percent of gold for a 14-karat gold alloy?

4. **Creating Data Tables** Create a data table that gives the approximate mass percent of gold for alloys with karat values of 10, 12, 14, 16, 18, 20, 22, and 24.

Karat Value of Gold

(Graph: Mass Percent of Gold (%) on y-axis, ranging 30 to 100; Gold Karat Value (K) on x-axis, ranging 8 to 24. A straight line rises from about 41% at 10 K to 100% at 24 K.)

Go Online

SciLINKS NSTA

For: Links on alloys
Visit: www.SciLinks.org
Web Code: scn-1142

Making and Using Alloys

Many alloys are made by melting metals and mixing them together in carefully measured amounts. Since the beginning of the Bronze Age, this technique has been used to make copper alloys. Some modern alloys are made by mixing the elements as powders and then heating them under high pressure. This process uses less energy because the metal powders blend at lower temperatures. The material then can be molded into the desired shape immediately. Using a more recent technique, titanium may be bombarded with nitrogen ions to make a strong alloy for artificial joints.

Steels When you want to describe something very hard or tough, you may use the expression "hard as steel." Steel is an alloy of iron with other elements. It is used for its strength, hardness, and resistance to corrosion. Without steel, automobiles, suspension bridges, skyscrapers, and surgical knives would not exist.

Not all steels are alike. Their properties depend on which elements are added to iron and in what amounts. Carbon steels are stronger and harder than wrought iron, which is almost pure iron.

FIGURE 9
Alloys have a wide variety of uses. **Making Generalizations**
How do the properties of bronze make it well-suited for its uses?

Common Alloys			
Alloy	**Elements**	**Properties**	**Uses**
Brass	Copper, zinc	Strong, resists corrosion, polishes well	Musical instruments, faucets, decorative hardware, jewelry
Bronze	Copper, tin	Hard, resists corrosion	Marine hardware, screws, grillwork
Stainless steel	Iron, carbon, nickel, chromium	Strong, resists corrosion	Tableware, cookware, surgical instruments
Carbon steel	Iron, carbon	Inexpensive, strong	Tools, auto bodies, machinery, steel girders, rails
Plumber's solder	Lead, tin	Low melting point	Sealer for joints and leaks in metal plumbing
Sterling silver	Silver, copper	Shiny, harder than pure silver	Jewelry, tableware
Dental amalgam	Mercury, silver, tin, copper, zinc	Low melting point, easily shaped	Dental fillings
Pewter	Tin, antimony, copper; sometimes lead*	Bright or satin finish, resists tarnish	Tableware, decorative objects
Wood's metal	Bismuth, lead, tin, cadmium	Low melting point	Fire sprinklers, electric fuses

*Pewter containing lead cannot be used with food.

Solder

FIGURE 10
Alloys in Daily Life
Solder is used by plumbers to seal leaking pipes. Brass is found in decorative objects, such as this door knocker. Stainless steel is often found in cookware, and pewter is used in some tableware.

▲ Brass

▲ Stainless steel

▲ Pewter

High-carbon steels contain 0.6 to 1.5 percent carbon. Tools, knives, and springs are just some of the uses for high-carbon steels. Low-carbon steels, with less than 0.2 percent carbon, are ductile and malleable and are used for nails, cables, and chains.

There are hundreds of different types of steels. Usually carbon is added to the iron plus one or more of the following metals: chromium, manganese, molybdenum, nickel, tungsten, and vanadium. Steels made with these metals are generally stronger, harder, and more corrosion-resistant than carbon steel. Depending on their properties, these steels may become bicycle frames, train rails, steel tubing, or construction equipment.

Other Alloys Bronze, brass, sterling silver, and solder (SAHD ur) are just a few examples of other kinds of alloys. Alloys are used to make items ranging from plumbing materials and sprinkler systems to tableware and doorknobs. Even your dentist uses alloys. Have you ever had a cavity in a tooth? A mixture of mercury with silver or gold (called an amalgam) makes a pasty solid. It hardens quickly, filling a hole in the tooth. Look at Figure 9 and see how many of the examples listed in the table are alloys you have seen or used.

 **Reading Checkpoint** Name three uses of high-carbon steels.

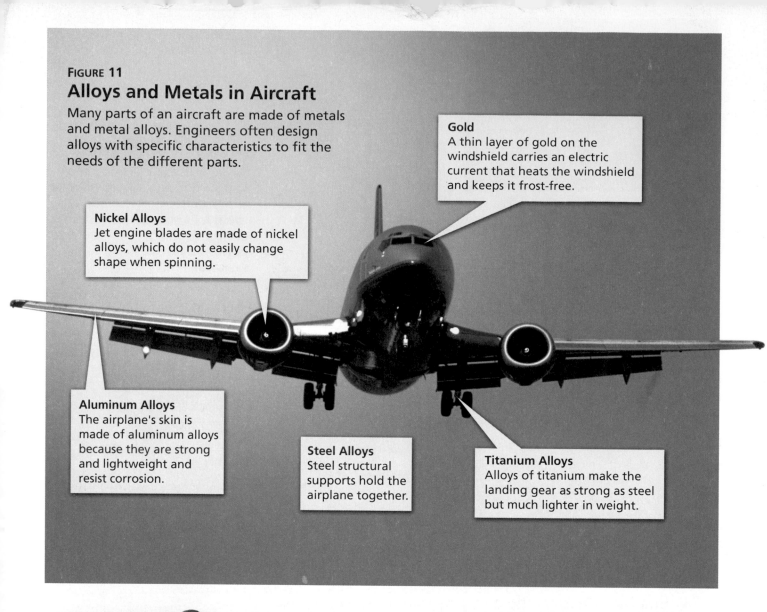

FIGURE 11
Alloys and Metals in Aircraft

Many parts of an aircraft are made of metals and metal alloys. Engineers often design alloys with specific characteristics to fit the needs of the different parts.

Gold
A thin layer of gold on the windshield carries an electric current that heats the windshield and keeps it frost-free.

Nickel Alloys
Jet engine blades are made of nickel alloys, which do not easily change shape when spinning.

Aluminum Alloys
The airplane's skin is made of aluminum alloys because they are strong and lightweight and resist corrosion.

Steel Alloys
Steel structural supports hold the airplane together.

Titanium Alloys
Alloys of titanium make the landing gear as strong as steel but much lighter in weight.

Section 2 Assessment

🔄 **Target Reading Skill** Outlining Use the information in your outline about metals and alloys to answer the questions.

Reviewing Key Concepts

1. a. **Listing** List three properties you would expect a pure metal object to have.
   b. **Reviewing** From what pure metals is bronze made?
   c. **Comparing and Contrasting** Compare and contrast the general properties of alloys and pure metals.

2. a. **Describing** Describe one way in which alloys are made.
   b. **Inferring** A steel suitable for making nails is malleable and ductile. What can you infer about the probable carbon content of the steel?
   c. **Interpreting Tables** Look at the table in Figure 9. What metal may be alloyed with silver to make tableware that is shiny and harder than pure silver?

Lab zone At-Home **Activity**

Finding Alloys Find items in your home that are made from metals or alloys. Look for cooking utensils, tools, toys, sports equipment, appliances, and other household items that are made with these materials. Discuss with members of your family how properties of the metals or alloys relate to the uses of the objects.

Ceramics and Glass

Reading Preview

Key Concepts
- What are the properties of ceramics?
- What are the properties of glass?

Key Terms
- ceramic • glass
- optical fiber

Target Reading Skill
Identifying Main Ideas As you read about ceramics, write the main idea in a graphic organizer like the one below. Then write three supporting details that give examples of the main idea.

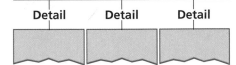

Main Idea

Ceramics are useful because they resist moisture.

Detail	Detail	Detail

Lab zone · Discover Activity

Does It Get Wet?
1. Find the masses of a glazed pottery flowerpot and an unglazed one of similar size. Record both values.
2. Place both pots in a basin of water for ten minutes.
3. Remove the pots from the water and gently blot dry with paper towels.
4. Find and record the masses of both flowerpots again.
5. Calculate the percent of change in mass for each pot.

Think It Over
Inferring Which pot had the greater change in mass? What can you infer about the effect that glazing has on the pot?

Have you ever heard the phrase "a bull in a china shop"? Imagine the damage! The phrase comes from the fact that ceramics and glass are brittle and can shatter when struck. In spite of this property, archaeologists have uncovered many ceramic and glass artifacts used by the Romans and other ancient civilizations. Because ceramics and glass resist moisture and don't react readily, some of these ancient objects remain in excellent condition even today.

Ceramics

Ceramics are hard, crystalline solids made by heating clay and other mineral materials to high temperatures. Clay is made of water and very small mineral particles containing mostly silicon, aluminum, and oxygen. Clay forms when the minerals in rock break down.

FIGURE 12
Homes Made of Clay
These homes in New Mexico were built with clay bricks hundreds of years ago.

Making Ceramics When a clay object is heated above 1,000°C, much of the water present in the clay evaporates, and the particles of clay stick together. This process forms hard ceramics such as bricks and flowerpots. These ceramics have tiny spaces in their structure that absorb and hold water. However, potters can cover a ceramic with a thin layer of silicon dioxide and heat it again. This process forms a glassy, waterproof coating called a glaze. You might see glazed pottery used to serve or store food. Potters often use colorful glazes to create artistic designs on their work.

Properties and Uses of Ceramics Despite their tendency to break, ceramics have several properties that make them useful. **Ceramics resist moisture, do not conduct electricity, and can withstand temperatures that would cause metals to melt.**

Ceramic pottery has been used for thousands of years to store food, protecting it from moisture and animals. Roofing tiles, bricks, and sewer pipes are all long-standing uses of ceramics. Ceramics also are used as insulators in electric equipment and light fixtures.

New uses for ceramics continue to be developed. Surgeons use bioceramic materials, for example, to replace human hips, knees, and other body parts. The catalytic converters in modern cars and trucks contain ceramics that help convert harmful exhaust gases to harmless carbon dioxide and water.

 **Reading Checkpoint** What are some uses of ceramics?

FIGURE 13
Making and Using Ceramics
Colorful glazes were used to decorate the ceramic plates below. **Predicting** *What will happen to the clay, right, when the potter heats it in a kiln, or hot oven?*

FIGURE 14
Ancient Glass
These glass objects, once used in ancient Rome, are on display at the Corning Museum in New York.

Glass

Thousands of years ago, people learned that sand mixed with limestone can be melted into a thick, hot liquid that flows like molasses. If this liquid cools quickly, it forms a clear, solid material with no crystal structure, called **glass**.

Making Glass Early glassmakers added calcium (in the form of limestone) and sodium (in the form of sodium carbonate) to the melting sand. This mixture melts at a lower temperature than sand alone, so it is easier to work with. Window glass, bottles, and jars are still made with this type of glass.

More than 2,000 years ago, glassmakers in ancient Syria invented glassblowing. A glassmaker would put a blob of melted glass on the end of an iron pipe. By blowing air through the pipe, the glassmaker could produce a hollow glass vessel. If the glass was blown inside a wooden mold, jars and vases in beautiful patterns and shapes could be created.

Properties and Uses of Glass Like ceramics, glass is brittle and can shatter when struck. Nonetheless, it has many useful properties. **Glass is clear, can be made in many shapes and colors, and can't be penetrated by liquids.**

Different materials may be added to glass to make it useful for particular purposes. Substituting lead oxide for limestone makes a glass that bends light in useful ways. This kind of glass is used to make lenses for eyeglasses, telescopes, and microscopes. Adding boron oxide creates a glass that resists heat better than ordinary glass. This type of glass is used for cookware and laboratory glassware that must be heated.

Lab zone Try This **Activity**

A Bright Idea
Model communication through glass.

1. Construct a barrier between you and a partner so that you cannot see each other.
2. Run a plastic optical fiber past the barrier. (Plastic fibers work similarly to glass fibers.)
3. Bring the bulb of a penlight flashlight close to your end of the fiber.
4. Using a single flash for "yes" and two flashes for "no," send your partner a message by responding to a series of yes and no questions he or she asks.
5. Change roles so that your partner has a chance to send signals in response to your questions.

Observing What happened when you and your partner sent signals to each other?

FIGURE 15
Light in Optical Fibers
Even if optical fibers are twisted into a loop, the light moves within the fibers.

Communication Through Glass There's a good chance that the next time you make a phone call, your message will travel through glass. An **optical fiber** is a threadlike piece of glass (or plastic) that can be used for transmitting light. When you speak into a telephone, the signal created by your voice is converted to light signals that travel through the glass fiber. At the other end, the light may be converted into electronic signals that can then be converted to sound.

A pair of optical fibers, each the thickness of a human hair, can carry 625,000 phone calls at one time. One quarter pound of glass fiber can replace more than 2 tons of copper wire. This difference is a big advantage when installing long lines like those that carry messages under the ocean. Another benefit of glass fiber is its stability. Since the glass does not corrode as metals do, the lines are easier to maintain.

 Reading Checkpoint **In what form is a signal transmitted through an optical fiber?**

Section 3 Assessment

Target Reading Skill Identifying Main Ideas Use your graphic organizer about ceramics to help you answer Question 1 below.

Reviewing Key Concepts

1. a. **Listing** What are the general properties of ceramics?
   b. **Explaining** Why are ceramics used in the manufacture of spark plugs and many other electrical devices?
   c. **Inferring** Before ceramics were invented, people stored food in containers such as baskets, leather bags, and wooden bowls. Why were ceramics an improvement as containers for food?
2. a. **Reviewing** What is the principal material used in making glass?
   b. **Describing** Describe how the composition of glass may be changed in order to make it useful in lenses.
   c. **Applying Concepts** What properties of glass make it particularly useful for communication via optical fibers?

Writing in Science

Letter It's Upper Egypt and the year is about 5000 B.C. You notice something strange that happens when your pottery furnace overheats. The presence of limestone containing sand and soda produces shiny coatings on your ceramic pots. Amazingly, the coatings render the pots waterproof! Write a letter to a relative describing your discovery.

Radioactive Elements

Reading Preview

Key Concepts
- How was radioactivity discovered?
- What types of particles and energy can radioactive decay produce?
- In what ways are radioactive isotopes useful?

Key Terms
- nuclear reaction
- radioactive decay
- radioactivity
- alpha particle
- beta particle
- gamma radiation
- half-life
- radioactive dating
- tracer

Target Reading Skill
Building Vocabulary A definition states the meaning of a word or phrase by explaining its most important feature or function. After you read the section, reread the paragraphs that contain definitions of Key Terms. Use all the information you have learned to write a definition of each Key Term in your own words.

Lab zone Discover **Activity**

How Much Goes Away?

1. Make a circle about 8–10 centimeters in diameter on a piece of paper. You can do this by tracing the rim of a round container.
2. Use a straightedge to draw a line dividing the circle in half. Then divide one half into quarters, then into eighths, and so on, as shown in the diagram.
3. With scissors, cut out your circle. Now cut away the undivided half circle. Next, cut away the undivided quarter circle. Continue until you are left with one segment.
4. Place the segments on your desktop in the order you cut them.

Think It Over
Drawing Conclusions How is the piece of paper changing each time? Suppose the original circle was a model for a sample of radioactive material, and the paper you cut away is material that became nonradioactive. What would eventually happen?

What if you could find a way to turn dull, cheap lead metal into valuable gold? More than a thousand years ago, many people thought it was a great idea, too. They tried everything they could think of. Of course, nothing worked. There is no chemical reaction that converts one element into another. Even so, elements do sometimes change into other elements. A uranium atom can become a thorium atom. Atoms of carbon can become atoms of nitrogen. (But lead never changes into gold, unfortunately!) How is it possible for these changes to happen?

FIGURE 16
Trying to Make Gold From Lead
This painting from 1570 shows people trying to change lead into gold. No such chemical reaction was ever accomplished.

FIGURE 17

Radiation From Uranium
As with Becquerel's discovery, radiation from the uranium-containing mineral has exposed the photographic film.

Radioactivity

You learned earlier that the number of protons in the nucleus of an atom determines its identity. Chemical change involves only an atom's electrons. Therefore, a chemical reaction will not convert one element into a different element. Such a change happens only during **nuclear reactions** (NOO klee ur)—reactions involving the particles in the nucleus of an atom.

Remember that atoms with the same number of protons and different numbers of neutrons are called isotopes. Some isotopes are unstable; that is, their nuclei do not hold together well. In a process called **radioactive decay,** the atomic nuclei of unstable isotopes release fast-moving particles and energy.

Discovery of Radioactivity In 1896, the French scientist Henri Becquerel discovered the effects of radioactive decay quite by accident while studying a mineral containing uranium. He observed that with exposure to sunlight, the mineral gave off a penetrating energy that could expose film. Becquerel assumed that sunlight was necessary for the energy release. So, when the weather turned cloudy, he put away his materials in a dark desk drawer, including a sample of the mineral placed next to a photographic plate wrapped in paper. Later, when Becquerel opened his desk to retrieve these items, he was surprised to discover an image of the mineral sample on the photographic plate. Sunlight wasn't necessary after all. Becquerel hypothesized that uranium spontaneously gives off energy, called radiation, all the time. But if so, what was the source of the energy?

Becquerel presented his findings to a young researcher, Marie Curie and her husband, Pierre. After further study, the Curies concluded that a reaction was taking place within the uranium nuclei. **Radioactivity** is the name that Marie gave to this spontaneous emission of radiation by an unstable atomic nucleus.

 **Reading Checkpoint** How is a nuclear reaction different from a chemical reaction?

FIGURE 18
Marie Curie
Marie Curie, her husband Pierre, and Henri Becquerel pioneered the study of radioactive elements.

Polonium and Radium Marie Curie was surprised to find that some minerals containing uranium were even more radioactive than pure uranium. Suspecting that the minerals contained small amounts of other, highly radioactive elements, the Curies set to work. They eventually isolated two new elements, which Marie named polonium and radium.

Types of Radioactive Decay

There are three major forms of radiation produced during the radioactive decay of an unstable nucleus. **Natural radioactive decay can produce alpha particles, beta particles, and gamma rays.** The particles and energy produced during radioactive decay are forms of nuclear radiation.

Alpha Decay An **alpha particle** consists of two protons and two neutrons and is positively charged. It is the same as a helium nucleus. The release of an alpha particle by an atom decreases the atomic number by 2 and the mass number by 4. For example, a thorium-232 nucleus decays to produce an alpha particle and a radium-228 nucleus.

Beta Decay Some atoms are unstable because they have too many neutrons. During beta decay, a neutron inside the nucleus of an unstable atom changes into a negatively charged beta particle and a proton. A **beta particle** is a fast-moving electron given off by a nucleus during radioactive decay. The new proton remains inside the nucleus. That means that the nucleus now has one less neutron and one more proton. Its mass number remains the same but its atomic number increases by 1. For example, a carbon-14 nucleus decays to produce a beta particle and a nitrogen-14 nucleus.

Gamma Radiation Alpha and beta decay are almost always accompanied by gamma radiation. **Gamma radiation** consists of high-energy waves, similar to X-rays. Gamma radiation (also called gamma rays) has no charge and does not cause a change in either the atomic mass or the atomic number.

FIGURE 19
Radioactive Decay
Radioactive elements give off particles and energy during radioactive decay. **Interpreting Diagrams** *Which type of radioactive decay produces a negatively charged particle?*

Alpha Decay

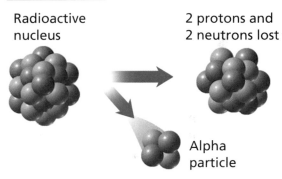

Radioactive nucleus → 2 protons and 2 neutrons lost — Alpha particle

Beta Decay

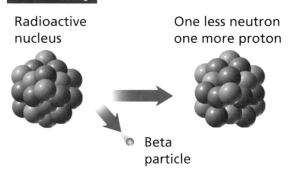

Radioactive nucleus → One less neutron one more proton — Beta particle

Gamma Decay

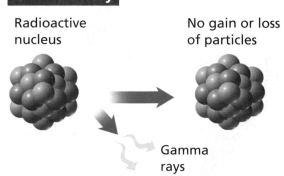

Radioactive nucleus → No gain or loss of particles — Gamma rays

FIGURE 20

The Penetrating Power of Nuclear Radiation
The three types of nuclear radiation were named based on how easily each one could be blocked. Alpha, beta, and gamma are the first three letters of the Greek alphabet.
Inferring *Which type of nuclear radiation is the most penetrating?*

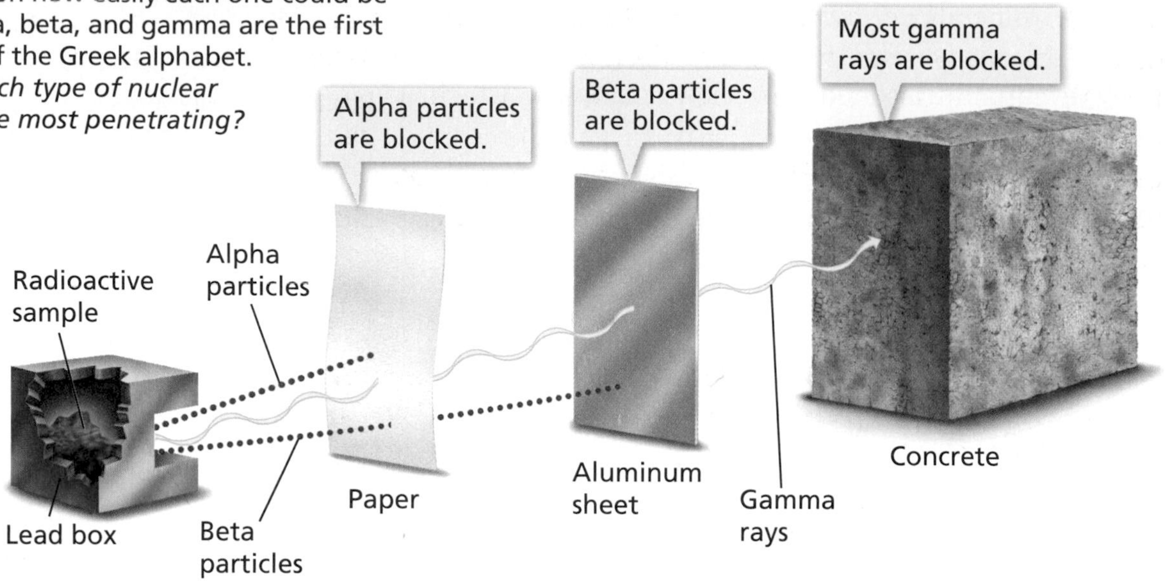

Most gamma rays are blocked.

Beta particles are blocked.

Alpha particles are blocked.

Radioactive sample

Alpha particles

Paper

Aluminum sheet

Gamma rays

Concrete

Lead box

Beta particles

Effects of Nuclear Radiation Although alpha particles move very fast, they are stopped by collisions with atoms. In Figure 20, you can see that alpha particles are blocked by a sheet of paper. Alpha radiation can cause an injury much like a bad burn.

Beta particles are much faster and more penetrating than alpha particles. They can pass through paper, but they are blocked by an aluminum sheet 5 millimeters thick. Beta particles can also travel into the human body and damage its cells.

Gamma rays are the most penetrating type of radiation. You would need a piece of lead several centimeters thick or a concrete wall about a meter thick to stop gamma rays. They can pass right through a human body, delivering intense energy to cells and causing severe damage.

 Reading Checkpoint) How can alpha radiation affect the body?

Lab zone Skills **Activity**

Calculating
Carbon-14 has a half-life of 5,730 years. Data from several newly discovered fossils shows that carbon-14 has undergone decay in the fossils for five half-lives. Calculate the age of the fossils.

Using Radioactive Isotopes

The decay of radioactive isotopes makes them useful in many ways. **Uses include determining the ages of natural materials on Earth, tracing the steps of chemical reactions and industrial processes, diagnosing and treating disease, and providing sources of energy.** These uses stem from two key properties of radioactive isotopes: First, radioactive isotopes change into different kinds of matter, and second, they give off detectable radiation.

Radioactive Dating When the atoms of a radioactive isotope decay, they can change into other kinds of atoms. However, not all the atoms of a radioactive sample decay at once. They decay randomly, one at a time. Although you can't predict when any particular nucleus will decay, the time it takes for half the atoms to change can be measured. The **half-life** of an isotope is the length of time needed for half of the atoms of a sample to decay. The half-life is different for each isotope. As you can see in Figure 21, half-lives can range from less than a second to billions of years!

Fossils are the traces or remains of living things that have been preserved. The half-lives of certain radioactive isotopes are useful in determining the ages of rocks and fossils. For example, as plants grow they use carbon dioxide (CO_2) from the air. Some carbon dioxide contains carbon-14, which becomes part of the plant's structures the same way carbon-12 does. After the plant dies, it stops taking in carbon dioxide. If the plant's remains are preserved as a fossil, the amount of carbon-14 present can be measured. From the data, scientists can calculate how many half-lives have passed since the plant was alive. In this way, they can estimate the age of the fossil and its surrounding rock. This process is called **radioactive dating**.

Because the half-life of carbon-14 is only 5,730 years, it cannot be used to find the ages of objects older than about 60,000 years. Other isotopes, such as potassium-40 and uranium-238, are used to study older fossils, rocks, and objects used by early humans.

FIGURE 21
The half-lives of radioactive isotopes vary greatly.

Half-Lives of Some Radioactive Isotopes	
Element	**Half-Life**
Polonium-216	0.16 second
Sodium-24	15 hours
Iodine-131	8.07 days
Phosphorus-32	14.3 days
Cobalt-60	5.26 years
Radium-226	1,600 years
Carbon-14	5,730 years
Chlorine-36	400,000 years
Uranium-235	710 million years
Uranium-238	4.5 billion years

FIGURE 22
Radioactive Dating
Using the known half-lives of certain radioactive isotopes, such as uranium-238, scientists can determine the age of ancient objects. This saber-toothed cat lived about 25 million years ago.

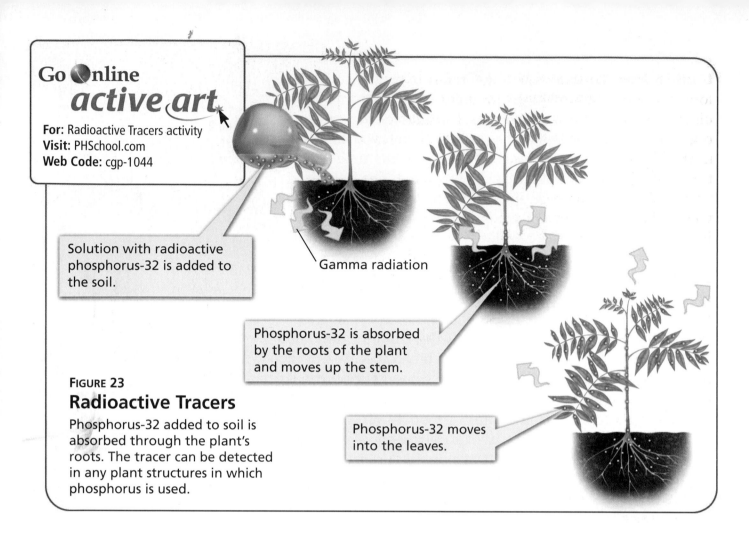

Go Online
active art

For: Radioactive Tracers activity
Visit: PHSchool.com
Web Code: cgp-1044

Solution with radioactive phosphorus-32 is added to the soil.

Gamma radiation

Phosphorus-32 is absorbed by the roots of the plant and moves up the stem.

FIGURE 23
Radioactive Tracers

Phosphorus-32 added to soil is absorbed through the plant's roots. The tracer can be detected in any plant structures in which phosphorus is used.

Phosphorus-32 moves into the leaves.

Uses in Science and Industry Like a lighthouse flashing in the night, a radioactive isotope "signals" where it is. **Tracers** are radioactive isotopes that can be followed through the steps of a chemical reaction or an industrial process. Tracers behave the same way as nonradioactive forms of an element. Scientists can follow tracers, using equipment that detects radiation. This technique is helpful for studying reactions in living organisms, as shown in Figure 23. Phosphorus is used by plants in small amounts for healthy growth. A plant will absorb radioactive phosphorus-32 added to the soil just as it does the nonradioactive form. Radiation will be present in any part of the plant that contains the isotope. In this way, biologists can learn where and how plants use phosphorus.

In industry, tracers are used to find weak spots in metal pipes, especially oil pipelines. When added to a liquid, tracers can be easily detected if they leak out of the pipes. Engineers use gamma radiation from radioactive isotopes to look for flaws in metal. Gamma rays can pass through metal and be detected on a photographic film. By looking at the gamma-ray images, structural engineers can detect small cracks in the metal of bridges and building frames. Without these images, a problem might not be discovered until a disaster occurs.

Uses in Medicine Doctors use radioactive isotopes to detect medical problems and to treat some diseases. Tracers injected into the body travel to organs and other structures where that chemical is normally used. Using equipment that detects radiation, technicians make images of the bone, blood vessel, or organ affected. For example, tracers made with technetium-99 are used to diagnose problems in the bones, liver, kidneys, and digestive system.

In a process called radiation therapy, radioactive elements are used to destroy unhealthy cells. For example, iodine-131 is given to patients with tumors of the thyroid gland—a gland in the neck that controls the rate at which nutrients are used. Because the thyroid gland uses iodine, the radioactive iodine-131 collects in the gland. Radiation from this isotope destroys unwanted cells in the gland without serious effects on other parts of the body.

Cancer tumors of different kinds often are treated from outside the body with high-energy gamma rays. Many hospitals use cobalt-60 for this purpose. When gamma radiation is directed toward a cancer tumor, it causes changes that kill the cancer cells.

Nuclear Power Some power plants use radioactive isotopes as fuel. The nuclei of certain radioactive isotopes are made to split into smaller fragments, releasing enormous amounts of energy. Carefully controlled reactions, most often using uranium-235, provide electric energy in many parts of the world. And nuclear reactions provide the energy for nuclear submarines and other types of ocean vessels.

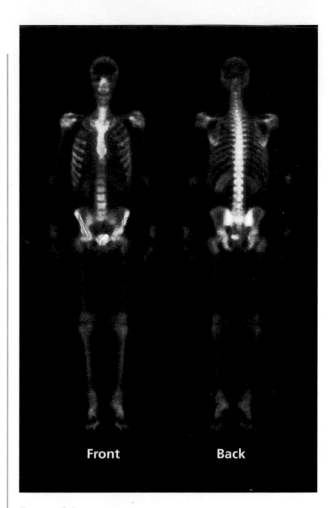

FIGURE 24
Radioactive Isotopes in Medicine
Front and back body scans of a healthy patient were made using a radioactive isotope.

Front   Back

 **Reading Checkpoint** What is the fuel source for nuclear power plants?

FIGURE 25
Nuclear Power
By using nuclear power, this submarine can operate for years without refueling. **Inferring** *Why is this an advantage for an ocean vessel?*

FIGURE 26
Radiation Protection
Clothing that protects against radiation must be worn by people working with highly radioactive materials.

Safe Use of Radioactive Materials Despite their usefulness, radioactive materials are dangerous. Radiation penetrates living tissue, knocking electrons from atoms. This process produces particles that then can interfere with chemical reactions in living cells. Illness, disease, and even death may result from overexposure to radiation.

The dangers of radioactive materials mean that their use must be carefully managed. People who work with these materials must wear protective clothing and use insulating shields. Radioactive wastes and contaminated equipment can't just be thrown away. These items must be disposed of properly.

Materials with low levels of radiation may be buried in landfills. Such landfills are carefully monitored to prevent contamination of the environment. Isotopes with long half-lives, however, will remain hazardous for hundreds or even thousands of years. One solution to this problem is to dispose of these kinds of materials in specially designed containers that are buried in very dry underground tunnels. In that way, the radioactive wastes can be isolated for many generations.

 **Reading Checkpoint** **What type of radioactive materials may be buried in landfills?**

Section 4 Assessment

Target Reading Skill **Building Vocabulary** Use your definitions to help answer the questions.

Reviewing Key Concepts

1. a. **Identifying** Under what circumstances did Becquerel first notice the effects of radioactivity?
   b. **Interpreting Photographs** Look at the photo in Figure 17. Explain in your own words what happened.
   c. **Applying Concepts** How did Becquerel's work lead to the discovery of two new elements?
2. a. **Listing** What are three products of radioactive decay?
   b. **Comparing and Contrasting** Contrast the penetrating power of the three major types of nuclear radiation.
   c. **Predicting** Predict the identity and mass number of the nucleus formed during the beta decay of magnesium-28.
3. a. **Explaining** How can radioactive isotopes be used as tracers?
   b. **Relating Cause and Effect** How is the use of radioactive isotopes in treating some forms of cancer related to certain properties of gamma radiation?

Writing in Science

Persuasive Speech N.I.M.B.Y. is short for the phrase "not in my backyard." It stands for the idea that people don't want unpleasant or possibly hazardous conditions near where they live. They would prefer to see radioactive wastes go elsewhere. Your local government has invited citizens to a meeting to discuss possible options for storing radioactive wastes from nearby medical or industrial sites. Write a one- or two-paragraph speech for the public meeting, expressing your opinion.

146 ◆ **K**

Lab zone Skills Lab

That's Half-Life!

Problem

How can you model the way a sample of radio-active waste decays to a nonhazardous level?

Skills Focus

making models, graphing, interpreting data

Materials

- 100 pennies
- graph paper
- container such as a jar or a box
- colored pencils (optional)

Procedure

1. Copy the data table into your notebook. Then place 100 pennies in a container.

2. Shake the pennies out onto the desktop. Separate the ones showing heads from those showing tails.

3. Count the number of pennies showing tails and count the number of pennies showing heads. Record both these values.

4. Put back only the pennies showing tails.

5. Repeat the process until there are two pennies or fewer left in the container.

6. Keep a tally of the total number of pennies removed from the container. Record this number after each trial.

Analyze and Conclude

1. **Making Models** What does each of the following represent: (a) each trial, (b) the pennies that came up heads, (c) the pennies that came up tails?

2. **Graphing** Make a graph of your data. Label the horizontal axis with the trial number. Label the vertical axis with the number of pennies left in the container after each trial. Connect the data points with a curved line. On the same set of axes, plot the total number of pennies removed from the container after each trial. Use a dotted line or different colored pencil to make this graph.

3. **Interpreting Data** What do the graphs show?

4. **Communicating** Suppose 2,560 grams of low-level radioactive waste is buried at a waste disposal site. Assume that 10 grams of radioactive material gives off an acceptable level of radiation and that one half-life is 5.26 years. Write a paragraph in which you explain to townspeople how much time must pass before there is an acceptable radiation level at the site.

More to Explore

How could you use this model to show the decay of a sample that has twice the mass as the sample you modeled in this lab? What would you do differently? Predict how you think the results would differ.

Data Table			
Trial	Tails Remaining	Heads Removed (each trial)	Total Pennies Removed
1			
2			
3			

① Polymers and Composites

Key Concepts

- Polymers form when chemical bonds link large numbers of monomers in a repeating pattern.
- Many composite materials include one or more polymers.
- Synthetic polymers are strong, inexpensive to make, and last a long time.
- It is often cheaper to throw plastics away and make new ones than it is to reuse them. As a result, plastics increase the volume of trash.

Key Terms
polymer
monomer
plastic
composite

② Metals and Alloys

Key Concepts

- Alloys are used much more than pure metals because they are generally stronger and less likely to react with air or water.
- Many alloys are made by melting metals and mixing them together in carefully measured amounts.

Key Term
alloy

③ Ceramics and Glass

Key Concepts

- Ceramics resist moisture, do not conduct electricity, and can withstand temperatures that would cause metals to melt.
- Glass is clear, can be made in many shapes and colors, and can't be penetrated by liquids.

Key Terms
ceramic
glass
optical fiber

④ Radioactive Elements

Key Concepts

- In 1896, the French scientist Henri Becquerel discovered the effects of radioactive decay while studying a mineral containing uranium.
- Natural radioactive decay can produce alpha particles, beta particles, and gamma rays.
- Among the many uses of the decay of radioactive isotopes are determining the ages of natural materials on Earth, tracing the steps of chemical reactions and industrial processes, diagnosing and treating disease, and providing sources of energy.

Key Terms
nuclear reaction
radioactive decay
radioactivity
alpha particle
beta particle
gamma radiation
half-life
radioactive dating
tracer

Review and Assessment

Organizing Information

Comparing and Contrasting Copy the table about polymers, alloys, ceramics, and glass onto a separate sheet of paper. Then fill in the empty spaces and add a title. (For more on Comparing and Contrasting tables, see the Skills Handbook.)

Material	Made From	How Made	How Used
Polymers	Monomers (carbon compounds)	a. ___?___	b. ___?___
Alloys	c. ___?___	Metals heated and mixed	d. ___?___
Ceramics	Clay; other materials	e. ___?___	f. ___?___
Glass	g. ___?___	Melted, then cooled in desired shapes	h. ___?___

Reviewing Key Terms

Choose the letter of the best answer.

1. Any large molecule made of many monomers is called a
   a. plastic.
   b. polymer.
   c. protein.
   d. chain.

2. Fiberglass is a type of
   a. polymer.
   b. alloy.
   c. ceramic.
   d. composite.

3. The properties of alloys most resemble those of
   a. ceramics.
   b. glass.
   c. metals.
   d. polymers.

4. Clean sand is heated to its melting point to make
   a. ceramics.
   b. glass.
   c. alloys.
   d. composites.

5. Unstable atomic nuclei that release fast-moving particles and energy are
   a. radioactive.
   b. alloys.
   c. isotopes.
   d. alpha particles.

If the statement is true, write *true*. If it is false, change the underlined word or words to make the statement true.

6. <u>Oxygen</u> is the element that forms the backbone of most polymers.

7. Cellulose is an example of a <u>synthetic</u> polymer.

8. A useful alloy of copper and tin is <u>steel</u>.

9. Roofing tiles and bricks are made with <u>ceramics</u>.

10. Alpha, beta, and gamma radiation form as the result of <u>chemical</u> reactions.

Writing in Science

Comparison Paragraph Write a paragraph comparing and contrasting natural and synthetic polymers. Give two examples of each.

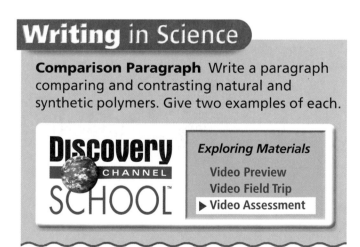
Discovery CHANNEL SCHOOL

Exploring Materials

Video Preview
Video Field Trip
▶ Video Assessment

Review and Assessment

Checking Concepts

11. Name some polymers that are produced in nature. Tell where they come from.

12. Explain why some advantages of using synthetic polymers can become disadvantages.

13. Why is gold mixed with other metals to make jewelry?

14. Describe the process that changes clay into ceramics.

15. Explain why a chemical reaction cannot change one element into another element.

16. What properties of radioactive isotopes make them useful?

Thinking Critically

17. **Comparing and Contrasting** Explain which material—steel, glass, or polystyrene foam—would be the best choice for each of the following uses: a hammer, the wall of a saltwater aquarium, an egg carton.

18. **Applying Concepts** The earliest ceramic pots absorbed moisture. Why are glazed pots better for storing food?

19. **Calculating** A wooden tool found in a cave has one fourth as much carbon-14 as a living tree. How old is the tool? (*Hint:* The half-life of carbon-14 is 5,730 years.)

20. **Interpreting Diagrams** Look at the diagram below. Identify what is happening. Then, draw a labeled diagram of how the next step in the process would look.

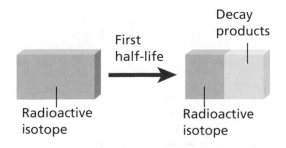

Applying Skills

Use the diagram to answer the questions.

The diagram below shows the first few steps of the radioactive decay of uranium-238.

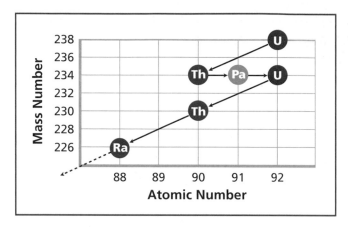

21. **Interpreting Data** How many elements are in the diagram? How many different isotopes of each element are there?

22. **Classifying** What type of radioactive decay resulted in uranium-238 becoming thorium-234? How do you know?

23. **Interpreting Diagrams** Describe how thorium-234 is changed into uranium-234.

24. **Inferring** How do you know from the diagram that thorium-230 is radioactive?

Lab zone Chapter **Project**

Performance Assessment Prepare a chart or poster to display the polymers you examined. Provide a sample of each polymer and include information such as its name, where it was found, what monomers it is made of (if known), and significant physical and chemical properties that you determined. Be prepared to compare the polymers with other types of materials such as glass, ceramics, and metals.

Standardized Test Prep

Choose the letter of the best answer.

1. Which of the following is *not* an example of an alloy?
   A brass
   B bronze
   C stainless steel
   D iron

Use the information and data table below to answer Questions 2–3.

Polymer Identification			
Test	**Cotton**	**Wool**	**Polyester**
Texture	Smooth	Rough	Smooth
Near flame	Does not bend or melt	Curls away from heat	Melts
In flame	Burns; smells like paper burning	Burns; smells like hair burning	Melts

2. A student has two pieces of fabric—one blue and one green. The student performs an investigation to identify the fabrics. What can the student conclude if the texture of both pieces of fabric is smooth?
   F Both fabrics must be cotton.
   G Both fabrics must be polyester.
   H One fabric must be cotton and the other must be polyester.
   J Neither piece is wool.

3. What should the student do before testing either piece of fabric near or in a flame?
   A Put on safety goggles and an apron and tie back long hair.
   B Crumple the fabric to make it burn more easily.
   C Wash his or her hands.
   D Determine the mass of the fabric

4. Radioactive isotopes give off radiation that can be detected. This property makes them useful in which of the following ways?
   F as tracers in chemical reactions
   G in detecting leaks in oil pipelines
   H in diagnosing certain medical problems
   J all of the above

Constructed Response

5. You are considering using either glass or disposable plastic to serve soft drinks at a party. Discuss how the beverage containers are similar and how they are different.

◀ A gold crown is a symbol of royalty.

Gold—The Noble Metal

You can find it —

on people's wrists, in your computer, on dinner plates, satellites, and in spacesuits

Because gold is both rare and beautiful, people have prized it since ancient times. Gold was so valuable that it was used to make crowns for rulers and coins for trade. In some cultures, people wear gold bracelets and necklaces to show their wealth.

In spite of its many uses, gold is scarce. For every 23,000 metric tons of rock and minerals from the Earth's crust, you could produce only about 14 grams of gold, enough to make a small ring. Today, gold is found in many parts of the world. But even rich gold fields produce only small amounts of gold. In fact, if all the gold mined over the years were gathered and melted down, you would have a cube only about 15 meters on a side—about the size of a four-story square building.

Wearing Gold
This woman from Ghana in Africa displays her wealth in gold jewelry.

Gold Nugget
A nugget is gold in one of its natural forms.

Properties of Gold

Why is gold used for everything from bracelets to space helmets to medicine? You'll find the answers in this precious metal's unusual chemical and physical properties. Gold is deep yellow in color and so shiny, or lustrous, that its Latin name, *aurum,* means "glowing dawn." Gold's chemical symbol—Au—comes from that Latin word. Gold is very heavy—one of the densest metals.

Gold is very soft and malleable. That is, it's easy to bend or hammer into shapes without breaking. It can be pounded into very thin sheets called gold leaf. Gold is also the most ductile metal. You can draw out 30 grams of gold into a fine thread as long as 8 kilometers without breaking it.

Gold is very stable. Unlike iron, gold doesn't rust. It also doesn't tarnish in air as silver does. Ancient chemists thought that gold was superior to other metals. They classified it as one of the "noble" metals.

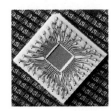

Ductile
Because gold is so ductile, it can be made into fine wires like the ones in this computer chip.

Malleable
A Korean delicacy is dried fish coated with gold leaf.

Stable and Lustrous
Hundreds of years ago, traders used these gold doubloons as money.

Science Activity

The gold hunters who flocked to California during the Gold Rush of 1849 were searching for gold in streams and rivers. Although they had very simple equipment, their technique worked because gold is so dense. Using pans, miners washed gold-bearing gravel in running water. Try your own gold panning.

Set up your own model of gold panning, using a large pan, a gravel mixture, and a very dense material as a substitute for gold. Use a sink trap. Under running water, shake and swirl the pan until the lighter materials wash away. What's left is your "gold."

• Why is "gold" left in the pan while other materials are washed away?

Golden Trade Routes

In West Africa nearly 1,000 years ago, salt was said to be worth its weight in gold. It may be hard to imagine how valuable this mineral was to people. But if you lived in a very hot, dry climate, you would need salt. It would be as valuable to you as gold. In West Africa, salt and gold were the most important goods traded.

Camel caravans crossed the desert going south, carrying slabs of salt from mines in the desert to trade centers, such as Jenne and Timbuktu. But several hundred kilometers south in the Kingdom of Ghana, salt was scarce and gold was plentiful. Salt traders from the north traveled into the forests of Ghana to trade salt for gold.

Around 1100, Arab travelers in Africa wrote about the fabulous wealth of the Kingdom of Ghana. The most popular tale was that the salt traders and gold miners never met, as a way of keeping secret the location of gold mines. Traders from the north left slabs of salt in an agreed-upon trading place, pounded their drums to indicate a trade, and then withdrew. Miners from the south arrived, left an amount of gold that seemed fair, and withdrew. The salt traders returned. If they thought the trade was fair, they took the gold and left. If they were not satisfied, the silent trade continued.

Salt Caravan
Camels carrying salt slabs
travel to Timbuktu.

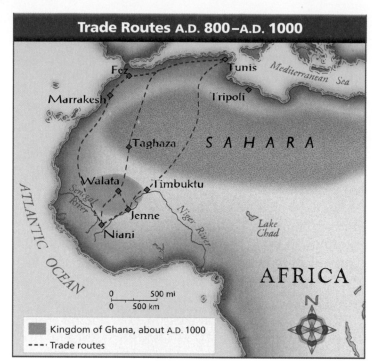

Gold Trade Routes
The map shows the busy north-south trade routes in West Africa about 1,000 years ago.

Social Studies Activity

How would you succeed as a gold or salt trader? Find out by carrying out your own silent trade. Work in teams of Salt Traders and Gold Miners. Before trading, each team should decide how much a bag of gold or a block of salt is worth. Then, for each silent trade, make up a situation that would change the value of gold or salt, such as, "Demand for gold in Europe increases."

• Suppose you are selling a product today. How would the supply of the product affect the value or sale price of the product?

Go for the Gold

What do these sayings have in common?

"It's worth its weight in gold."

"Speech is silver, silence is golden."

"All that glitters is not gold."

"Go for the gold!"

All of these sayings use gold as a symbol of excellence, richness, and perfection—things that people want and search for. When writers use *gold* or *golden,* they are referring to something desirable, of value or worth. These words may also represent the beauty of gold.

In literature, writers and poets often use *gold* to make a comparison in a simile or metaphor. Similes and metaphors are figures of speech.

- A simile makes a comparison between two things, using *like* or *as* in the comparison. Here's an example: "An honest person's promise is as good as gold."

- A metaphor is a comparison without the use of like or as, such as, "When you're in trouble, true friends are golden."

Look for similes and metaphors in the poem by Florence Converse. What similes or metaphors has Converse made? What would this poem be like without the comparisons?

Rune of Riches*

I have a golden ball,
A big, bright, shining one,
Pure gold; and it is all
Mine—It is the sun.

I have a silver ball
A white and glistening stone
That other people call
The moon;—my very own!

The jewel things that prick
My cushion's soft blue cover
Are mine,—my stars, thick, thick,
Scattered the sky all over.

And everything that's mine
Is yours, and yours, and yours,—
The shimmer and the shine!—
Let's lock our wealth out-doors!

—Florence Converse

*A rune is a song or poem.

Language Arts Activity

What does gold symbolize for you? Think of some comparisons of your own in which you use gold in a simile or metaphor. After jotting down all of your ideas, choose one (or more) and decide what comparison you will make. Write a short saying, a proverb, or a short poem that includes your own simile or metaphor.

- How does your comparison make your saying or poem more interesting?

Measuring Gold

People often say that something is "worth its weight in gold." But modern-day jewelry is seldom made of pure gold. Because gold is so soft, it is usually mixed with another metal to form an alloy—a mixture of two or more metals. Most commonly the other metal in a gold alloy is copper, although alloys of gold can also contain silver, zinc, or other metals.

Suppose you are shopping for a gold chain. You see two chains that look the same and are exactly the same size. How do you decide which one to buy? If you look closely at the gold jewelry, you'll probably see in small print the numbers "20K," "18K," "14K," or "12K." The "K" is the abbreviation for karat, which is the measure of how pure an alloy of gold is. Pure gold is 24 karat. Gold that is 50 percent pure is $\frac{12}{24}$ gold, or 12 karat. The greater the amount of gold in a piece of jewelry, the higher the value.

You look again at the two gold chains and decide that your favorite is the 18-karat gold chain. It has copper in it. What percent of the 18 K gold chain is gold? What percent is copper?

Weighing Gold
A worker in the Federal Reserve Bank of the United States weighs dense ingots, or bars, of pure gold.

❶ Read and Understand

You know that pure gold is $\frac{24}{24}$ gold,

and an 18 karat chain is $\frac{18}{24}$ gold.

❷ Plan and Solve

In order to find out what percent of an 18 K chain is gold, you need to write a proportion.

$$\frac{\text{Number of gold parts} \rightarrow 18}{\text{Number of parts in the whole} \rightarrow 24}$$

Then simplify the fraction and convert it to a percentage.

$$\frac{18}{24} = \frac{3}{4} = 75\%$$

❸ Look Back and Check

If 75% of the chain is gold, then 25% of the chain must be copper.

How would you choose a gold ring? To decide, you might determine what percent of each ring is gold.

- What percent of a 14 K gold ring is gold? What percent is another metal? Round decimals to the nearest hundredth.

- What percent of a 12 K ring is gold? What percent of the 20 K ring is gold?

- Which ring would you like to own— the 12 K or the 20 K? Why?

Gold Mask
This gold mask was found in the tomb of a ruler of Mycenae, a city in ancient Greece. The mask is about 3,500 years old.

Tie It Together

Gold Producers

South Africa	United States	Russia
Australia	Canada	China

A Treasure Hunt

Work in small groups to make a World Treasure Map of one of the countries where gold is mined today. Use the library to learn about the gold-producing countries listed above.

On a large map of the world, use push pins to mark the locations of the gold sites. In the United States and Canada, mark the states and provinces that are the largest producers. Make up fact sheets to answer questions such as:

- Where are gold sites located in each country?

- When was gold first discovered there?

- Did a gold rush influence the history of that area?

If possible, collect photographs to illustrate gold products in each country. Post your pictures and fact sheets at the side of the World Treasure Map.

Think Like a Scientist

Scientists have a particular way of looking at the world, or scientific habits of mind. Whenever you ask a question and explore possible answers, you use many of the same skills that scientists do. Some of these skills are described on this page.

Observing

When you use one or more of your five senses to gather information about the world, you are **observing.** Hearing a dog bark, counting twelve green seeds, and smelling smoke are all observations. To increase the power of their senses, scientists sometimes use microscopes, telescopes, or other instruments that help them make more detailed observations.

An observation must be an accurate report of what your senses detect. It is important to keep careful records of your observations in science class by writing or drawing in a notebook. The information collected through observations is called evidence, or data.

Inferring

When you interpret an observation, you are **inferring,** or making an inference. For example, if you hear your dog barking, you may infer that someone is at your front door. To make this inference, you combine the evidence—the barking dog—and your experience or knowledge—you know that your dog barks when strangers approach—to reach a logical conclusion.

Notice that an inference is not a fact; it is only one of many possible interpretations for an observation. For example, your dog may be barking because it wants to go for a walk. An inference may turn out to be incorrect even if it is based on accurate observations and logical reasoning. The only way to find out if an inference is correct is to investigate further.

Predicting

When you listen to the weather forecast, you hear many predictions about the next day's weather—what the temperature will be, whether it will rain, and how windy it will be. Weather forecasters use observations and knowledge of weather patterns to predict the weather. The skill of **predicting** involves making an inference about a future event based on current evidence or past experience.

Because a prediction is an inference, it may prove to be false. In science class, you can test some of your predictions by doing experiments. For example, suppose you predict that larger paper airplanes can fly farther than smaller airplanes. How could you test your prediction?

Activity

Use the photograph to answer the questions below.

Observing Look closely at the photograph. List at least three observations.

Inferring Use your observations to make an inference about what has happened. What experience or knowledge did you use to make the inference?

Predicting Predict what will happen next. On what evidence or experience do you base your prediction?

Classifying

Could you imagine searching for a book in the library if the books were shelved in no particular order? Your trip to the library would be an all-day event! Luckily, librarians group together books on similar topics or by the same author. Grouping together items that are alike in some way is called **classifying.** You can classify items in many ways: by size, by shape, by use, and by other important characteristics.

Like librarians, scientists use the skill of classifying to organize information and objects. When things are sorted into groups, the relationships among them become easier to understand.

Activity

Classify the objects in the photograph into two groups based on any characteristic you choose. Then use another characteristic to classify the objects into three groups.

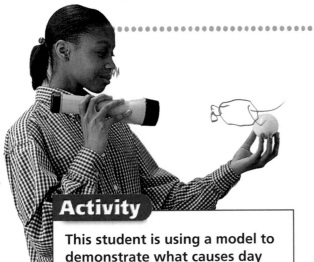

Making Models

Have you ever drawn a picture to help someone understand what you were saying? Such a drawing is one type of model. A model is a picture, diagram, computer image, or other representation of a complex object or process. **Making models** helps people understand things that they cannot observe directly.

Scientists often use models to represent things that are either very large or very small, such as the planets in the solar system, or the parts of a cell. Such models are physical models—drawings or three-dimensional structures that look like the real thing. Other models are mental models—mathematical equations or words that describe how something works.

Activity

This student is using a model to demonstrate what causes day and night on Earth. What do the flashlight and the tennis ball in the model represent?

Communicating

Whenever you talk on the phone, write a report, or listen to your teacher at school, you are communicating. **Communicating** is the process of sharing ideas and information with other people. Communicating effectively requires many skills, including writing, reading, speaking, listening, and making models.

Scientists communicate to share results, information, and opinions. Scientists often communicate about their work in journals, over the telephone, in letters, and on the Internet.

They also attend scientific meetings where they share their ideas with one another in person.

Activity

On a sheet of paper, write out clear, detailed directions for tying your shoe. Then exchange directions with a partner. Follow your partner's directions exactly. How successful were you at tying your shoe? How could your partner have communicated more clearly?

Making Measurements

By measuring, scientists can express their observations more precisely and communicate more information about what they observe.

Measuring in SI

The standard system of measurement used by scientists around the world is known as the International System of Units, which is abbreviated as SI (**Système International d'Unités,** in French). SI units are easy to use because they are based on multiples of 10. Each unit is ten times larger than the next smallest unit and one tenth the size of the next largest unit. The table lists the prefixes used to name the most common SI units.

Common SI Prefixes		
Prefix	Symbol	Meaning
kilo-	k	1,000
hecto-	h	100
deka-	da	10
deci-	d	0.1 (one tenth)
centi-	c	0.01 (one hundredth)
milli-	m	0.001 (one thousandth)

Length To measure length, or the distance between two points, the unit of measure is the **meter (m).** The distance from the floor to a doorknob is approximately one meter. Long distances, such as the distance between two cities, are measured in kilometers (km). Small lengths are measured in centimeters (cm) or millimeters (mm). Scientists use metric rulers and meter sticks to measure length.

Common Conversions	
1 km	= 1,000 m
1 m	= 100 cm
1 m	= 1,000 mm
1 cm	= 10 mm

Liquid Volume To measure the volume of a liquid, or the amount of space it takes up, you will use a unit of measure known as the **liter (L).** One liter is the approximate volume of a medium-size carton of milk. Smaller volumes are measured in milliliters (mL). Scientists use graduated cylinders to measure liquid volume.

Activity

The larger lines on the metric ruler in the picture show centimeter divisions, while the smaller, unnumbered lines show millimeter divisions. How many centimeters long is the shell? How many millimeters long is it?

Activity

The graduated cylinder in the picture is marked in milliliter divisions. Notice that the water in the cylinder has a curved surface. This curved surface is called the *meniscus.* To measure the volume, you must read the level at the lowest point of the meniscus. What is the volume of water in this graduated cylinder?

Common Conversion
1 L = 1,000 mL

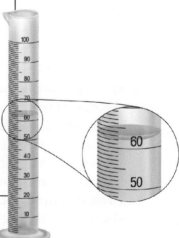

Mass To measure mass, or the amount of matter in an object, you will use a unit of measure known as the **gram (g).** One gram is approximately the mass of a paper clip. Larger masses are measured in kilograms (kg). Scientists use a balance to find the mass of an object.

Common Conversion

1 kg = 1,000 g

Activity

The mass of the potato in the picture is measured in kilograms. What is the mass of the potato? Suppose a recipe for potato salad called for one kilogram of potatoes. About how many potatoes would you need?

0.25 KG

Temperature To measure the temperature of a substance, you will use the **Celsius scale.** Temperature is measured in degrees Celsius (°C) using a Celsius thermometer. Water freezes at 0°C and boils at 100°C.

Time The unit scientists use to measure time is the **second (s).**

Activity

What is the temperature of the liquid in degrees Celsius?

Converting SI Units

To use the SI system, you must know how to convert between units. Converting from one unit to another involves the skill of **calculating,** or using mathematical operations. Converting between SI units is similar to converting between dollars and dimes because both systems are based on multiples of ten.

Suppose you want to convert a length of 80 centimeters to meters. Follow these steps to convert between units.

1. Begin by writing down the measurement you want to convert—in this example, 80 centimeters.

2. Write a conversion factor that represents the relationship between the two units you are converting. In this example, the relationship is 1 meter = 100 centimeters. Write this conversion factor as a fraction, making sure to place the units you are converting from (centimeters, in this example) in the denominator.

3. Multiply the measurement you want to convert by the fraction. When you do this, the units in the first measurement will cancel out with the units in the denominator. Your answer will be in the units you are converting to (meters, in this example).

Example

80 centimeters = ■ meters

$$80 \text{ centimeters} \times \frac{1 \text{ meter}}{100 \text{ centimeters}} = \frac{80 \text{ meters}}{100}$$

$$= 0.8 \text{ meters}$$

Activity

Convert between the following units.
1. 600 millimeters = ■ meters
2. 0.35 liters = ■ milliliters
3. 1,050 grams = ■ kilograms

Conducting a Scientific Investigation

In some ways, scientists are like detectives, piecing together clues to learn about a process or event. One way that scientists gather clues is by carrying out experiments. An experiment tests an idea in a careful, orderly manner. Although experiments do not all follow the same steps in the same order, many follow a pattern similar to the one described here.

Posing Questions

Experiments begin by asking a scientific question. A scientific question is one that can be answered by gathering evidence. For example, the question "Which freezes faster—fresh water or salt water?" is a scientific question because you can carry out an investigation and gather information to answer the question.

Developing a Hypothesis

The next step is to form a hypothesis. A **hypothesis** is a possible explanation for a set of observations or answer to a scientific question. In science, a hypothesis must be something that can be tested. A hypothesis can be worded as an *If . . . then . . .* statement. For example, a hypothesis might be *"If I add salt to fresh water, then the water will take longer to freeze."* A hypothesis worded this way serves as a rough outline of the experiment you should perform.

Designing an Experiment

Next you need to plan a way to test your hypothesis. Your plan should be written out as a step-by-step procedure and should describe the observations or measurements you will make.

Two important steps involved in designing an experiment are controlling variables and forming operational definitions.

Controlling Variables In a well-designed experiment, you need to keep all variables the same except for one. A **variable** is any factor that can change in an experiment. The factor that you change is called the **manipulated variable**. In this experiment, the manipulated variable is the amount of salt added to the water. Other factors, such as the amount of water or the starting temperature, are kept constant.

The factor that changes as a result of the manipulated variable is called the **responding variable.** The responding variable is what you measure or observe to obtain your results. In this experiment, the responding variable is how long the water takes to freeze.

An experiment in which all factors except one are kept constant is called a **controlled experiment.** Most controlled experiments include a test called the control. In this experiment, Container 3 is the control. Because no salt is added to Container 3, you can compare the results from the other containers to it. Any difference in results must be due to the addition of salt alone.

Forming Operational Definitions Another important aspect of a well-designed experiment is having clear operational definitions. An **operational definition** is a statement that describes how a particular variable is to be measured or how a term is to be defined. For example, in this experiment, how will you determine if the water has frozen? You might decide to insert a stick in each container at the start of the experiment. Your operational definition of "frozen" would be the time at which the stick can no longer move.

Experimental Procedure
1. Fill 3 containers with 300 milliliters of cold tap water.
2. Add 10 grams of salt to Container 1; stir. Add 20 grams of salt to Container 2; stir. Add no salt to Container 3.
3. Place the 3 containers in a freezer.
4. Check the containers every 15 minutes. Record your observations.

Interpreting Data

The observations and measurements you make in an experiment are called **data.** At the end of an experiment, you need to analyze the data to look for any patterns or trends. Patterns often become clear if you organize your data in a data table or graph. Then think through what the data reveal. Do they support your hypothesis? Do they point out a flaw in your experiment? Do you need to collect more data?

Drawing Conclusions

A **conclusion** is a statement that sums up what you have learned from an experiment. When you draw a conclusion, you need to decide whether the data you collected support your hypothesis or not. You may need to repeat an experiment several times before you can draw any conclusions from it. Conclusions often lead you to pose new questions and plan new experiments to answer them.

Activity

Is a ball's bounce affected by the height from which it is dropped? Using the steps just described, plan a controlled experiment to investigate this problem.

Technology Design Skills

Engineers are people who use scientific and technological knowledge to solve practical problems. To design new products, engineers usually follow the process described here, even though they may not follow these steps in the exact order. As you read the steps, think about how you might apply them in technology labs.

Identify a Need

Before engineers begin designing a new product, they must first identify the need they are trying to meet. For example, suppose you are a member of a design team in a company that makes toys. Your team has identified a need: a toy boat that is inexpensive and easy to assemble.

Research the Problem

Engineers often begin by gathering information that will help them with their new design. This research may include finding articles in books, magazines, or on the Internet. It may also include talking to other engineers who have solved similar problems. Engineers often perform experiments related to the product they want to design.

For your toy boat, you could look at toys that are similar to the one you want to design. You might do research on the Internet. You could also test some materials to see whether they will work well in a toy boat.

Drawing for a boat design ▼

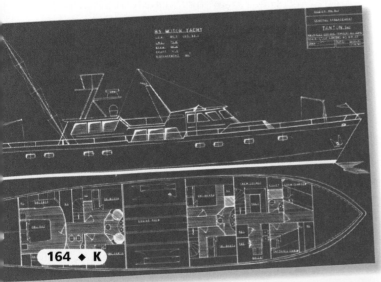

Design a Solution

Research gives engineers information that helps them design a product. When engineers design new products, they usually work in teams.

Generating Ideas Often design teams hold brainstorming meetings in which any team member can contribute ideas. **Brainstorming** is a creative process in which one team member's suggestions often spark ideas in other group members. Brainstorming can lead to new approaches to solving a design problem.

Evaluating Constraints During brainstorming, a design team will often come up with several possible designs. The team must then evaluate each one.

As part of their evaluation, engineers consider constraints. **Constraints** are factors that limit or restrict a product design. Physical characteristics, such as the properties of materials used to make your toy boat, are constraints. Money and time are also constraints. If the materials in a product cost a lot, or if the product takes a long time to make, the design may be impractical.

Making Trade-offs Design teams usually need to make trade-offs. In a **trade-off,** engineers give up one benefit of a proposed design in order to obtain another. In designing your toy boat, you will have to make trade-offs. For example, suppose one material is sturdy but not fully waterproof. Another material is more waterproof, but breakable. You may decide to give up the benefit of sturdiness in order to obtain the benefit of waterproofing.

Build and Evaluate a Prototype

Once the team has chosen a design plan, the engineers build a prototype of the product. A **prototype** is a working model used to test a design. Engineers evaluate the prototype to see whether it works well, is easy to operate, is safe to use, and holds up to repeated use.

Think of your toy boat. What would the prototype be like? Of what materials would it be made? How would you test it?

Troubleshoot and Redesign

Few prototypes work perfectly, which is why they need to be tested. Once a design team has tested a prototype, the members analyze the results and identify any problems. The team then tries to **troubleshoot,** or fix the design problems. For example, if your toy boat leaks or wobbles, the boat should be redesigned to eliminate those problems.

Communicate the Solution

A team needs to communicate the final design to the people who will manufacture and use the product. To do this, teams may use sketches, detailed drawings, computer simulations, and word descriptions.

Activity

You can use the technology design process to design and build a toy boat.

Research and Investigate

1. Visit the library or go online to research toy boats.

2. Investigate how a toy boat can be powered, including wind, rubber bands, or baking soda and vinegar.

3. Brainstorm materials, shapes, and steering for your boat.

Design and Build

4. Based on your research, design a toy boat that
   • is made of readily available materials
   • is no larger than 15 cm long and 10 cm wide
   • includes a power system, a rudder, and an area for cargo
   • travels 2 meters in a straight line carrying a load of 20 pennies

5. Sketch your design and write a step-by-step plan for building your boat. After your teacher approves your plan, build your boat.

Evaluate and Redesign

6. Test your boat, evaluate the results, and troubleshoot any problems.

7. Based on your evaluation, redesign your toy boat so it performs better.

Creating Data Tables and Graphs

**How can you make sense of the data in a science experiment?
The first step is to organize the data to help you understand them.
Data tables and graphs are helpful tools for organizing data.**

Data Tables

You have gathered your materials and set up your experiment. But before you start, you need to plan a way to record what happens during the experiment. By creating a data table, you can record your observations and measurements in an orderly way.

Suppose, for example, that a scientist conducted an experiment to find out how many Calories people of different body masses burn while doing various activities. The data table shows the results.

Notice in this data table that the manipulated variable (body mass) is the heading of one column. The responding variable (for

Calories Burned in 30 Minutes			
Body Mass	Experiment 1: Bicycling	Experiment 2: Playing Basketball	Experiment 3: Watching Television
30 kg	60 Calories	120 Calories	21 Calories
40 kg	77 Calories	164 Calories	27 Calories
50 kg	95 Calories	206 Calories	33 Calories
60 kg	114 Calories	248 Calories	38 Calories

Experiment 1, the number of Calories burned while bicycling) is the heading of the next column. Additional columns were added for related experiments.

Bar Graphs

To compare how many Calories a person burns doing various activities, you could create a bar graph. A bar graph is used to display data in a number of separate, or distinct, categories. In this example, bicycling, playing basketball, and watching television are the three categories.

To create a bar graph, follow these steps.

1. On graph paper, draw a horizontal, or *x-*, axis and a vertical, or *y-*, axis.

2. Write the names of the categories to be graphed along the horizontal axis. Include an overall label for the axis as well.

3. Label the vertical axis with the name of the responding variable. Include units of measurement. Then create a scale along the axis by marking off equally spaced numbers that cover the range of the data collected.

4. For each category, draw a solid bar using the scale on the vertical axis to determine the height. Make all the bars the same width.

5. Add a title that describes the graph.

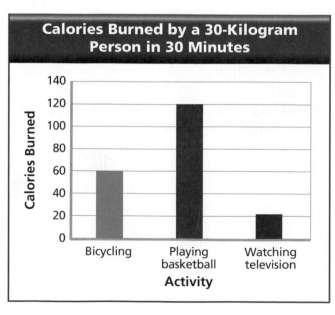

Line Graphs

To see whether a relationship exists between body mass and the number of Calories burned while bicycling, you could create a line graph. A line graph is used to display data that show how one variable (the responding variable) changes in response to another variable (the manipulated variable). You can use a line graph when your manipulated variable is **continuous,** that is, when there are other points between the ones that you tested. In this example, body mass is a continuous variable because there are other body masses between 30 and 40 kilograms (for example, 31 kilograms). Time is another example of a continuous variable.

Line graphs are powerful tools because they allow you to estimate values for conditions that you did not test in the experiment. For example, you can use the line graph to estimate that a 35-kilogram person would burn 68 Calories while bicycling.

To create a line graph, follow these steps.

1. On graph paper, draw a horizontal, or *x*-, axis and a vertical, or *y*-, axis.

2. Label the horizontal axis with the name of the manipulated variable. Label the vertical axis with the name of the responding variable. Include units of measurement.

3. Create a scale on each axis by marking off equally spaced numbers that cover the range of the data collected.

4. Plot a point on the graph for each piece of data. In the line graph above, the dotted lines show how to plot the first data point (30 kilograms and 60 Calories). Follow an imaginary vertical line extending up from the horizontal axis at the 30-kilogram mark. Then follow an imaginary horizontal line extending across from the vertical axis at the 60-Calorie mark. Plot the point where the two lines intersect.

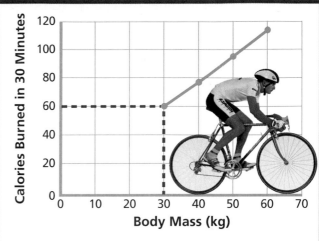

Effect of Body Mass on Calories Burned While Bicycling

5. Connect the plotted points with a solid line. (In some cases, it may be more appropriate to draw a line that shows the general trend of the plotted points. In those cases, some of the points may fall above or below the line. Also, not all graphs are linear. It may be more appropriate to draw a curve to connect the points.)

6. Add a title that identifies the variables or relationship in the graph.

Activity

Create line graphs to display the data from Experiment 2 and Experiment 3 in the data table.

Activity

You read in the newspaper that a total of 4 centimeters of rain fell in your area in June, 2.5 centimeters fell in July, and 1.5 centimeters fell in August. What type of graph would you use to display these data? Use graph paper to create the graph.

Circle Graphs

Like bar graphs, circle graphs can be used to display data in a number of separate categories. Unlike bar graphs, however, circle graphs can only be used when you have data for *all* the categories that make up a given topic. A circle graph is sometimes called a pie chart. The pie represents the entire topic, while the slices represent the individual categories. The size of a slice indicates what percentage of the whole a particular category makes up.

The data table below shows the results of a survey in which 24 teenagers were asked to identify their favorite sport. The data were then used to create the circle graph at the right.

Favorite Sports	
Sport	Students
Soccer	8
Basketball	6
Bicycling	6
Swimming	4

To create a circle graph, follow these steps.

1. Use a compass to draw a circle. Mark the center with a point. Then draw a line from the center point to the top of the circle.

2. Determine the size of each "slice" by setting up a proportion where *x* equals the number of degrees in a slice. (*Note:* A circle contains 360 degrees.) For example, to find the number of degrees in the "soccer" slice, set up the following proportion:

$$\frac{\text{Students who prefer soccer}}{\text{Total number of students}} = \frac{x}{\text{Total number of degrees in a circle}}$$

$$\frac{8}{24} = \frac{x}{360}$$

Cross-multiply and solve for x.

$$24x = 8 \times 360$$
$$x = 120$$

The "soccer" slice should contain 120 degrees.

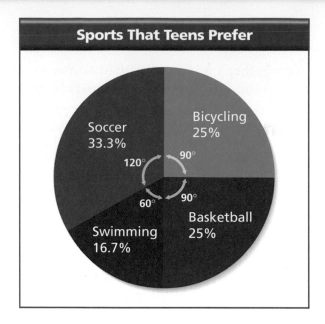

Sports That Teens Prefer

Soccer 33.3% · Bicycling 25% · Basketball 25% · Swimming 16.7% · 120° · 90° · 60° · 90°

3. Use a protractor to measure the angle of the first slice, using the line you drew to the top of the circle as the 0° line. Draw a line from the center of the circle to the edge for the angle you measured.

4. Continue around the circle by measuring the size of each slice with the protractor. Start measuring from the edge of the previous slice so the wedges do not overlap. When you are done, the entire circle should be filled in.

5. Determine the percentage of the whole circle that each slice represents. To do this, divide the number of degrees in a slice by the total number of degrees in a circle (360), and multiply by 100%. For the "soccer" slice, you can find the percentage as follows:

$$\frac{120}{360} \times 100\% = 33.3\%$$

6. Use a different color for each slice. Label each slice with the category and with the percentage of the whole it represents.

7. Add a title to the circle graph.

Activity

In a class of 28 students, 12 students take the bus to school, 10 students walk, and 6 students ride their bicycles. Create a circle graph to display these data.

Math Review

Scientists use math to organize, analyze, and present data.
This appendix will help you review some basic math skills.

Mean, Median, and Mode

The **mean** is the average, or the sum of the data divided by the number of data items. The middle number in a set of ordered data is called the **median.** The **mode** is the number that appears most often in a set of data.

Example

A scientist counted the number of distinct songs sung by seven different male birds and collected the data shown below.

Male Bird Songs							
Bird	A	B	C	D	E	F	G
Number of Songs	36	29	40	35	28	36	27

To determine the mean number of songs, add the total number of songs and divide by the number of data items—in this case, the number of male birds.

$$\text{Mean} = \frac{231}{7} = 33 \text{ songs}$$

To find the median number of songs, arrange the data in numerical order and find the number in the middle of the series.

27 28 29 35 36 36 40

The number in the middle is 35, so the median number of songs is 35.

The mode is the value that appears most frequently. In the data, 36 appears twice, while each other item appears only once. Therefore, 36 songs is the mode.

Practice

Find out how many minutes it takes each student in your class to get to school. Then find the mean, median, and mode for the data.

Probability

Probability is the chance that an event will occur. Probability can be expressed as a ratio, a fraction, or a percentage. For example, when you flip a coin, the probability that the coin will land heads up is 1 in 2, or $\frac{1}{2}$, or 50 percent.

The probability that an event will happen can be expressed in the following formula.

$$P(\text{event}) = \frac{\text{Number of times the event can occur}}{\text{Total number of possible events}}$$

Example

A paper bag contains 25 blue marbles, 5 green marbles, 5 orange marbles, and 15 yellow marbles. If you close your eyes and pick a marble from the bag, what is the probability that it will be yellow?

$$P(\text{yellow marbles}) = \frac{15 \text{ yellow marbles}}{50 \text{ marbles total}}$$

$$P = \frac{15}{50}, \text{ or } \frac{3}{10}, \text{ or } 30\%$$

Practice

Each side of a cube has a letter on it. Two sides have A, three sides have B, and one side has C. If you roll the cube, what is the probability that A will land on top?

Area

The **area** of a surface is the number of square units that cover it. The front cover of your textbook has an area of about 600 cm².

Area of a Rectangle and a Square To find the area of a rectangle, multiply its length times its width. The formula for the area of a rectangle is

$$A = \ell \times w, \text{ or } A = \ell w$$

Since all four sides of a square have the same length, the area of a square is the length of one side multiplied by itself, or squared.

$$A = s \times s, \text{ or } A = s^2$$

Example

A scientist is studying the plants in a field that measures 75 m × 45 m. What is the area of the field?

$$A = \ell \times w$$
$$A = 75 \text{ m} \times 45 \text{ m}$$
$$A = 3{,}375 \text{ m}^2$$

Area of a Circle The formula for the area of a circle is

$$A = \pi \times r \times r, \text{ or } A = \pi r^2$$

The length of the radius is represented by r, and the value of π is approximately $\frac{22}{7}$.

Example

Find the area of a circle with a radius of 14 cm.

$$A = \pi r^2$$
$$A = 14 \times 14 \times \frac{22}{7}$$
$$A = 616 \text{ cm}^2$$

Practice

Find the area of a circle that has a radius of 21 m.

Circumference

The distance around a circle is called the circumference. The formula for finding the circumference of a circle is

$$C = 2 \times \pi \times r, \text{ or } C = 2\pi r$$

Example

The radius of a circle is 35 cm. What is its circumference?

$$C = 2\pi r$$
$$C = 2 \times 35 \times \frac{22}{7}$$
$$C = 220 \text{ cm}$$

Practice

What is the circumference of a circle with a radius of 28 m?

Volume

The volume of an object is the number of cubic units it contains. The volume of a wastebasket, for example, might be about 26,000 cm³.

Volume of a Rectangular Object To find the volume of a rectangular object, multiply the object's length times its width times its height.

$$V = \ell \times w \times h, \text{ or } V = \ell w h$$

Example

Find the volume of a box with length 24 cm, width 12 cm, and height 9 cm.

$$V = \ell w h$$
$$V = 24 \text{ cm} \times 12 \text{ cm} \times 9 \text{ cm}$$
$$V = 2{,}592 \text{ cm}^3$$

Practice

What is the volume of a rectangular object with length 17 cm, width 11 cm, and height 6 cm?

Fractions

A **fraction** is a way to express a part of a whole. In the fraction $\frac{4}{7}$, 4 is the numerator and 7 is the denominator.

Adding and Subtracting Fractions To add or subtract two or more fractions that have a common denominator, first add or subtract the numerators. Then write the sum or difference over the common denominator.

To find the sum or difference of fractions with different denominators, first find the least common multiple of the denominators. This is known as the least common denominator. Then convert each fraction to equivalent fractions with the least common denominator. Add or subtract the numerators. Then write the sum or difference over the common denominator.

> **Example**
>
> $$\frac{5}{6} - \frac{3}{4} = \frac{10}{12} - \frac{9}{12} = \frac{10 - 9}{12} = \frac{1}{12}$$

Multiplying Fractions To multiply two fractions, first multiply the two numerators, then multiply the two denominators.

> **Example**
>
> $$\frac{5}{6} \times \frac{2}{3} = \frac{5 \times 2}{6 \times 3} = \frac{10}{18} = \frac{5}{9}$$

Dividing Fractions Dividing by a fraction is the same as multiplying by its reciprocal. Reciprocals are numbers whose numerators and denominators have been switched. To divide one fraction by another, first invert the fraction you are dividing by—in other words, turn it upside down. Then multiply the two fractions.

> **Example**
>
> $$\frac{2}{5} \div \frac{7}{8} = \frac{2}{5} \times \frac{8}{7} = \frac{2 \times 8}{5 \times 7} = \frac{16}{35}$$

> **Practice**
>
> Solve the following: $\frac{3}{7} \div \frac{4}{5}$.

Decimals

Fractions whose denominators are 10, 100, or some other power of 10 are often expressed as decimals. For example, the fraction $\frac{9}{10}$ can be expressed as the decimal 0.9, and the fraction $\frac{7}{100}$ can be written as 0.07.

Adding and Subtracting With Decimals To add or subtract decimals, line up the decimal points before you carry out the operation.

> **Example**
>
> $$\begin{array}{r} 27.4 \\ + \ 6.19 \\ \hline 33.59 \end{array} \qquad \begin{array}{r} 278.635 \\ - \ 191.4 \\ \hline 87.235 \end{array}$$

Multiplying With Decimals When you multiply two numbers with decimals, the number of decimal places in the product is equal to the total number of decimal places in each number being multiplied.

> **Example**
>
> $$\begin{array}{r} 46.2 \ \text{(one decimal place)} \\ \times \ 2.37 \ \text{(two decimal places)} \\ \hline 109.494 \ \text{(three decimal places)} \end{array}$$

Dividing With Decimals To divide a decimal by a whole number, put the decimal point in the quotient above the decimal point in the dividend.

> **Example**
>
> $$15.5 \div 5$$
> $$\begin{array}{r} 3.1 \ \ \\ 5\overline{)15.5} \end{array}$$

To divide a decimal by a decimal, you need to rewrite the divisor as a whole number. Do this by multiplying both the divisor and dividend by the same multiple of 10.

> **Example**
>
> $$1.68 \div 4.2 = 16.8 \div 42$$
> $$\begin{array}{r} 0.4 \ \ \\ 42\overline{)16.8} \end{array}$$

> **Practice**
>
> Multiply 6.21 by 8.5.

Ratio and Proportion

A **ratio** compares two numbers by division. For example, suppose a scientist counts 800 wolves and 1,200 moose on an island. The ratio of wolves to moose can be written as a fraction, $\frac{800}{1,200}$, which can be reduced to $\frac{2}{3}$. The same ratio can also be expressed as 2 to 3 or 2 : 3.

A **proportion** is a mathematical sentence saying that two ratios are equivalent. For example, a proportion could state that $\frac{800 \text{ wolves}}{1,200 \text{ moose}} = \frac{2 \text{ wolves}}{3 \text{ moose}}$. You can sometimes set up a proportion to determine or estimate an unknown quantity. For example, suppose a scientist counts 25 beetles in an area of 10 square meters. The scientist wants to estimate the number of beetles in 100 square meters.

Example

1. Express the relationship between beetles and area as a ratio: $\frac{25}{10}$, simplified to $\frac{5}{2}$.

2. Set up a proportion, with x representing the number of beetles. The proportion can be stated as $\frac{5}{2} = \frac{x}{100}$.

3. Begin by cross-multiplying. In other words, multiply each fraction's numerator by the other fraction's denominator.

   $5 \times 100 = 2 \times x$, or $500 = 2x$

4. To find the value of x, divide both sides by 2. The result is 250, or 250 beetles in 100 square meters.

Practice

Find the value of x in the following proportion: $\frac{6}{7} = \frac{x}{49}$.

Percentage

A **percentage** is a ratio that compares a number to 100. For example, there are 37 granite rocks in a collection that consists of 100 rocks. The ratio $\frac{37}{100}$ can be written as 37%. Granite rocks make up 37% of the rock collection.

You can calculate percentages of numbers other than 100 by setting up a proportion.

Example

Rain falls on 9 days out of 30 in June. What percentage of the days in June were rainy?

$$\frac{9 \text{ days}}{30 \text{ days}} = \frac{d\%}{100\%}$$

To find the value of d, begin by cross-multiplying, as for any proportion:

$9 \times 100 = 30 \times d$ $d = \frac{900}{30}$ $d = 30$

Practice

There are 300 marbles in a jar, and 42 of those marbles are blue. What percentage of the marbles are blue?

Significant Figures

The **precision** of a measurement depends on the instrument you use to take the measurement. For example, if the smallest unit on the ruler is millimeters, then the most precise measurement you can make will be in millimeters.

The sum or difference of measurements can only be as precise as the least precise measurement being added or subtracted. Round your answer so that it has the same number of digits after the decimal as the least precise measurement. Round up if the last digit is 5 or more, and round down if the last digit is 4 or less.

Example

Subtract a temperature of 5.2°C from the temperature 75.46°C.

75.46 − 5.2 = 70.26

5.2 has the fewest digits after the decimal, so it is the least precise measurement. Since the last digit of the answer is 6, round up to 3. The most precise difference between the measurements is 70.3°C.

Practice

Add 26.4 m to 8.37 m. Round your answer according to the precision of the measurements.

Significant figures are the number of nonzero digits in a measurement. Zeroes between nonzero digits are also significant. For example, the measurements 12,500 L, 0.125 cm, and 2.05 kg all have three significant figures. When you multiply and divide measurements, the one with the fewest significant figures determines the number of significant figures in your answer.

Example

Multiply 110 g by 5.75 g.

110 × 5.75 = 632.5

Because 110 has only two significant figures, round the answer to 630 g.

Scientific Notation

A **factor** is a number that divides into another number with no remainder. In the example, the number 3 is used as a factor four times.

An **exponent** tells how many times a number is used as a factor. For example, $3 \times 3 \times 3 \times 3$ can be written as 3^4. The exponent ^{4} indicates that the number 3 is used as a factor four times. Another way of expressing this is to say that 81 is equal to 3 to the fourth power.

Example

$$3^4 = 3 \times 3 \times 3 \times 3 = 81$$

Scientific notation uses exponents and powers of ten to write very large or very small numbers in shorter form. When you write a number in scientific notation, you write the number as two factors. The first factor is any number between 1 and 10. The second factor is a power of 10, such as 10^3 or 10^6.

Example

The average distance between the planet Mercury and the sun is 58,000,000 km. To write the first factor in scientific notation, insert a decimal point in the original number so that you have a number between 1 and 10. In the case of 58,000,000, the number is 5.8.

To determine the power of 10, count the number of places that the decimal point moved. In this case, it moved 7 places.

$$58,000,000 \text{ km} = 5.8 \times 10^7 \text{ km}$$

Practice

Express 6,590,000 in scientific notation.

Reading Comprehension Skills

Each section in your textbook introduces a Target Reading Skill.
You will improve your reading comprehension by using the
Target Reading Skills described below.

Using Prior Knowledge

Your prior knowledge is what you already know before you begin to read about a topic. Building on what you already know gives you a head start on learning new information. Before you begin a new assignment, think about what you know. You might look at the headings and the visuals to spark your memory. You can list what you know. Then, as you read, consider questions like these.

• How does what you learn relate to what you know?

• How did something you already know help you learn something new?

• Did your original ideas agree with what you have just learned?

Asking Questions

Asking yourself questions is an excellent way to focus on and remember new information in your textbook. For example, you can turn the text headings into questions. Then your questions can guide you to identify the important information as you read. Look at these examples:

Heading: Using Seismographic Data

Question: How are seismographic data used?

Heading: Kinds of Faults

Question: What are the kinds of faults?

You do not have to limit your questions to text headings. Ask questions about anything that you need to clarify or that will help you understand the content. *What* and *how* are probably the most common question words, but you may also ask *why, who, when,* or *where* questions.

Previewing Visuals

Visuals are photographs, graphs, tables, diagrams, and illustrations. Visuals contain important information. Before you read, look at visuals and their labels and captions. This preview will help you prepare for what you will be reading.

Often you will be asked what you want to learn about a visual. For example, after you look at the normal fault diagram below, you might ask: What is the movement along a normal fault? Questions about visuals give you a purpose for reading—to answer your questions.

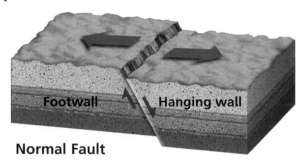

Footwall   **Hanging wall**

Normal Fault

Outlining

An outline shows the relationship between main ideas and supporting ideas. An outline has a formal structure. You write the main ideas, called topics, next to Roman numerals. The supporting ideas, called subtopics, are written under the main ideas and labeled A, B, C, and so on. An outline looks like this:

Technology and Society
I. Technology through history
II. The impact of technology on society
A.
B.

Identifying Main Ideas

When you are reading science material, it is important to try to understand the ideas and concepts that are in a passage. Each paragraph has a lot of information and detail. Good readers try to identify the most important—or biggest—idea in every paragraph or section. That's the main idea. The other information in the paragraph supports or further explains the main idea.

Sometimes main ideas are stated directly. In this book, some main ideas are identified for you as key concepts. These are printed in bold-face type. However, you must identify other main ideas yourself. In order to do this, you must identify all the ideas within a paragraph or section. Then ask yourself which idea is big enough to include all the other ideas.

Comparing and Contrasting

When you compare and contrast, you examine the similarities and differences between things. You can compare and contrast in a Venn diagram or in a table.

Venn Diagram A Venn diagram consists of two overlapping circles. In the space where the circles overlap, you write the characteristics that the two items have in common. In one of the circles outside the area of overlap, you write the differing features or characteristics of one of the items. In the other circle outside the area of overlap, you write the differing characteristics of the other item.

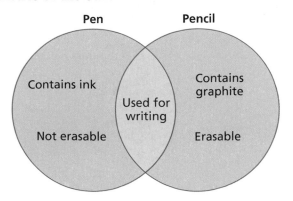

Table In a compare/contrast table, you list the characteristics or features to be compared across the top of the table. Then list the items to be compared in the left column. Complete the table by filling in information about each characteristic or feature.

Blood Vessel	Function	Structure of Wall
Artery	Carries blood away from heart	
Capillary		
Vein		

Identifying Supporting Evidence

A hypothesis is a possible explanation for observations made by scientists or an answer to a scientific question. Scientists must carry out investigations and gather evidence that either supports or disproves the hypothesis.

Identifying the supporting evidence for a hypothesis or theory can help you understand the hypothesis or theory. Evidence consists of facts—information whose accuracy can be confirmed by testing or observation.

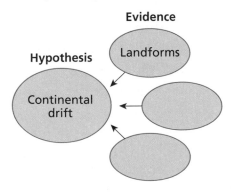

Sequencing

A sequence is the order in which a series of events occurs. A flowchart or a cycle diagram can help you visualize a sequence.

Flowchart To make a flowchart, write a brief description of each step or event in a box. Place the boxes in order, with the first event at the top of the page. Then draw an arrow to connect each step or event to the next.

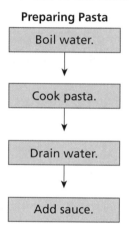

Preparing Pasta

Boil water.

↓

Cook pasta.

↓

Drain water.

↓

Add sauce.

Cycle Diagram A cycle diagram shows a sequence that is continuous, or cyclical. A continuous sequence does not have an end because when the final event is over, the first event begins again. To create a cycle diagram, write the starting event in a box placed at the top of a page in the center. Then, moving in a clockwise direction, write each event in a box in its proper sequence. Draw arrows that connect each event to the one that occurs next.

Seasons of the Year

Winter → Spring → Summer → Fall → Winter

Relating Cause and Effect

Science involves many cause-and-effect relationships. A cause makes something happen. An effect is what happens. When you recognize that one event causes another, you are relating cause and effect.

Words like *cause, because, effect, affect,* and *result* often signal a cause or an effect. Sometimes an effect can have more than one cause, or a cause can produce several effects.

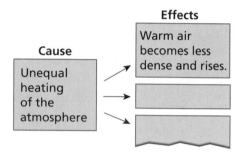

Cause

Unequal heating of the atmosphere

Effects

Warm air becomes less dense and rises.

Concept Mapping

Concept maps are useful tools for organizing information on any topic. A concept map begins with a main idea or core concept and shows how the idea can be subdivided into related subconcepts or smaller ideas.

You construct a concept map by placing concepts (usually nouns) in ovals and connecting them with linking words (usually verbs). The biggest concept or idea is placed in an oval at the top of the map. Related concepts are arranged in ovals below the big idea. The linking words connect the ovals.

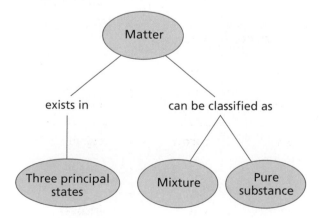

Matter

exists in — Three principal states

can be classified as — Mixture — Pure substance

Building Vocabulary

Knowing the meaning of these prefixes, suffixes, and roots will help you understand the meaning of words you do not recognize.

Word Origins Many science words come to English from other languages, such as Greek and Latin. By learning the meaning of a few common Greek and Latin roots, you can determine the meaning of unfamiliar science words.

Prefixes A prefix is a word part that is added at the beginning of a root or base word to change its meaning.

Suffixes A suffix is a word part that is added at the end of a root word to change the meaning.

Greek and Latin Roots		
Greek Roots	**Meaning**	**Example**
ast-	star	astronaut
geo-	Earth	geology
metron-	measure	kilometer
opt-	eye	optician
photo-	light	photograph
scop-	see	microscope
therm-	heat	thermostat
Latin Roots	**Meaning**	**Example**
aqua-	water	aquarium
aud-	hear	auditorium
duc-, duct-	lead	conduct
flect-	bend	reflect
fract-, frag-	break	fracture
ject-	throw	reject
luc-	light	lucid
spec-	see	inspect

Prefixes and Suffixes		
Prefix	**Meaning**	**Example**
com-, con-	with	communicate, concert
de-	from; down	decay
di-	two	divide
ex-, exo-	out	exhaust
in-, im-	in, into; not	inject, impossible
re-	again; back	reflect, recall
trans-	across	transfer
Suffix	**Meaning**	**Example**
-al	relating to	natural
-er, -or	one who	teacher, doctor
-ist	one who practices	scientist
-ity	state of	equality
-ology	study of	biology
-tion, -sion	state or quality of	reaction, tension

Safety Symbols

These symbols warn of possible dangers in the laboratory and remind you to work carefully.

 Safety Goggles Wear safety goggles to protect your eyes in any activity involving chemicals, flames or heating, or glassware.

 Lab Apron Wear a laboratory apron to protect your skin and clothing from damage.

 Breakage Handle breakable materials, such as glassware, with care. Do not touch broken glassware.

 Heat-Resistant Gloves Use an oven mitt or other hand protection when handling hot materials such as hot plates or hot glassware.

 Plastic Gloves Wear disposable plastic gloves when working with harmful chemicals and organisms. Keep your hands away from your face, and dispose of the gloves according to your teacher's instructions.

 Heating Use a clamp or tongs to pick up hot glassware. Do not touch hot objects with your bare hands.

 Flames Before you work with flames, tie back loose hair and clothing. Follow instructions from your teacher about lighting and extinguishing flames.

 No Flames When using flammable materials, make sure there are no flames, sparks, or other exposed heat sources present.

 Corrosive Chemical Avoid getting acid or other corrosive chemicals on your skin or clothing or in your eyes. Do not inhale the vapors. Wash your hands after the activity.

 Poison Do not let any poisonous chemical come into contact with your skin, and do not inhale its vapors. Wash your hands when you are finished with the activity.

 Fumes Work in a ventilated area when harmful vapors may be involved. Avoid inhaling vapors directly. Only test an odor when directed to do so by your teacher, and use a wafting motion to direct the vapor toward your nose.

 Sharp Object Scissors, scalpels, knives, needles, pins, and tacks can cut your skin. Always direct a sharp edge or point away from yourself and others.

 Animal Safety Treat live or preserved animals or animal parts with care to avoid harming the animals or yourself. Wash your hands when you are finished with the activity.

 Plant Safety Handle plants only as directed by your teacher. If you are allergic to certain plants, tell your teacher; do not do an activity involving those plants. Avoid touching harmful plants such as poison ivy. Wash your hands when you are finished with the activity.

 Electric Shock To avoid electric shock, never use electrical equipment around water, or when the equipment is wet or your hands are wet. Be sure cords are untangled and cannot trip anyone. Unplug equipment not in use.

 Physical Safety When an experiment involves physical activity, avoid injuring yourself or others. Alert your teacher if there is any reason you should not participate.

 Disposal Dispose of chemicals and other laboratory materials safely. Follow the instructions from your teacher.

 Hand Washing Wash your hands thoroughly when finished with the activity. Use antibacterial soap and warm water. Rinse well.

 General Safety Awareness When this symbol appears, follow the instructions provided. When you are asked to develop your own procedure in a lab, have your teacher approve your plan before you go further.

Science Safety Rules

General Precautions

Follow all instructions. Never perform activities without the approval and supervision of your teacher. Do not engage in horseplay. Never eat or drink in the laboratory. Keep work areas clean and uncluttered.

Dress Code

Wear safety goggles whenever you work with chemicals, glassware, heat sources such as burners, or any substance that might get into your eyes. If you wear contact lenses, notify your teacher.

Wear a lab apron or coat whenever you work with corrosive chemicals or substances that can stain. Wear disposable plastic gloves when working with organisms and harmful chemicals. Tie back long hair. Remove or tie back any article of clothing or jewelry that can hang down and touch chemicals, flames, or equipment. Roll up long sleeves. Never wear open shoes or sandals.

First Aid

Report all accidents, injuries, or fires to your teacher, no matter how minor. Be aware of the location of the first-aid kit, emergency equipment such as the fire extinguisher and fire blanket, and the nearest telephone. Know whom to contact in an emergency.

Heating and Fire Safety

Keep all combustible materials away from flames. When heating a substance in a test tube, make sure that the mouth of the tube is not pointed at you or anyone else. Never heat a liquid in a closed container. Use an oven mitt to pick up a container that has been heated.

Using Chemicals Safely

Never put your face near the mouth of a container that holds chemicals. Never touch, taste, or smell a chemical unless your teacher tells you to.

Use only those chemicals needed in the activity. Keep all containers closed when chemicals are not being used. Pour all chemicals over the sink or a container, not over your work surface. Dispose of excess chemicals as instructed by your teacher.

Be extra careful when working with acids or bases. When mixing an acid and water, always pour the water into the container first and then add the acid to the water. Never pour water into an acid. Wash chemical spills and splashes immediately with plenty of water.

Using Glassware Safely

If glassware is broken or chipped, notify your teacher immediately. Never handle broken or chipped glass with your bare hands.

Never force glass tubing or thermometers into a rubber stopper or rubber tubing. Have your teacher insert the glass tubing or thermometer if required for an activity.

Using Sharp Instruments

Handle sharp instruments with extreme care. Never cut material toward you; cut away from you.

Animal and Plant Safety

Never perform experiments that cause pain, discomfort, or harm to animals. Only handle animals if absolutely necessary. If you know that you are allergic to certain plants, molds, or animals, tell your teacher before doing an activity in which these are used. Wash your hands thoroughly after any activity involving animals, animal parts, plants, plant parts, or soil.

During field work, wear long pants, long sleeves, socks, and closed shoes. Avoid poisonous plants and fungi as well as plants with thorns.

End-of-Experiment Rules

Unplug all electrical equipment. Clean up your work area. Dispose of waste materials as instructed by your teacher. Wash your hands after every experiment.

The laboratory balance is an important tool in scientific investigations. You can use a balance to determine the masses of materials that you study or experiment with in the laboratory.

Different kinds of balances are used in the laboratory. One kind of balance is the triple-beam balance. The balance that you may use in your science class is probably similar to the balance illustrated in this Appendix. To use the balance properly, you should learn the name, location, and function of each part of the balance you are using. What kind of balance do you have in your science class?

The Triple-Beam Balance

The triple-beam balance is a single-pan balance with three beams calibrated in grams. The back, or 100-gram, beam is divided into ten units of 10 grams each. The middle, or 500-gram, beam is divided into five units of 100 grams each. The

front, or 10-gram, beam is divided into ten major units of 1 gram each. Each of these units is further divided into units of 0.1 gram. What is the largest mass you could find with a triple-beam balance?

The following procedure can be used to find the mass of an object with a triple-beam balance:

1. Place the object on the pan.
2. Move the rider on the middle beam notch by notch until the horizontal pointer drops below zero. Move the rider back one notch.
3. Move the rider on the back beam notch by notch until the pointer again drops below zero. Move the rider back one notch.
4. Slowly slide the rider along the front beam until the pointer stops at the zero point.
5. The mass of the object is equal to the sum of the readings on the three beams.

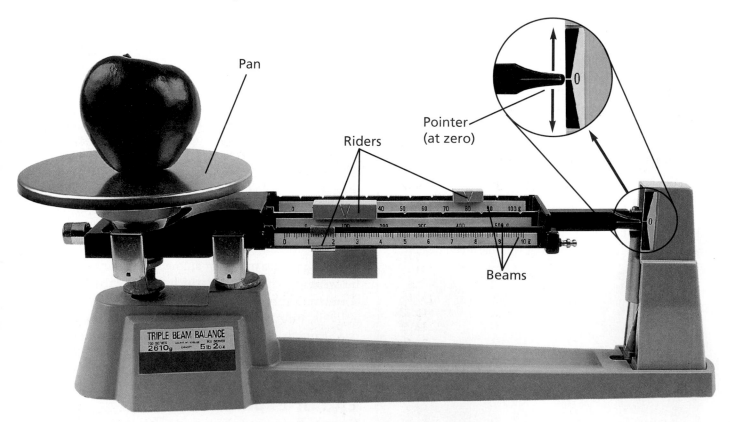

Triple-Beam Balance

Name	Symbol	Atomic Number	Atomic Mass†
Actinium	Ac	89	(227)
Aluminum	Al	13	26.982
Americium	Am	95	(243)
Antimony	Sb	51	121.75
Argon	Ar	18	39.948
Arsenic	As	33	74.922
Astatine	At	85	(210)
Barium	Ba	56	137.33
Berkelium	Bk	97	(247)
Beryllium	Be	4	9.0122
Bismuth	Bi	83	208.98
Bohrium	Bh	107	(264)
Boron	B	5	10.81
Bromine	Br	35	79.904
Cadmium	Cd	48	112.41
Calcium	Ca	20	40.08
Californium	Cf	98	(251)
Carbon	C	6	12.011
Cerium	Ce	58	140.12
Cesium	Cs	55	132.91
Chlorine	Cl	17	35.453
Chromium	Cr	24	51.996
Cobalt	Co	27	58.933
Copper	Cu	29	63.546
Curium	Cm	96	(247)
Darmstadtium	Ds	110	(269)
Dubnium	Db	105	(262)
Dysprosium	Dy	66	162.50
Einsteinium	Es	99	(252)
Erbium	Er	68	167.26
Europium	Eu	63	151.96
Fermium	Fm	100	(257)
Fluorine	F	9	18.998
Francium	Fr	87	(223)
Gadolinium	Gd	64	157.25
Gallium	Ga	31	69.72
Germanium	Ge	32	72.59
Gold	Au	79	196.97
Hafnium	Hf	72	178.49
Hassium	Hs	108	(265)
Helium	He	2	4.0026
Holmium	Ho	67	164.93
Hydrogen	H	1	1.0079
Indium	In	49	114.82
Iodine	I	53	126.90
Iridium	Ir	77	192.22
Iron	Fe	26	55.847
Krypton	Kr	36	83.80
Lanthanum	La	57	138.91
Lawrencium	Lr	103	(262)
Lead	Pb	82	207.2
Lithium	Li	3	6.941
Lutetium	Lu	71	174.97
Magnesium	Mg	12	24.305
Manganese	Mn	25	54.938
Meitnerium	Mt	109	(268)
Mendelevium	Md	101	(258)

Name	Symbol	Atomic Number	Atomic Mass†
Mercury	Hg	80	200.59
Molybdenum	Mo	42	95.94
Neodymium	Nd	60	144.24
Neon	Ne	10	20.179
Neptunium	Np	93	(237)
Nickel	Ni	28	58.71
Niobium	Nb	41	92.906
Nitrogen	N	7	14.007
Nobelium	No	102	(259)
Osmium	Os	76	190.2
Oxygen	O	8	15.999
Palladium	Pd	46	106.4
Phosphorus	P	15	30.974
Platinum	Pt	78	195.09
Plutonium	Pu	94	(244)
Polonium	Po	84	(209)
Potassium	K	19	39.098
Praseodymium	Pr	59	140.91
Promethium	Pm	61	(145)
Protactinium	Pa	91	231.04
Radium	Ra	88	(226)
Radon	Rn	86	(222)
Rhenium	Re	75	186.21
Rhodium	Rh	45	102.91
Rubidium	Rb	37	85.468
Ruthenium	Ru	44	101.07
Rutherfordium	Rf	104	(261)
Samarium	Sm	62	150.4
Scandium	Sc	21	44.956
Seaborgium	Sg	106	(263)
Selenium	Se	34	78.96
Silicon	Si	14	28.086
Silver	Ag	47	107.87
Sodium	Na	11	22.990
Strontium	Sr	38	87.62
Sulfur	S	16	32.06
Tantalum	Ta	73	180.95
Technetium	Tc	43	(98)
Tellurium	Te	52	127.60
Terbium	Tb	65	158.93
Thallium	Tl	81	204.37
Thorium	Th	90	232.04
Thulium	Tm	69	168.93
Tin	Sn	50	118.69
Titanium	Ti	22	47.90
Tungsten	W	74	183.85
Ununbium	Uub	112	(277)
Ununquadium	Uuq	114	*
Unununium	Uuu	111	(272)
Uranium	U	92	238.03
Vanadium	V	23	50.941
Xenon	Xe	54	131.30
Ytterbium	Yb	70	173.04
Yttrium	Y	39	88.906
Zinc	Zn	30	65.38
Zirconium	Zr	40	91.22

†Numbers in parentheses give the mass number of the most stable isotope.

*Newly discovered

Key

C	Solid
Br	Liquid
H	Gas
Tc	Not found in nature

1

1
H
Hydrogen
1.0079

2

2	
3 **Li** Lithium 6.941	**4** **Be** Beryllium 9.0122
11 **Na** Sodium 22.990	**12** **Mg** Magnesium 24.305

3	**4**	**5**	**6**	**7**	**8**	**9**
21 **Sc** Scandium 44.956	**22** **Ti** Titanium 47.90	**23** **V** Vanadium 50.941	**24** **Cr** Chromium 51.996	**25** **Mn** Manganese 54.938	**26** **Fe** Iron 55.847	**27** **Co** Cobalt 58.933
39 **Y** Yttrium 88.906	**40** **Zr** Zirconium 91.22	**41** **Nb** Niobium 92.906	**42** **Mo** Molybdenum 95.94	**43** **Tc** Technetium (98)	**44** **Ru** Ruthenium 101.07	**45** **Rh** Rhodium 102.91
71 **Lu** Lutetium 174.97	**72** **Hf** Hafnium 178.49	**73** **Ta** Tantalum 180.95	**74** **W** Tungsten 183.85	**75** **Re** Rhenium 186.21	**76** **Os** Osmium 190.2	**77** **Ir** Iridium 192.22
103 **Lr** Lawrencium (262)	**104** **Rf** Rutherfordium (261)	**105** **Db** Dubnium (262)	**106** **Sg** Seaborgium (263)	**107** **Bh** Bohrium (264)	**108** **Hs** Hassium (265)	**109** **Mt** Meitnerium (268)

Rows 4–7 group 1–2:

4		
19 **K** Potassium 39.098	**20** **Ca** Calcium 40.08	
37 **Rb** Rubidium 85.468	**38** **Sr** Strontium 87.62	
55 **Cs** Cesium 132.91	**56** **Ba** Barium 137.33	
87 **Fr** Francium (223)	**88** **Ra** Radium (226)	

Lanthanides

57 **La** Lanthanum 138.91	**58** **Ce** Cerium 140.12	**59** **Pr** Praseodymium 140.91	**60** **Nd** Neodymium 144.24	**61** **Pm** Promethium (145)	**62** **Sm** Samarium 150.4

Actinides

89 **Ac** Actinium (227)	**90** **Th** Thorium 232.04	**91** **Pa** Protactinium 231.04	**92** **U** Uranium 238.03	**93** **Np** Neptunium (237)	**94** **Pu** Plutonium (244)

Key

■	Metal
□	Metalloid
▨	Nonmetal
▨	Properties not established

18

| 2 **He** Helium 4.0026 |

13	**14**	**15**	**16**	**17**	
5 **B** Boron 10.81	6 **C** Carbon 12.011	7 **N** Nitrogen 14.007	8 **O** Oxygen 15.999	9 **F** Fluorine 18.998	10 **Ne** Neon 20.179
13 **Al** Aluminum 26.982	14 **Si** Silicon 28.086	15 **P** Phosphorus 30.974	16 **S** Sulfur 32.06	17 **Cl** Chlorine 35.453	18 **Ar** Argon 39.948

10	**11**	**12**						
28 **Ni** Nickel 58.71	29 **Cu** Copper 63.546	30 **Zn** Zinc 65.38	31 **Ga** Gallium 69.72	32 **Ge** Germanium 72.59	33 **As** Arsenic 74.922	34 **Se** Selenium 78.96	35 **Br** Bromine 79.904	36 **Kr** Krypton 83.80
46 **Pd** Palladium 106.4	47 **Ag** Silver 107.87	48 **Cd** Cadmium 112.41	49 **In** Indium 114.82	50 **Sn** Tin 118.69	51 **Sb** Antimony 121.75	52 **Te** Tellurium 127.60	53 **I** Iodine 126.90	54 **Xe** Xenon 131.30
78 **Pt** Platinum 195.09	79 **Au** Gold 196.97	80 **Hg** Mercury 200.59	81 **Tl** Thallium 204.37	82 **Pb** Lead 207.2	83 **Bi** Bismuth 208.98	84 **Po** Polonium (209)	85 **At** Astatine (210)	86 **Rn** Radon (222)
110 **Ds** Darmstadtium (269)	111 ***Uuu** Unununium (272)	112 ***Uub** Ununbium (277)		114 ***Uuq** Ununquadium				

*Name not officially assigned
(Atomic masses in parentheses are those of the most stable isotope.)

63 **Eu** Europium 151.96	64 **Gd** Gadolinium 157.25	65 **Tb** Terbium 158.93	66 **Dy** Dysprosium 162.50	67 **Ho** Holmium 164.93	68 **Er** Erbium 167.26	69 **Tm** Thulium 168.93	70 **Yb** Ytterbium 173.04

95 **Am** Americium (243)	96 **Cm** Curium (247)	97 **Bk** Berkelium (247)	98 **Cf** Californium (251)	99 **Es** Einsteinium (252)	100 **Fm** Fermium (257)	101 **Md** Mendelevium (258)	102 **No** Nobelium (259)

English and Spanish Glossary

A

alkali metal An element in Group 1 of the periodic table. (p. 90)
metal alcalino Elemento en el Grupo 1 de la tabla periódica.

alkaline earth metal An element in Group 2 of the periodic table. (p. 91)
metal alcalinotérreo Elemento en el Grupo 2 de la tabla periódica.

alloy A mixture of two or more elements, one of which is a metal. (pp. 92, 130)
aleación Mezcla de dos o más elementos, uno de los cuales es un metal.

alpha particle A type of nuclear radiation consisting of two protons and two neutrons. (p. 141)
partícula alfa Tipo de radiación nuclear que consiste de dos protones y dos neutrones.

amorphous solid A solid made up of particles that are not arranged in a regular pattern. (p. 44)
sólido amorfo Sólido constituido por partículas que no están dispuestas en un patrón regular.

atom The basic particle from which all elements are made. (p. 11)
átomo Partícula básica de la que están formados todos los elementos.

atomic mass The average mass of all the isotopes of an element. (p. 81)
masa atómica Promedio de la masa de todos los isótopos de un elemento.

atomic number The number of protons in the nucleus of an atom. (p. 78)
número atómico Número de protones en el núcleo de un átomo.

B

beta particle A fast-moving electron that is given off as nuclear radiation. (p. 141)
partícula beta Electrón de rápido movimiento que se produce como radiación nuclear.

boiling The process that occurs when vaporization takes place inside a liquid as well as on the surface. (p. 51)
ebullición Proceso que se da cuando la vaporización se efectúa dentro de un líquido, además de en la superficie.

boiling point The temperature at which a substance changes from a liquid to a gas; the same as the condensation point, or temperature at which a gas changes to a liquid. (p. 51)
punto de ebullición Temperatura a la que una sustancia cambia de líquido a gas; es lo mismo que el punto de condensación (la temperatura a la que un gas se vuelve líquido).

Boyle's law A principle that describes the relationship between the pressure and volume of a gas at constant temperature. (p. 58)
ley de Boyle Principio que describe la relación entre la presión y el volumen de un gas a temperatura constante.

C

ceramic A hard, crystalline solid made by heating clay and other mineral materials to high temperatures. (p. 135)
cerámica Sólido cristalino duro hecho al calentar a altas temperaturas arcilla y otros materiales minerales.

Charles's law A principle that describes the relationship between the temperature and volume of a gas at constant pressure. (p. 60)
ley de Charles Principio que describe la relación entre la temperatura y el volumen de un gas a presión constante.

chemical bond The force that holds two atoms together. (p. 11)
enlace químico Fuerza que mantiene juntos a dos átomos.

chemical change A change in which one or more substances combine or break apart to form new substances. (p. 24)
cambio químico Cambio en el cual una o más sustancias se combinan o se rompen para formar nuevas sustancias.

chemical energy A form of potential energy that is stored in chemical bonds between atoms. (p. 32)
energía química Forma de energía potencial almacenada en los enlaces químicos entre átomos.

chemical formula A formula that gives the elements in a compound and the ratio of atoms. (p. 12)
fórmula química Fórmula que da los elementos en un compuesto y la razón de los átomos.

chemical property A characteristic of a pure substance that describes its ability to change into a different substance. (p. 9)
propiedad química Característica de una sustancia pura que describe su capacidad para cambiar a una sustancia diferente.

chemical symbol A one- or two-letter representation of an element. (p. 83)
símbolo químico Representación con una o dos letras de un elemento.

chemistry The study of the properties of matter and how matter changes. (p. 7)
química Estudio de las propiedades de la materia y de cómo cambia.

composite A combination of two or more substances that creates a new material with different properties. (p. 122)
material compuesto Combinación de dos o más sustancias que crea un nuevo material con propiedades diferentes.

compound A pure substance made of two or more elements chemically combined. (p. 12)
compuesto Sustancia pura formada por dos o más elementos combinados químicamente.

condensation The change of state from a gas to a liquid. (p. 52)
condensación Cambio del estado gaseoso a líquido.

conductivity The ability of an object to transfer heat or electricity to another object. (p. 89)
conductividad Capacidad de un objeto para transferir calor o electricidad a otro objeto.

corrosion The gradual wearing away of a metal element due to a chemical reaction. (p. 89)
corrosión Desgaste gradual de un elemento metal debido a una reacción química.

crystalline solid A solid that is made up of crystals in which particles are arranged in a regular, repeating pattern. (p. 44)
sólido cristalino Sólido constituido por cristales en los que las partículas están dispuestas en un patrón regular repetitivo.

D

density The measurement of how much mass of a substance is contained in a given volume. (p. 19)
densidad Medida de cuánta masa de una sustancia hay contenida en un volumen dado.

diatomic molecule A molecule consisting of two atoms. (p. 101)
molécula diatómica Molécula que tiene dos átomos.

directly proportional A term used to describe the relationship between two variables whose graph is a straight line passing through the point (0, 0). (p. 64)
directamente proporcional Término empleado para describir la relación entre dos variables cuya gráfica forma una recta que pasa por el punto (0, 0).

ductile A term used to describe a material that can be pulled out into a long wire. (p. 88)
dúctil Término usado para describir un material que se puede estirar hasta convertirlo en un alambre largo.

E

electrical energy The energy of electrically charged particles moving from one place to another. (p. 32)
energía eléctrica Energía de las partículas con carga eléctrica cuando se mueven de un lugar a otro.

electrode A metal strip that conducts electricity. (p. 32)
electrodo Tira de metal que conduce la electricidad.

electromagnetic energy A form of energy that travels through space as waves. (p. 32)
energía electromagnética Forma de energía que viaja a través del espacio en forma de ondas.

English and Spanish Glossary

electron A tiny, negatively charged particle that moves around the nucleus of an atom. (p. 75)
electrón Partícula diminuta con carga negativa, que se mueve alrededor del núcleo de un átomo.

element A pure substance that cannot be broken down into other substances by chemical or physical means. (p. 10)
elemento Sustancia pura que no se puede descomponer en otras sustancias por medios químicos o físicos.

endothermic change A change in which energy is taken in. (p. 26)
cambio endotérmico Cambio en el que se absorbe energía.

energy The ability to do work or cause change. (p. 26)
energía Capacidad de realizar trabajo o causar un cambio.

evaporation The process that occurs when vaporization takes place only on the surface of a liquid. (p. 50)
evaporación Proceso que se da cuando la vaporización se efectúa únicamente en la superficie de un líquido.

exothermic change A change in which energy is given off. (p. 26)
cambio exotérmico Cambio en el que se libera energía.

 F

fluid Any substance that can flow. (p. 45)
fluid Cualquier sustancia que puede fluir.

freezing The change in state from a liquid to a solid. (p. 50)
congelación Cambio del estado líquido al sólido.

 G

gamma radiation A type of nuclear radiation made of high-energy waves. (p. 141)
radiación gamma Tipo de radiación nuclear hecha de ondas de alta energía.

gas A state of matter with no definite shape or volume. (p. 47)
gas Estado de la materia sin forma ni volumen definidos.

glass A clear, solid material with no crystal structure, created by heating sand to a very high temperature. (p. 137)
vidrio Material sólido y transparente que no tiene estructura de cristal, creado al calentar arena a temperaturas muy altas.

graph A diagram that shows how two variables are related. (p. 62)
gráfica Diagrama que muestra la relación entre dos variables.

group Elements in the same vertical column of the periodic table; also called family. (p. 87)
grupo Elementos en la misma columna vertical de la tabla periódica; también llamado familia.

 H

half-life The length of time needed for half of the atoms of a sample of a radioactive isotope to decay. (p. 143)
vida media Tiempo que necesita la mitad de los átomos de una muestra de un isótopo radiactivo para desintegrarse.

halogen An element found in Group 17 of the periodic table. (p. 103)
halógeno Elemento que se encuentra en el Grupo 17 de la tabla periódica.

heterogeneous mixture A mixture in which pure substances are unevenly distributed throughout the mixture. (p. 13)
mezcla heterogénea Mezcla en la cual las sustancias puras están distribuidas desigualmente.

homogeneous mixture A mixture in which substances are evenly distributed throughout the mixture. (p. 13)
mezcla homogénea Mezcla en la cual las sustancias químicas están distribuidas uniformemente.

International System of Units The system of units (SI) used by scientists to measure the properties of matter. (p. 17)
Sistema Internacional de Unidades Sistema de unidades (SI) usado por los científicos para medir las propiedades de la materia.

isotope An atom with the same number of protons and a different number of neutrons from other atoms of the same element. (p. 78)
isótopo Átomo con el mismo número de protones y un número diferente de neutrones que otros átomos del mismo elemento.

kinetic energy The energy of matter in motion. (p. 31)
energía cinética Energía de la materia en movimiento.

law of conservation of mass The principle that the total amount of matter is neither created nor destroyed during any chemical or physical change. (p. 25)
ley de conservación de la masa Principio que enuncia que la cantidad de materia total no se crea ni se destruye durante cambios químicos o físicos.

liquid A state of matter that·has no definite shape but has a definite volume. (p. 45)
líquido Estado de la materia que no tiene forma definida pero sí volumen definido.

malleable A term used to describe material that can be pounded into shapes. (p. 88)
maleable Término usado para describir el material al que se le puede dar forma.

mass A measure of how much matter is in an object. (p. 17)
masa Medida de cuánta materia hay en un objeto.

mass number The sum of protons and neutrons in the nucleus of an atom. (p. 78)
número de masa Suma de protones y neutrones en el núcleo de un átomo.

matter Anything that has mass and occupies space. (p. 6)
materia Cualquier cosa que tiene masa y ocupa un espacio.

melting The change in state from a solid to a liquid. (p. 49)
fusión Cambio del estado sólido a líquido.

melting point The temperature at which a substance changes from a solid to a liquid; the same as the freezing point, or temperature at which a liquid changes to a solid. (p. 49)
punto de fusión Temperatura a la que una sustancia cambia de estado sólido a líquido; es lo mismo que el punto de congelación (la temperatura a la que un líquido se vuelve sólido).

metal A class of elements characterized by physical properties that include shininess, malleability, ductility, and conductivity. (p. 88)
metal Clase de elementos caracterizados por las propiedades físicas que incluye brillo, maleabilidad, ductilidad y conductividad.

metalloid An element that has some characteristics of both metals and nonmetals. (p. 105)
metaloide Elemento que tiene algunas características de los metales y de los no metales.

mixture Two or more substances that are mixed together but not chemically combined. (p. 13)
mezcla Dos o más sustancias que están mezcladas, pero que no están combinadas químicamente.

model In science, a diagram, a mental picture, a mathematical statement, or an object that helps explain ideas about the natural world. (p. 79)
modelo En ciencias, un diagrama, una imagen mental, un enunciado matemático o un objeto que ayuda a explicar ideas sobre el mundo natural.

molecule A particle made of two or more atoms bonded together. (p. 11)
molécula Partícula formada de dos o más átomos unidos.

monomer One of the smaller molecules from which polymers are built. (p. 119)
monómero Una de las moléculas más pequeñas que componen un polímero.

English and Spanish Glossary

nebula The cloudlike region of gases left over in the remains of a shrinking, sun-sized star. (p. 110)
nebulosa Región de gases parecida a una nube que queda como resto de una estrella del tamaño del Sol en proceso de reducción.

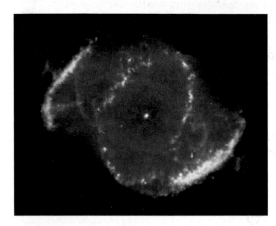

neutron A small particle in the nucleus of the atom, with no electrical charge. (p. 75)
neutrón Partícula pequeña en el núcleo del átomo, que no tiene carga eléctrica.

noble gas An element in Group 18 of the periodic table. (p. 104)
gas noble Elemento del Grupo 18 de la tabla periódica.

nonmetal An element that lacks most of the properties of a metal. (p. 99)
no metal Elemento que carece de la mayoría de las propiedades de un metal.

nuclear fusion The process in which two atomic nuclei combine to form a larger nucleus, forming a heavier element and releasing huge amounts of energy. (p. 109)
fusión nuclear Proceso en el cual dos núcleos atómicos se combinan para formar un núcleo mayor; forman un elemento más pesado y liberan grandes cantidades de energía.

nuclear reaction A reaction involving the particles in the nucleus of an atom that can change one element into another element. (p. 140)
reacción nuclear Reacción de las partículas en el núcleo de un átomo que puede transformar un elemento a otro.

nucleus The central core of an atom containing protons and usually neutrons. (p. 75)
núcleo Parte central del átomo que contiene protones y normalmente neutrones.

optical fiber A threadlike piece of glass (or plastic) that can be used for transmitting messages in the form of light. (p. 138)
fibra óptica Pieza de vidrio (o plástico) parecido a hilo que se puede usar para transmitir mensajes en forma de luz.

origin The (0, 0) point on a line graph. (p. 64)
origen Punto (0, 0) en una gráfica lineal.

particle accelerator A machine that moves atomic nuclei at higher and higher speeds until they crash into one another, sometimes forming heavier elements. (p. 94)
acelerador de partículas Máquina que mueve los núcleos atómicos a velocidades cada vez más altas hasta que chocan entre ellas, a veces forman elementos más pesados.

period A horizontal row of elements in the periodic table. (p. 86)
período Fila horizontal de los elementos en la tabla periódica.

periodic table A chart of the elements showing the repeating pattern of their properties. (p. 82)
tabla periódica Tabla de los elementos que muestra el patrón repetido de sus propiedades.

physical change A change in a substance that does not change its identity. (p. 23)
cambio físico Cambio en una sustancia que no cambia su identidad.

physical property A characteristic of a pure substance that can be observed without changing it into another substance. (p. 8)
propiedad física Característica de una sustancia pura que se puede observar sin convertirla en otra sustancia.

plasma A gas-like state of matter consisting of a mixture of free electrons and atoms that are stripped of their electrons. (p. 109)
plasma Estado de la materia similar al gas que consiste en la mezcla de electrones libres y átomos desprovistos de sus electrones.

plastic A synthetic polymer that can be molded or shaped. (p. 121)
plástico Polímero sintético que se puede moldear o se le puede dar forma.

polymer A large, complex molecule built from smaller molecules joined together in a repeating pattern. (p. 118)
polímero Molécula grande y compleja formada por moléculas más pequeñas que se unen en un patrón que se repite.

potential energy The energy an object has because of its position; also the internal stored energy of an object, such as energy stored in chemical bonds. (p. 31)
energía potencial Energía que tiene un objeto por su posición; también es la energía interna almacenada de un objeto, como la energía almacenada en los enlaces químicos.

pressure The force pushing on a surface divided by the area of that surface. (p. 57)
presión Fuerza que actúa contra una superficie, dividida entre el área de esa superficie.

proton A small, positively charged particle in the nucleus of the atom. (p. 75)
protón Partícula pequeña con carga positiva, que se encuentra en el núcleo del átomo.

R

radioactive dating The process of determining the age of an object using the half-life of one or more radioactive isotopes. (p. 143)
datación radiactiva Proceso para determinar la edad de un objeto que usa la vida media de uno o más isótopos radiactivos.

radioactive decay The process in which the atomic nuclei of unstable isotopes release fast-moving particles and energy. (p. 140)
desintegración radiactiva Proceso por el cual los núcleos atómicos de isótopos inestables liberan partículas de rápido movimiento y gran cantidad de energía.

radioactivity The spontaneous emission of radiation by an unstable atomic nucleus. (p. 140)
radiactividad Emisión espontánea de radiación por un núcleo atómico inestable.

reactivity The ease and speed with which an element combines, or reacts, with other elements and compounds. (p. 89)
reactividad Facilidad y rapidez con las que un elemento se combina, o reacciona, con otros elementos y compuestos.

S

semiconductor A substance that can conduct electricity under some conditions. (p. 105)
semiconductor Sustancia que puede conducir electricidad bajo algunas condiciones.

solid A state of matter that has a definite shape and a definite volume. (p. 43)
sólido Estado de la materia con forma y volumen definidos.

solution An example of a homogeneous mixture; forms when substances dissolve. (p. 13)
solución Ejemplo de una mezcla homogénea; se forma cuando las sustancias se disuelven.

sublimation The change in state from a solid directly to a gas without passing through the liquid state. (p. 53)
sublimación Cambio del estado sólido directamente a gas, sin pasar por el estado líquido.

substance A single kind of matter that is pure and has a specific set of properties. (p. 7)
sustancia Tipo único de materia que es pura y tiene un conjunto de propiedades específicas.

supernova An explosion of a massive star. (p. 111)
supernova Explosión de una estrella gigantesca.

surface tension The result of an inward pull among the molecules of a liquid that brings the molecules on the surface closer together; causes the surface to act as if it has a thin skin. (p. 46)
tensión superficial Resultado de la atracción hacia el centro entre las moléculas de un líquido, que hace que las moléculas de la superficie se junten más; hace que la superficie actúe como si tuviera una piel delgada.

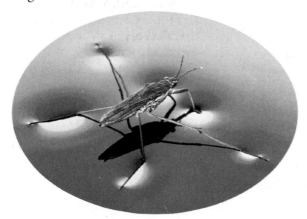

 T

temperature A measure of the average energy of motion of the particles of a substance. (p. 26)
temperatura Medida de la energía promedio de movimiento de las partículas de una sustancia.

thermal energy The total energy of all the particles of an object. (p. 26)
energía térmica Energía total de las partículas de un objeto.

tracer A radioactive isotope that can be followed through the steps of a chemical reaction or industrial process. (p. 144)
trazador Isótopo radiactivo que se puede seguir mediante los pasos de una reacción química o proceso industrial.

transition metal One of the elements in Groups 3 through 12 of the periodic table. (p. 92)
metal de transición Uno de los elementos en los Grupos 3 a 12 de la tabla periódica.

 V

vaporization The change of state from a liquid to a gas. (p. 50)
vaporización Cambio del estado de líquido a gas.

vary inversely A term used to describe the relationship between two variables whose graph forms a curve that slopes downward. (p. 65)
variar inversamente Término empleado para describir la relación entre dos variables cuya gráfica forma una curva con pendiente hacia abajo.

viscosity A liquid's resistance to flowing. (p. 46)
viscosidad Resistencia a fluir que presenta un líquido.

volume The amount of space that matter occupies. (p. 18)
volumen Cantidad de espacio que ocupa la materia.

W

weight A measure of the force of gravity on an object. (p. 17)
peso Medida de la fuerza de gravedad sobre un objeto.

Page numbers for key terms are printed in **boldface** type.
Page numbers for illustrations, maps, and charts are printed in *italics*.

Index

A

actinides 94
air
as mixture of gases 47, 99
nitrogen in 10, 101, 102
oxygen in 10, 102
as solution **13**
air pressure, boiling point and 51
alkali metals *90*
alkaline earth metals *91*
alloys **92**, 130–134
in aircraft *134*
common *132*
making and using 132–133, *134*
properties of 131
alpha particle *141*, 142
aluminum 10, 91, 92
amalgam *132*, 133
americium-241 94
amino acids 120
amorphous solids *44*
area 170
astatine 103
atmosphere. *See* air
atomic mass **81**
average 83
atomic mass units (amu) 77
atomic number **78**
measure of an atom's positive
charge 82
in periodic table 83
atoms *11*, 74
ability to form chemical bond
11
cloud of electrons in 32, 76
elements and 11, 78
mass of 77
modeling *11*, 74–75, 79
particles in 75–77
structure of 75–77
volume of 76
average atomic mass 83
axes on graph 62

B

bacteria, nitrogen fixation by 101
Becquerel, Henri 140
behavior of gases. *See* gas
behavior
beryllium 110
beta particle *141*, 142
bioceramic materials 136

Bohr, Niels 77
boiling *51*
in distillation 14
boiling point **51**
boron 105
Boyle, Robert 58, 61
Boyle's law **58**
graphing 64–65
brainstorming **164**
brass, as solution 13
bromine 86, 99, 103
Bronze Age 130, 132

C

calcium 86, 91
calculating, skill of **161**
cancer, radiation therapy for 145
carbon 98, 99
atomic number of 78
bonds 119
chains and rings 119
isotopes of **78**
model of atom *11*, *75*
nuclear fusion in sun producing
110
carbon-14 *78*, 141, 143
carbon compounds, polymers as
118, 119
carbon dioxide
as product of
chemical change 24, 25
chemical formula 12
dry ice as solid 53
molecule of *11*
carbon family 87, 100
carbon monoxide 12
carbon steels 131, 132–133
Cat's Eye Nebula *110*
cellulose 120, 123
Celsius
degrees, conversion to kelvins
from 63
scale **161**
ceramics **135**–136
making 136
properties and uses of 136
Chadwick, James 77
changes in matter 22–27
chemical **24**–25, 32, 33
forms of energy related to
30–33
physical **23**, 32
thermal energy and **26**, 30, 32,
48, 49

changes of state **23**, 48–53
between liquid and gas 23, 50–52
between solid and gas 53
between solid and liquid 48,
49–50
Charles, Jacques 60, 61
Charles's law *60*–61, 63
graph of 64
chemical bond **11**
internal energy stored in 32
chemical change **24**–25
conservation of mass, law of **25**
electromagnetic energy and **32**
electrons and 140
transforming energy in 33
chemical energy 31, **32**
produced by photosynthesis 33
chemical engineer x–3
chemical formula **12**
chemical property(ies) 7, **9**. *See
also* reactivity
of matter 7, **9**
of metals 89, 90
of nonmetals 100
chemical reaction. *See* chemical
change
chemical symbol **83**
chemistry **7**
chlorine 81, *100*, 103, 119
classifying, skill of **159**
clay 135, 136
coal 100
cobalt-60 145
color, as physical property 8
combustion 24
as exothermic change **26**
communicating, skill of **159**
communication through glass
138
composites **122**
polymers and 122–124
uses of 124
compounds *12*
alkali metals in **90**
alkaline earth metals in **91**
mixtures compared to **13**, 14
nonmetals forming 100, 103
conclusion (of an experiment) **163**
condensation *52*
conductivity **89**

Index

Index

Page numbers for key terms are printed in **boldface** type.
Page numbers for illustrations, maps, and charts are printed in *italics*.

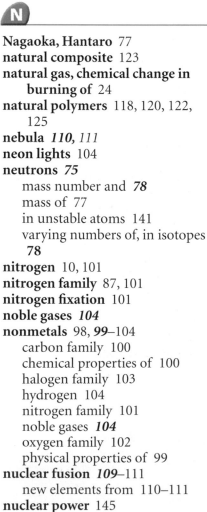

Acknowledgments

Acknowledgment for page 155: "Rune of Riches" by Florence Converse from *Sung Under the Silver Umbrella: Poems for Young Children*. Copyright © 1937 by The Macmillan Company. Reprinted by permission of the Association for Childhood Education International.

Staff Credits

Diane Alimena, Scott Andrews, Jennifer Angel, Michele Angelucci, Laura Baselice, Carolyn Belanger, Barbara A. Bertell, Suzanne Biron, Peggy Bliss, Stephanie Bradley, James Brady, Anne M. Bray, Sarah M. Carroll, Kerry Cashman, Jonathan Cheney, Joshua D. Clapper, Lisa J. Clark, Bob Craton, Patricia Cully, Patricia M. Dambry, Kathy Dempsey, Leanne Esterly, Emily Ellen, Thomas Ferreira, Jonathan Fisher, Patricia Fromkin, Paul Gagnon, Kathy Gavilanes, Holly Gordon, Robert Graham, Ellen Granter, Diane Grossman, Barbara Hollingdale, Linda Johnson, Anne Jones, John Judge, Kevin Keane, Kelly Kelliher, Toby Klang, Sue Langan, Russ Lappa, Carolyn Lock, Rebecca Loveys, Constance J. McCarty, Carolyn B. McGuire, Ranida Touranont McKneally, Anne McLaughlin, Eve Melnechuk, Natania Mlawer, Janet Morris, Karyl Murray, Francine Neumann, Baljit Nijjar, Marie Opera, Jill Ort, Kim Ortell, Joan Paley, Dorothy Preston, Maureen Raymond, Laura Ross, Rashid Ross, Siri Schwartzman, Melissa Shustyk, Laurel Smith, Emily Soltanoff, Jennifer A. Teece, Elizabeth Torjussen, Amanda M. Watters, Merce Wilczek, Amy Winchester, Char Lyn Yeakley. **Additional Credits:** Tara Alamilla, Louise Gachet, Allen Gold, Andrea Golden, Terence Hegarty, Etta Jacobs, Meg Montgomery, Stephanie Rogers, Kim Schmidt, Adam Teller, Joan Tobin.

Illustration

All art development by Morgan Cain and Associates.

Photography

Photo Research Sue McDermott
Cover image top, Thom Lang/Corbis; **bottom,** Arnold Fisher/Photo Researchers, Inc.

Page vi t, Brand X Pictures/Getty Images, Inc.; **vi bl,** Richard Megna/Fundamental Photographs; **vi bm,** Charles D. Winters/Photo Researchers, Inc.; **vi br,** Layne Kennedy/Corbis; **vii,** Richard Haynes; **viii,** Richard Haynes; **x inset,** Courtesy of Dr. Rathin Datta; **x,** Charlie Waite/Getty Images, Inc.; **1 both,** Courtesy of Dr. Rathin Datta; **2b,** Lisa Blumenfeld/Getty Images, Inc.; **2t,** Laszlo Selly/Getty Images, Inc.; **3tl,** Photo courtesy of Cargill Dow LLC; **3ml,** Photodisc/Getty Images, Inc.; **3bl,** Royalty-Free/Corbis; **3tr,** Photodisc/Getty Images, Inc.; **3br,** Courtesy of Dr. Rathin Datta; **3 car,** Alamy Images; **3 Rathin,** Courtesy of Dr. Rathin Datta.

Chapter 1
Pages 4–5, (c) Lawrence Migdale/PIX; **5 inset,** Richard Haynes; **6b,** Russ Lappa; **6t,** Richard Haynes; **7,** Russ Lappa; **8bl,** Norbert Wu/DRK Photo; **8r,** Richard Haynes; **8t,** Ted Kinsman/Photo Researchers, Inc.; **9l,** Walter Hodges/Getty Images, Inc.; **9m,** Mary Ellen Bartley/PictureArts/Corbis; **9r,** Layne Kennedy/Corbis; **10bl,** MVR Photo; **10r,** Corbis; **10tl,** Mahaux Photography/Getty Images, Inc.; **11,** Tim Ridley/Dorling Kindersley; **12tl,** Andrew Lambert Photography/SPL/Photo Researchers, Inc.; **12tr,** Ed Degginger/Color-Pic, Inc.; **12b,** Grant V. Faint/Getty Images, Inc.; **13b,** graficart.net/Alamy Images; **13t,** Michael Newman/PhotoEdit; **14 all,** Richard Haynes; **15 all,** Richard Haynes; **16 both,** Richard Haynes; **17l,** Russ Lappa; **17r,** Richard Haynes; **18,** Russ Lappa; **20,** Dorling Kindersely; **22,** Frans Lemmens/Getty Images, Inc.; **23bl,** Tony Freeman/PhotoEdit; **23br,** Photo Researchers, Inc.; **23t,** Richard Megna/Fundamental Photographs; **24,** Art Montes de Oca; **25,** Brand X pictures/Getty Images, Inc.; **26b,** Snaevarr Gudmundsson/Nordic Photos/Alamy Images; **26t,** Victoria Pearson/Getty Images, Inc.; **28–29,** Digital Vision/Getty Images, Inc.; **30,** Russ Lappa; **31l,** Richard R. Hansen/Photo Researchers, Inc.; **31r,** Mark Richards/PhotoEdit; **32,** Russ Lappa; **33,** Adam Jones/Photographer's Choice/Getty Images, Inc.; **34,** Richard Haynes; **35,** Richard Haynes; **36,** Corbis.

Chapter 2
Pages 40–41, Steve Bloom; **41 inset,** Richard Haynes; **42b,** LWA-Dann Tardif/Corbis; **42t,** Richard Haynes; **43,** James A. Sugar/Corbis; **44b,** Patrick J. LaCroix/Getty Images, Inc.; **44t,** S. Stammer/Photo Researchers Inc.; **45 all,** Richard Haynes; **46b,** Herman Eisenbeiss /Photo Researchers, Inc.; **46t,** Breck Kent/Earth Scenes; **48b,** Hubert Camille/Getty Images, Inc.; **48t,** Richard Haynes; **49l,** Breck P. Kent/Earth Scenes; **49m,** Chuck O'Rear/Corbis; **49r,** Leslie Harris/Index Stock; **50 both,** Richard Haynes; **51 both,** Dorling Kindersley/Science Museum; **52,** Tony Freeman/PhotoEdit; **53,** Charles D. Winters/Photo Researchers Inc.; **54,** Russ Lappa; **55,** Carl & Ann Purcell/Corbis; **56b,** MVR Photo; **56t,** Richard Hutchings/Corbis; **57 both,** Richard Haynes; **58,** Richard Haynes; **60 all,** Dorling Kindersley; **61,** Eye Ubiquitous/Corbis; **66,** Russ Lappa; **67,** Richard Haynes; **68b,** Eye Ubiquitous/Corbis; **68t,** S. Stammer/Photo Researchers, Inc.

Chapter 3
Pages 72–73, Greg Elms/Lonely Planet Images; **73 inset,** Richard Haynes; **74 both,** 1998, The Art Institute of Chicago; **76l,** Royalty-Free/Corbis; **76r,** Russ Lappa; **77l,** Dorling Kindersley; **77m,** Dorling Kindersley; **77r,** Frank Cezus/FPG International; **79,** courtesy of the National Institute of Science and Technology; **80b,** Richard Haynes; **80t,** Russ Lappa; **81bl,** Richard Megna/Fundamental Photographs; **81br,** Richard Megna/Fundamental Photographs; **81m,** Robert Mathena/Fundamental Photographs; **81t,** Philip Coblentz/Alamy Images; **83,** Photodisc/Getty Images, Inc.; **87,** Richard Megna/Fundamental Photos; **88,** Richard Haynes; **89b,** Cameron Davidson/Getty Images, Inc.; **89m,** Jeffrey L. Rotman/Corbis; **89t,** Dorling Kindersley; **90l,** Richard Megna/Fundamental Photographs; **90m,** Dorling Kindersley; **90r,** Eyewire/Getty Images, Inc.; **91,** Jeff Greenberg/PhotoEdit; **93b,** Richard Haynes; **93ml,** Christie's Images; **93mr,** Russ Lappa; **93t,** Richard Haynes; **94,** NASA/Johnson Space Center; **95l,** Stephen Marks/Getty Images, Inc.; **95r,** David Parker/Photo Researchers, Inc.; **96b,** Russ Lappa; **96t,** Richard Haynes; **97 both,** Richard Haynes; **98,** Kathy Bushue/Getty Images, Inc.; **99bl,** Lawrence Migdale/Science Source/Photo Researchers Inc.; **99br,** Dennis McDonald/PhotoEdit; **99t,** Bettmann/Corbis; **100b,** Charles D. Winters/Photo Researchers Inc.; **100t,** Grant Heilman Photography, Inc.; **101 inset,** Michael Newman/PhotoEdit; **101l,** David Porter/Index Stock; **101r,** Joseph Devenney/Getty Images, Inc.; **102l,** Novovitch/Liaison International; **102r,** Pete Oxford/Minden Pictures; **103l,** Mary Kate Denny/PhotoEdit; **103r,** Richard Megna/Fundamental Photographs; **104b,** A & L Sinibaldi/Getty Images, Inc.; **104t,** Michael Dalton/Fundamental Photographs; **105,** Andrew Syred/SPL/Photo Researchers Inc.; **107,** Grant V. Faint/Getty Images, Inc.; **108–09,** NASA; **109,** Celestron International; **110,** J.P. Harrington & K.J. Borkowski/NASA; **111,** NC: Science VU/ESO/Visuals Unlimited; **112,** Richard Megna/Fundamental Photographs.

Chapter 4
Pages 116–17, Paul Chesley/Getty Images, Inc.; **117 inset,** Jon Chomitz; **118,** John Terence Turner; **119,** Russ Lappa; **120l,** Joe McDonald/Corbis; **120m,** Royalty-Free/Corbis; **120r,** Larry Ulrich/DRK Photo; **121,** Superstock; **122l,** Corbis-Bettmann; **122m,** Chris Rogers/Corbis; **122r,** Terry Wild Studio/Uniphoto; **123l,** David Young-Wolfe/PhotoEdit; **123m,** Jeffry W. Myers/Corbis; **123r,** Courtesy of Dow Corporation; **124l,** Ariel Skelley/Corbis; **124r,** David Stoecklein/Corbis; **125,** Fred Habegger/Grant Heilman Photography; **126,** Daemmrich/Uniphoto; **127,** Richard Haynes; **128,** Richard Haynes; **129b,** Richard Megna/Fundamental Photographs; **129t,** 2004 Richard Megna/Fundamental Photographs; **130b,** Photodisc; **130t,** Russ Lappa; **131l,** Diana Calder/The Stock Market; **131r,** Royalty-Free/Corbis; **133bl,** Marc Pokempner/Corbis; **133bm,** Richard Haynes; **133br,** Dorling Kindersley; **133t,** William Hopkins; **134,** Chris Sorensen; **135,** M. Borchi White Star/Photo Researchers Inc.; **136l,** Dan McCoy/Rainbow; **136r,** Jacky Chapman/Alamy Images; **137,** James L. Amos/Peter Arnold; **138,** Ted Horowitz/Corbis; **139,** Jan Van Der Straet/Granger Collection; **140b,** Bettmann/Corbis; **140t,** Paul Silverman/Fundamental Photographs; **143,** T.A. Wiewandt/DRK Photo; **145b,** Reuters NewMedia Inc./Corbis; **145t,** RVI Medical Physics, Newcastle/Simon, Fraser/Science Photo Library; **146,** Robert Patrick/Corbis Sygma; **147,** Richard Megna/Fundamental Photographs; **148bl,** Photodisc/Getty Images, Inc.; **148br,** Robert Patrick/Corbis Sygma; **148t,** Superstock; **152b,** Colin Keates/Dorling Kindersley; **152t,** Steve Gorton/Dorling Kindersley; **152–53,** Bob Burch/Index Stock Imagery; **153b,** The British Museum/Dorling Kindersley; **153m,** Kim Jae-Hwan/AFP/Corbis; **153t,** Rosenfeld Imaged Ltd/Rainbow; **154–55,** Ali Murat Atay/Atlas Geographic; **155,** Index Stock Imagery; **156t,** Winfield I. Parks/National Geographic Image Collection; **156b,** Photodisc/Getty Images, Inc.; **157b,** C.M. Dixon; **157t,** Royalty-Free/Corbis; **158,** Tony Freeman/PhotoEdit; **159b,** Russ Lappa; **159m,** Richard Haynes; **159t,** Russ Lappa; **160,** Richard Haynes; **162,** Richard Haynes; **164,** Morton Beebe/Corbis; **165,** Richard Haynes; **167b,** Richard Haynes; **167t,** Dorling Kinderlsey; **169,** Image Stop/Phototake; **172,** Richard Haynes; **179,** Richard Haynes; **180,** Richard Haynes; **184,** Dan McCoy/Rainbow; **185,** Tony Freeman/PhotoEdit; **186,** Snaevarr Gudmundsson/Nordic Photos/Alamy Images; **187,** Andrew Syred/SPL/Photo Researchers Inc.; **188b,** Tony Freeman/PhotoEdit **188t,** J.P. Harrington & K.J. Borkowski/NASA; **189,** Charles D. Winters/Photo Researchers, Inc.; **190,** Herman Eisenbeiss/Photo Researchers, Inc.